ASPECTS OF SAXO-NORMAN LONDON: III

THE BRIDGEHEAD AND BILLINGSGATE TO 1200

ASPECTS OF SAXO-NORMAN LONDON: III

THE BRIDGEHEAD AND BILLINGSGATE TO 1200

by Ken Steedman, Tony Dyson and John Schofield

with contributions by Jennifer Hillam and Alan Vince

London & Middlesex Archaeological Society
Special Paper 14

Published by the London and Middlesex
Archaeological Society

First published 1992

Series editor: Francis Grew

Graphic design: David Bentley and Alison Hawkins
Drawings by Melanie Connell

Book design and production: Melissa Denny of Diptych

Typeset and printed by BAS Printers Limited,
Over Wallop, Hampshire

The cover illustration, by Martin Bentley, shows the
late 10th/early 11th-century jetty at New Fresh Wharf
(Period 2.2), with the breached Roman riverside wall
behind.

ISBN 0 903290 40 5

**The Society is grateful to English Heritage for
a grant towards the publication of this report.**

CONTENTS

CONVENTIONS USED IN THE FIGURES

The line drawings follow conventions which have been developed and standardised by the Department of Urban Archaeology; for ease of comparison, both symbols and scales are consistent with those used in other DUA publications.

Most figures fall into one of the following categories: location maps (1:20000 and 1:2500), phase plans (1:200) or summary maps (1:1200). The symbols for these are listed in the Key (facing page). All phase plans are oriented with OS north at the top of the page; where the viewpoint of photographs is unclear, it has been marked by a 'view' symbol (see Key). The extent to which features are conjectured has been standardised. On phase plans, structural elements such as buildings and drains have been extrapolated a notional 0.5m beyond their last recorded limit; however, they have been extended still further when, for instance, floors are recorded beyond the walls of a building or when walls are implied by the position of an external surface. If walls have been retained in a later phase of building, they are shown (both found and conjectured portions) by the 'retained' symbol. Structural elements, shown in black, represent only the lowest *in situ* portion; collapsed or partially collapsed structural features have normally been omitted for clarity. Where relevant, evidence recorded in section has been extrapolated and drawn in plan as a notional 0.2m-wide strip, using the same conventions as if it had been recorded in plan.

Specialised conventions used on the sections and historical maps (scale 1:1250) are identified by separate keys or in the captions. However, the following conventions have been used in all the sections (Figs 54, 56, 59): *blacked in* Roman riverside wall = wall found in excavation; *hatched* riverside wall = position conjectured from timber pile foundations; *stippled* deposits = result of natural silting. On the historical maps (Figs 4, 43) *dashed lines* = parish boundaries; *darker grey* = churches drawn by Leake (1666).

KEY

--------- limit of excavation

——————— outline of site

Location maps (1:2500)

 area of investigation (hatched) showing trench (black) and ground plan of former property

Site plans (1:200)

Structures

 surviving waterfront/building

 conjectured

 retained – still in use

 surviving – not in use

 other surviving timbers

 vertical posts / stakes

 threshold

23◊ photographic viewpoint and figure reference number

Deposits

 found and conjectured extent of dumped embankment material with found edge

 conjectured extent of areas of internal occupation

Other features

 pits/cuts

 embankment slope, found and conjectured

 tenement boundary

 hearth with found and conjectured edge

Summary plans (1:625)

 building and waterfront structures (surviving and conjectured)

 tenement access through riverside wall

 projected tenement boundary

 embankment showing high water level

ABSTRACT

This volume describes features dating to the period c.400 to c.1200 from four waterfront excavations of 1974-82 in the City of London; two (New Fresh Wharf and Billingsgate Lorry Park) immediately below the late Saxon and medieval bridge, and two (Swan Lane and Seal House) just above it. In conjunction with a review of the available documentary evidence, the archaeological findings provide an outline of development for the area around the northern bridgehead and the harbour of Billingsgate (first mentioned c.1000) in the late Saxon and early medieval period.

During the period 400-900 the evidence on these four sites confirms recent suggestions that the Roman city was largely deserted; the Roman waterfront was gradually obscured by silts of the rising river, and the Roman bridge, if it still survived, probably did not form a focus of activity or public resort. There is archaeological evidence for a shift in the location of settlement from the Strand to within the Roman walls, some time in the late 9th or early 10th century. Documentary evidence demonstrates that at least one block of land near the waterfront, south of St Paul's, was laid out in the last decade of the 9th century; and in all likelihood its occupiers were engaging in trade, perhaps through a beach-market on the site of Queenhithe. There is, however, evidence that during the 10th and early 11th centuries London looked inland rather than abroad for its commercial well-being, and this local or at best inter-regional trading network has parallels elsewhere in Europe.

The earliest post-Roman structural activities discovered between Billingsgate and London bridge were the jetty and associated rubble bank at New Fresh Wharf, dated to the late 10th or early 11th century. On three of the four sites there followed embankments of clay and timber during the first half of the 11th century; at New Fresh Wharf the embankments were constructed in parts which became individual medieval properties by 1200, suggesting that they may have been in individual ownership from the beginning. The embankments would have been suitable for the berthing of the smaller kind of shipping then prevalent, and they probably formed part of London's expanding harbour facilities in the 11th century. The relationship of the various embankments to the rising river level is also considered.

The development of the waterfront area south of Thames Street, between the bridge and Billingsgate, can be seen within the context of the late 10th- and early 11th-century development of the immediate neighbourhood and of the city as a whole. The waterfront ends of north-south streets served as localised minor markets, situated at the only places on the foreshore to which there was public access and initially co-existing with the major harbours at Queenhithe, Billingsgate and Botolph Wharf. The building of the bridge by 1000 (though the precise date is not yet certain) symbolises not only London's re-established role as a distributive centre for imports or a collection-point for exports, but also its nodal position in the local and regional road network.

Development of the two sites above the bridge after 1050 was comparatively unspectacular, but below the bridge two further phases can be seen: by about 1100, the final demolition of the Roman riverside wall and the construction of the churches of St Magnus and St Botolph south of the new thoroughfare, Thames Street; secondly, the erection of stone buildings on the reclaimed land during the 12th and early 13th centuries, concomitant with the crystallisation of St Botolph's Wharf as a an entry-point of civic and greater significance, a place where royal customs were received in 1200-1.

The study also comprises detailed tables describing the dating evidence (including dendrochronology) and summaries of the artefacts.

1. INTRODUCTION

The evolution of the historic waterfront of the City of London has been the major topic of investigation by the Department of Urban Archaeology of the Museum of London since its inception in 1973. This has been primarily a result of the wholesale redevelopment of the land on both sides of Thames Street, but principally to the south of the street and bordering on the present river. From 1972 to the end of 1989, 46 excavations took place in this zone, and major publications have already appeared, both on the Roman waterfront (Tatton-Brown 1974; Hill, Millett & Blagg 1980; Milne 1985; Miller, Schofield & Rhodes 1986; Brigham 1990) and on the medieval reclamation process (Tatton-Brown 1975; Milne & Milne 1981). The present study attempts to fill the gap between these two fields of research by reporting those features and layers on four waterfront excavations of 1974-82 which can be attributed to the period c.400-c.1200, with associated documentary research.

The study falls into two distinct but related geographical areas (Figs 1 and 2):
(i) New Fresh Wharf and Billingsgate Lorry Park, directly adjacent to and downstream of modern London Bridge
(ii) Swan Lane and Seal House, situated on either side of a narrow street leading from Thames Street to the present riverfront immediately upstream of the Bridge.

Two of these sites, New Fresh Wharf and Seal House, both excavated in 1974, were among the earliest to be investigated by the DUA. Along with Baynard's Castle and Custom House, undertaken by or on behalf of Guildhall Museum in 1972 and 1973, they were also the first archaeological excavations to take place south of Thames Street, offering opportunities not previously available of examining the waterfront zone itself, the focus of London's longstanding prominence as a port. Baynard's Castle was primarily of late- and post-medieval interest; Custom House and New Fresh Wharf on the other hand revealed entire sequences of stratigraphy from the Roman period

to the 14th century and later, though at Custom House an apparent hiatus between the 4th and late 13th centuries was not at first fully understood. Also of great importance was the watching brief maintained over a disconnected series of contractor's trenches at the Public Cleansing Depot at Dowgate in 1959-61. This yielded evidence of activity on the foreshore from the 11th century onwards but was recorded in a less detailed and coherent fashion than would have been the case had a systematic archaeological excavation been possible.

Supplemented by Swan Lane (1981) and Billingsgate Lorry Park (1982-3), these sites were the only ones sufficiently close to the south side of Thames Street to bear upon the evolution of the late Saxon and early medieval foreshore, and all were to have been included in this report as first envisaged. However major investigations in comparable locations at Thames Exchange (Malvern House) and Vintry House in the Vintry area, and at Cannon Street railway station to the east of Dowgate, in 1988-9 resulted in a change of specification. The four sites in the bridgehead area (from west to east: Swan Lane, Seal House, New Fresh Wharf and Billingsgate Lorry Park), representing a natural grouping, would appear as before, but the Public Cleansing Depot evidence would be reserved for a second report covering the equally coherent group of recent excavations some distance upstream in the central sector of the waterfront.

Each group of sites is nevertheless part of the evidence for the development of the London waterfront as a whole. To keep this broader perspective in view it was also decided to hold to the original intention of including here a general survey of the historical evidence (Part 2). This will serve as an introduction both to the present sites and the Vintry-Dowgate group, and to two forthcoming reports on more specialised aspects of the later medieval waterfront: a study and catalogue of medieval revetment structures, medieval carpentry and previous uses of timbers (for instance,

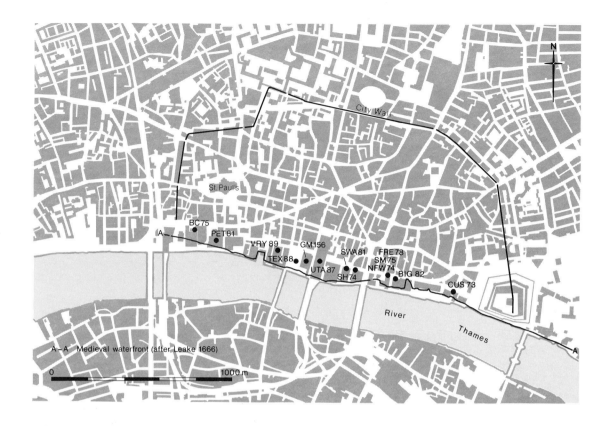

in near-contemporary houses) (*Medieval waterfront structures*; Milne in prep); and a study of tenements and buildings on the four bridgehead sites (*Medieval waterfront tenements*, by John Schofield and Tony Dyson). In effect the latter will be the direct continuation of the present report, the dividing line between them being set at about 1200.

Detailed summaries of the relevant parts of the sequence from each of the study sites, and relevant documentary evidence, are presented in Part 3. The dating used in this study (summarised in Fig 3) is based predominantly on dendrochronologically dated timbers from within the waterfront structures and on the assigning of pottery assemblages recovered from waterfront deposits to particular Ceramic Phases. These Ceramic Phases (abbreviated to CP hereafter) are defined by Vince (1991), and the dendrochronological dates, particularly those from Billingsgate Lorry Park, have been used in refining them. The dating evidence is presented in detail in Appendix 1, whilst the results of dendrochronology from the sites is given in Appendix 2.

Parts 4-5 comprise discussion of this evidence. In Part 4 the development of the waterfront in

1. Plan of the City, showing sites mentioned in the text. The site codes refer to excavations as follows: from west to east, Baynards Castle (BC75), Peter's Hill (PET81), Vintry House (VRY88), Thames Exchange (TEX88), Public Cleansing Depot (1959; shown as GM156), Cannon Street Station (south side; UTA87), Swan Lane (SWA81), Seal House (SH74), New Fresh Wharf (NFW74, SM75, FRE78), Billingsgate Lorry Park (BIG82), and Custom House (CUS73). Scale 1:20000.

the bridgehead area is summarised, parallels sought and its evolution within the developing city outlined. In Part 5 the construction and purpose of the embankments is examined from the point of view of their relation to the river and the rising water level.

Part 6 broadens the scope of the study to the entire early medieval waterfront, viewed from a further particular standpoint, a topographical study of the evolution of Thames Street and the lanes to north and south. The division between the present study and its successor, at around 1200, roughly corresponds to differences in the type and extent of the evidence, both excavated and written. In the subsequent period the archaeological evidence for buildings is fuller and more clearly and consistently identifiable with distinct

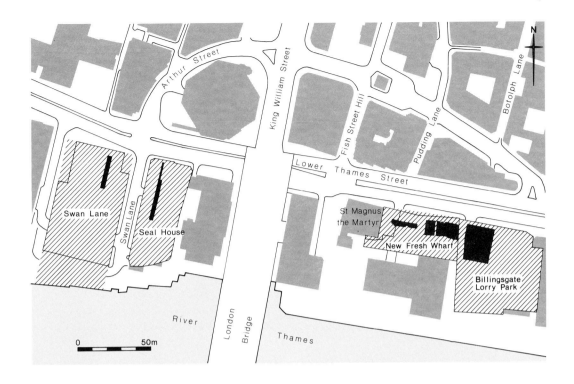

2. *The area around the north end of the modern London Bridge, showing the four study sites. Site limits are hatched, with areas of controlled excavation in black. Scale 1 :2500.*

tenements, whose separate development can be traced in greater detail. The same is largely true of the documentary evidence, systematically collected for the seventeen intramural waterfront parishes up to *c.*1550; as far as individual tenements are concerned, such evidence is rarely available before the mid 13th century, so that detailed comparison with the archaeological findings is usually possible only subsequently, and then not always to any great extent. There are however certain respects in which documents, even of substantially later date, can make an important contribution to the understanding of the earlier period covered by this report. One of these is in the recording of the early names of places, streets and wharves, and Part 6, based on such evidence, shows how the development of the waterfront was closely related to, and inseparable from, the formation of the southern half of London's street system. Thus in reporting one group of sites, the present volume also attempts to establish the basic outline and context of the London waterfront in the late Saxon and early medieval period, to a point where it is best considered further in the form of separate

monographs concerned with particular topics already introduced here, or with further groups of sites.

The concluding Part 7 summarises the development of London's waterfront in the period 400-1200, and points to the most significant trends, especially for the period 1000-1200 and in the stretch of foreshore between the medieval bridge and Billingsgate, which have been identified by the present work.

It is a pleasure to acknowledge the assistance of many institutions and individuals in the preparation of this study. Negotiation for the sites was conducted by Brian Hobley with David Browne (New Fresh Wharf and Seal House), Charles Hill (New Fresh Wharf Area III) and John Schofield (Swan Lane and Billingsgate Lorry Park). The excavation work and much of the post-excavation analysis was funded by the Department of Environment (from 1984, the Historic Buildings and Monuments Commission), with substantial grants also from the Corporation of the City of London and the City of London Archaeological Trust at Billingsgate Lorry Park, and Edger Investments and the Archaeological Trust at Swan Lane. For permissions and assistance during the site work the Museum is indebted to the Engineer's, Surveyor's and Planning Departments of the Corporation, the Worshipful

Company of Fishmongers, National Carparks, Higgs & Hill, John Mowlem, Mott Hay & Anderson, and Seifert and Partners. The documentary work has been undertaken largely in the City of London Records Office, Guildhall Library and the Public Record Office, and the ready assistance of the staffs of these and other institutions is gratefully acknowledged. Parts 2 and 6 were written by Tony Dyson; parts 3 and 4 by Ken Steedman and John Schofield, with the documentary work by Tony Dyson; parts 5 and 6 by Ken Steedman; and part 7 by John Schofield.

The archive reports and finds from these sites are housed in the Museum of London.

SWAN LANE	SEAL HOUSE
Groups 20-1: *silting over Roman quay* pottery: Roman residual only	**Period II:** *silting over Roman quay* pottery: 3rd-12th century
Groups 22-4: *first embankment (W6)* pottery: CP3(1020-50)	
Groups 25-6: *second embankment (W7)* pottery: CP4(1050-80)	
Group 27: *Waterfronts 8, 9* timber (W8): 1042+ ?early 12th century	**Period III:** *Waterfront 1, Building A* timbers: 1133-70 pottery: CP5(1080-1150)
Groups 29-33: *Waterfront 10* timbers: 1123+ pottery: ?late 12th century	**Period IV:** *Waterfront II* timbers: 1163-92 pottery: CP6(1150-80)
Groups 34-5: *reclamation behind W9-10* timber: 1142+ pottery: 12th century	
Group 45: *occupation contemporary with W7-10 (ie late 11th to late 12th century)* no dating evidence	

3. Summary of dating of the periods on the four study sites.

NEW FRESH WHARF	BILLINGSGATE	Conclusions	Ceramic Phase
Period 2.1: *silting over Roman quay* contaminated from Period 2.3	**Period III:** *silting over Roman quay* pottery: 3rd-11th century	silting of robbed Roman quay no activity on foreshore bridge is broken	**1** (850-1020)
Period 2.2: *rubble bank and grid of stakes* radiocarbon: 760-980, 855-1019 boat timbers: 915-55 pottery: Roman residual only		jetty and bank, *c*.1000 bridge rebuilt by 1000	**2** (1000-1020)
Period 2.3: *foreshore* pottery: CP3(1020-50)		private embankments except at St Botolph's Wharf, first half 11th century	**3** (1020-1050)
Period 2.4: *clay embankments* timbers: 1014+	**Period IV:** *Waterfronts 2-4* timbers: 1039/40 pottery during use: CP4(1050-80)		**4** (1050-1080)
Period 3.1: *silting* pottery: CP4(1050-80)	**Period IV:** *Waterfronts 3, 5* timbers: 1055 pottery during use: CP5(1080-1150)		
Period 3.2: *revetments* timbers: 1055+, 1084+ pottery: CP5(1080-1150)	**Period V:** *Waterfronts 6-7* timbers (W6): 1080+ timbers (W7): 1056-1101 pottery: CP5-6(1080-1180)	repairs and extensions to private properties, mid/late 11th century	**5** (1080-1150)
Period 3.3: *silting* pottery: CP5(1080-1150)	**Period VI:** *Waterfronts 8-9* timbers (W8) in inlet: 1060+, 1108(+1-2 years) timbers (W9): 1108-25 pottery (W8/W9): CP6 (1150-80)	?St Botolph's church founded by 1100 to north of Billingsgate excavation	
Period 3.4: *revetments, Buildings A-E* timber: 1166-1211 pottery: CP5(1080-1150) and early/mid 13th century link with documentary evidence: 1107/8-67 Building C built in mid 13th century	**Period VII:** *Waterfronts 10-11, Building 1* timbers (W10) blocking inlet: 1144-83 timber (W11): 1172-1216 Building 1, contemporary with modifications to W11, ?c.1200 St Botolph's church south wall: 13th century	further revetments and buildings, some of stone, on reclaimed land, 12th to mid 13th century St Botolph's church extended to south in mid 13th century	**6** (1150-1180)
Period 3.5: *silting* pottery: mid 12th-mid 13th century			

2. THE LONDON WATERFRONT 400-1000

The earliest post-Roman structures so far discovered in the City date, with very rare exceptions, from c.900, and on most sites permanent occupation can be reliably dated only from the mid to late 10th century. The earliest evidence of this kind for continuous activity on the waterfront in particular occurs rather later: from the turn of the 10th and 11th centuries. Both inland and on the waterfront the structures are readily distinguishable from the preceding strata. Inland, they are normally founded upon a thick accumulation of dark earth which, from as early as the mid 2nd century, in many instances replaced small-scale properties of mixed domestic and commercial character, some of them deliberately demolished beforehand. This accumulation persisted into the late Roman and early and mid Saxon periods as virtually their sole stratigraphical representation. Comparable changes are apparent on the waterfront, though from a century later. While the timber quays of the 1st and 2nd centuries at New Fresh Wharf were replaced and enlarged by ambitious new extensions early in the 3rd century (Miller, Schofield & Rhodes 1986, 72) there is little to show that they saw much subsequent use. Instead they soon fell into neglect and decay, especially after the river wall was constructed across their heads in the mid 3rd century to complete the City's defences.

Though still a centre of continuing importance, as is shown by the attention lavished on its defences in the 3rd and 4th centuries and by the notably more spacious and luxurious character of its buildings, late Roman London was clearly much less dependent than it had once been on commerce, overseas trade and a large population. This raises the questions how truly urban London was on the departure of the Romans in the 5th century, how really abrupt the transition from late Roman to post-Roman and, consequently, just how powerful — or negligible — an impression London made on the earliest English settlers. All the evidence is that it made next to none, except perhaps on long-distance travellers passing through on the major roads which converged upon its site (Dyson & Schofield 1984, 287-9). Most of the gates appear to have survived, but between them the main streets seem to have followed the Roman lines only coincidentally, their degraded courses showing more concern for direct and rapid transit than for any settled occupation alongside them. The later record of such rare name forms as *Hwaetmundestan* (889) and *Wifladeston* (12th century) appear to denote the survival of individual Roman stone buildings in some visible form; the former on the site of the Huggin Hill bath-house immediately north of Queenhithe, and the latter on a comparable waterfront location some 200m downstream of the Billingsgate bath-house. But names of this kind also suggest that the survival and adaptation of such buildings was exceptional rather than general. The significance of the site of the Roman City as a whole was certainly not lost, and must have been an important factor in the building of St Paul's cathedral within its walls in 604 as the seat of the local bishopric, and in Pope Gregory's original intention that it should serve a southern English archdiocese (Colgrave & Mynors 1969, 104-7). In 839 Bishop Helmstan of Winchester wrote of his recent consecration 'in the illustrious place built by the skill of the ancient Romans, called throughout the world the great city of London' (Birch 1885, no. 424). On the evidence available to us the description cannot have been warranted by much more than the surviving walls and gates: perhaps it was inspired as much by a sense of occasion or even by a reading of Bede's *History*.

Against the consistent archaeological evidence of abandonment and neglect in the post-Roman centuries before c.900 has to be set the contradictory historical evidence which is available from the 7th century. The references in question, though few, brief and incidental, are sufficient to show that the London of this period was nevertheless seen as a place of considerable importance, at least by the standards of the time and certainly to an extent that could not be suspected on the basis of the physical evidence. Almost all these notices lay special emphasis on the town's role as a port and market. As early as the 670s London was casually described in the text of a Chertsey charter as a port where ships tie up, without any suggestion that this was a novelty (Dyson 1980, 83-90). From the next decade, law codes of the Kentish kings reveal the existence of a hall where merchants could obtain warranty for the goods they purchased, and also the presence of a royal reeve (Thorpe 1840, 14-5) who would doubtless uphold the king's fiscal interests. By the 730s Bede could refer to the town as a mart of many nations coming by land and sea (Colgrave & Mynors 1969, 142-3). Although 'nations' in this context need mean little more than the several Anglo-Saxon kingdoms of the day, his mention of the sale of slaves to Frisian traders (*ibid*, 404-5), as well as the evidence of coins (Dolley 1976, 351-2), shows that London attracted a much wider overseas clientele. Under the Mercian king Ethelbald in the 730s and 740s, its importance as a trading centre is underlined by a short series of charters issued in favour of the bishops of Rochester and Worcester and of the abbess of Minster in Thanet, granting them customs levied on cargoes arriving at the port in specific shiploads (Sawyer 1968, nos 86, 88, 98). Ethelbald's successor, Offa, was especially concerned with the promotion of trade, both internal as shown by his currency reforms and external as revealed by his commercial treaties with Charlemagne. In this last respect London must have been of special importance as the only major south-eastern port under his direct control. By 811 it could be described, without any reference to the Romans, as a famous place and a (Mercian) royal town (*vicus*) (*ibid*, no. 168).

Until six years ago, the great problem of post-Roman London was how to reconcile this consistent historical testimony to a flourishing mid Saxon trading centre with the persistent dearth of contemporary archaeological evidence, structural and artefactual, from the intramural City (Dyson & Schofield 1984, 285, 294-5). As the current programme proceeded it became increasingly difficult to maintain that excavation was still insufficiently extensive to rule out the possibility of a small, compact nucleus of settlement in some neglected corner of the city – though it remains the case that relatively little work has been done in the area south of St Paul's and upstream of Queenhithe. But speculation of this kind was to be overtaken by a revelation which followed the thorough reassessment of the dating, identification and distribution of finds previously recovered from the areas adjoining the walled city. This led to the conclusion that the population and commercial centre of the 7th to late 9th century had lain not within the walls but in the district to the west, between the River Fleet and Westminster (Vince 1984, 431-9; 1991, 412-18). From here, along the primary axis of the street called the Strand, close to the contemporary bank of the Thames and extending some unknown distance inland, could now be recognized an incidence of finds (and to a lesser extent structures) of mid Saxon date sufficient in range, quantity and breadth of distribution to resolve the archaeological problem of pre-Alfredian London and to vindicate the historical record.

In its desertion of an ancient, defended centre in favour of a new, unprotected settlement along the Strand, London is seen to have conformed to a common practice on the part of contemporary trading stations around the coasts of the North Sea, many of them, like London, distinguished by the suffix *wic* (Biddle 1976a, 114-5). The form *Lundenwic* first occurs in the 680s (Thorpe 1840, 14-5) and persists into the mid 9th century, and it has not escaped attention that half-way along the Strand there occurs the place-name 'Aldwych', or 'old *wic*', first recorded in the late 12th century (Biddle 1984, 25-6). One analogy outside London to the duality of ancient walled town and new extramural settlement appears to be the association between Winchester and the port of *Hamwic*, twelve miles further down the unnavigable River Itchen on the eastern outskirts of the later Southampton (Biddle 1976a, 112-4). From the late 7th to mid 9th centuries Winchester appears to have retained its royal, administrative and ecclesiastical functions within its walls, just as St Paul's cathedral was built within the walls of London, while the outlying port of *Hamwic*, like the settlement on the Strand, served as the focus of true urban activity. At both Winchester and London also, the ancient sites were to re-emerge as urban centres in the fullest sense upon their refoundation and resettlement at the end of the 9th century. Another parallel with the Strand *wic*, and in many ways a closer one, may well be the mid Saxon settlement recently located at York on the Gilbertine priory site alongside the Ouse, just outside the medieval defences, and tentatively identified as *Eoforwic* (*Medieval Archaeol*, **31**, 1987, 170; Hall 1988, 128-9).

The reasons for the widespread abandonment of the older towns are not clear. It has been suggested that the new *wics* were set up in response to the needs of a developing long distance trade, offering more favourable conditions and special immunities (Biddle 1984, 26-7; Hodges 1982, 52-5, 65). Very little is definitely known of the organisation of trade in either the old locations or the new. The main vested interests at both would have been those of the local kings or their delegates, and Ethelbald's charters for London reveal a well developed system for the collection of taxes on individual shiploads. Though changing conditions might well have called for a fresh start, the real obstacles may have been more physical than institutional or legal. The prime advantage of *Hamwic* to Winchester, like that of Fordwich to Canterbury, was access to navigable water. Similarly the problem at London is likely to have been the state of the intramural waterfront: littered with the half-submerged debris of Roman revetment timbers, cut off from the rest of the City by the riverside wall and in places severely limited by the natural terrain, it could have had little appeal, especially at a period when some ships were perhaps still designed for mooring on beaches. In that sense at least there may well have been restrictions from which the post-Roman traders would have been glad to escape to the more gently shelving and open foreshore from which the Strand was to take its name.

THE ALFREDIAN PORT

After the mid 9th century, according to the available archaeological evidence, occupation in the Strand district ceased. From the end of that century and the beginning of the 10th it was resumed, tentatively at first, within the walls of the largely deserted Roman city (Vince 1984, 435-6). The best explanation for the comprehensive reversion to the ancient site of London is the persistent series of Danish raids and invasions which occurred throughout the period. The Strand settlement is likely to have lacked any formal defences, at least on the scale of the Roman walls. Under repeated attack from as early as 841, 'London' was occupied by the Danes during the winter of 872/3, as was Fulham in 879/80. The nature and duration of this occupation, or series of occupations, are uncertain: we only know that, apparently after some fighting, London was recaptured by King Alfred in 886, was placed in the custody of the Mercian ealdorman Ethelred and was subsequently strengthened and restored (Keynes & Lapidge 1983, 97-8). Whereas in the past it was unclear precisely what was meant by this restoration, and what it implied of the previous condition of the City, recent advances in our understanding of mid Saxon London suggest that what was at issue was the reconditioning of the site of the Roman city that had not been extensively inhabited for at least four centuries. This in turn places in better perspective the one aspect of the Alfredian restoration of which there is a detailed record: the establishment of the harbour at Queenhithe. Just as the character of the Strand settlement, and the contemporary historical records, emphasise the dominant importance of riverborne trade in London, so the innovations at Queenhithe can now be seen as playing a central part in the resumption of that trade in a new physical and political context.

The evidence for Alfred's activity at Queenhithe derives from the texts of two grants which together provide a detailed insight into the workings of his policy of urban renovation. The documents are so wholly consistent with the physical evidence revealed by archaeology throughout England during the last few decades as to outweigh the suspicions of forgery invited by the late date and corrupt form of the surviving copies (discussed more fully in Dyson 1978, 200-15). In the earlier of the two, dated 889, Alfred awarded to the bishop of Worcester a measured plot of land adjoining the trading shore (*ripa emtoralis*) for use as a market, together with its profits (Sawyer 1968, no. 346). In the later, dated 898 or 899, the king awarded to the same bishop and also to the archbishop of Canterbury a plot of land each, adjacent to each other and defined by streets on all sides but the south, where the beneficiaries were further entitled to moor ships (*ibid*, no. 1628). The two plots were stated to be at 'Ethelred's hithe', identified in the 12th century with Queenhithe, and the likelihood that the same Worcester plot was involved on both occa-

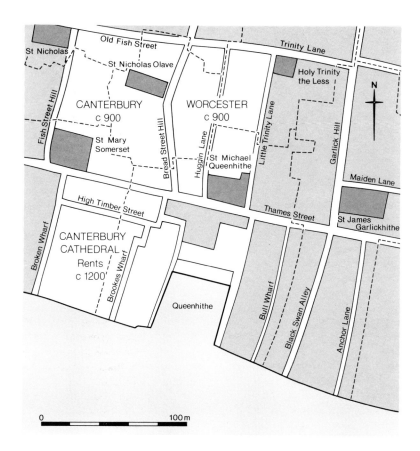

4. Plan of the Queenhithe-Timberhithe area based on the street outline of Leake's map of 1666 (simplified south of Thames Street). It shows, to the north of Thames Street, the two market plots of c.900, divided from each other by Bread Street; and, to the south, the area covered by the Canterbury cathedral rentals of c.1200, and the position of High Timber Street in relation to those features. The Canterbury rents are shown with the river frontage of 1666; in earlier centuries the frontage would have lain somewhere between this line and Timberhithe (High Timber Street). Parish boundaries are shown as dashed lines. For location of this area see Fig 65. (Based on the 1980 Ordnance Survey 1:1250 map, and reproduced with the permission of the Controller of Her Majesty's Stationery Office: Crown Copyright.) Scale 1:2500.

sions is strengthened by the measurements supplied with the earlier grant, which correspond most closely with the area on the opposite side of Thames Street from Queenhithe between Bread Street Hill (not Huggin Lane, as stated in Horsman, Milne & Milne 1988, 112) to the west, Little Trinity Lane to the east and Trinity Lane (later Knightrider Street) to the north (Fig 4). The Canterbury plot, described in 898/9 as lying to the west of the Worcester plot, must therefore have lain between Bread Street Hill to the east

and, presumably, Old Fish Street Hill to the west, opposite which area Canterbury cathedral priory owned a series of rents along the waterfront in the 12th and early 13th centuries (see below, p.19). The purpose of the second grant was evidently to confirm both Worcester and Canterbury in their existing market privileges, of which only Worcester's original award survives in the form of the 889 text. It also enhanced both beneficiaries' status by giving them the use of mooring on the foreshore, which had been specifically excluded from the earlier Worcester grant. Thus, in addition to the plots to the north, where Worcester and presumably Canterbury already held a market, both now acquired exclusive control over the riverborne traffic which supplied them.

As well as providing evidence of the restoration of trade in London, Alfred's grants are important for the light they throw on the development of the local street system as a direct consequence of the establishment of Queenhithe. Whereas the earlier text made use of measurements to define the precise location, the later text was able to depend wholly upon the existence of streets between the two plots and along their outer limits.

The natural inference from this is that Little Trinity Lane, Bread Street Hill and, probably, Old Fish Street Hill had emerged only between the dates of the two grants, 889 and 898/9, as if in conformity with another of the essential characteristics of Alfred's defended towns (Biddle 1976a, 129-30). Of these new streets, Old Fish Street Hill and Little Trinity Lane are likely to have been of only incidental importance in the development of Queenhithe, defining and articulating the settlement of the immediate area. Bread Street Hill, on the other hand, was of much broader significance for the growth of London as a whole. To re-establish trade and occupation within the ancient city in place of the settlement on the Strand, it would hardly have sufficed to leave the new harbour in a vacuum. It would also have been necessary to provide access to and from the interior of the city by extending at least one of the Queenhithe side roads further to the north. The medieval street plan, which until recently survived relatively intact in this area, shows that Bread Street, in 898/9 constituting the boundary between the Canterbury plot to the west and the Worcester plot to the east, continued as far north as Cheapside in a direct and unbroken line.

In doing so, it strongly contrasts with all but one of the neighbouring streets which run from the river to Cheapside but which are either terminated altogether by the lines of intervening east-west streets, or are staggered to the east or west beyond the point of intersection. The single exception is the line of Bow Lane and Garlick Hill, the whole of which was known in the medieval period as *Corveser* or Cordwainer Street. Like Bread Street, this too is unbroken in its course; and recent excavations at Well Court near its northern end have shown that both the earliest street levels and the earliest occupation on its eastern side date, as does Queenhithe, from the turn of the 9th and 10th centuries (Schofield, Allen & Taylor in prep). Taken together, Bread Street and Garlick Hill/Bow Lane seem to present a matching pair, the one meeting the waterfront just to the west of Queenhithe and the other meeting it a little to the east. It seems reasonable to conclude that the arrangement was deliberately designed for optimum communication with the new harbour when no other means of access was available. The two streets would also have formed the framework for an initial nucleus of settlement and activity which could readily be extended and replicated to east and west as the need arose. Both were important enough to lend their names to City wards (Bread Street and Cordwainer), and

Bread Street, commemorating one of the most basic of commodities, very probably reflects the early importance of grain, which was certainly a prominent import at Queenhithe in later centuries. Bread ovens were in evidence in the earliest occupation of Bow Lane, the grain which supplied them presumably being imported. Like the Oxford district pottery which was so prevalent in late 9th and early 10th-century London (Vince 1991, 40-1), the grain probably came from the upper Thames basin at this earlier date also.

Some idea of the special status of the harbour at Queenhithe is given by its early name of 'Ethelred's hithe', clearly borrowed from the Mercian leader who acted as Alfred's vice-regent in London. At the same time, the use of the term *ripa emtoralis* in the earlier grant, and the careful definition of mooring rights (*statio navis*) in the later, seems to imply that riverborne trade was officially confined to this particular section of the waterfront and that it was not permissible at any other. The award of a riverside market and shortly afterwards of exclusive landing rights should also be seen as marks of special confidence in Ethelred's two fellow Mercians, Bishop Werferth of Worester and Archbishop Plegmund of Canterbury, who are best known for their literary and propagandist services to Alfred (Keynes & Lapidge 1983, 92-3, 259). In effect, Werferth and Plegmund were made responsible for the running of the hithe, with the incentive of a definite stake in its profits. Whereas, a century and a half earlier, most of these would have fallen to King Ethelbald through his reeves and tax collectors in the hithe and *portus* of London, in Alfred's day a partnership appears to have been established between king, ealdorman and trusted ecclesiastics, comparable with a similar division of interests between Alfred, Ethelred and Werferth at Worcester (Dyson 1978, 211). An arrangement of this kind, which was essentially personal, is unlikely to have survived much longer than the participants, all of whom were dead by 923. Neither Canterbury nor Worcester was to retain these plots as such: the fact that the Canterbury clerks of the 13th century took their Ethelred's hithe text to concern Rotherhithe is a sure sign of the oblivion into which the Alfredian scheme had fallen — and also of the fundamental credibility of the grant.

Both Worcester and Canterbury were however to retain some property or rents within their respective areas into the early medieval period. Worcester's interests, represented in the mid 12th century by the bishop's soke (Loyd & Stenton

1950, no. 123) and in the late 13th by a small rent payment from the parish of Holy Trinity the Less (*Taxatio*, 13) had no doubt been largely supplanted by those of Henry I's queen Matilda, after whom Queenhithe was renamed. The Canterbury holdings on the other hand survived a little more intact, and were represented by the archbishop's waterfront soke recorded in the 1240s (Chew & Weinbaum 1970, no. 262) and also by a series of properties on the south side of Thames Street in the parish of St Mary Somerset, which are listed in the late 12th- and early 13th-century rentals of Canterbury cathedral priory (Bateson 1902, 483-4; Keene & Harding 1985, no. 129). This line of properties extended from Queenhithe in the east roughly as far as Broken Wharf in the west (Fig 4), and coincided with the width of the plot to the north between Bread and Fish Street Hills which Archbishop Plegmund held in 898/9. The correspondence with the archbishop's plot is further underlined by references in the Canterbury rentals to the existence of a street (*vicus*) called *Tymberhethe* which traversed the line of properties from east to west. Referred to in 13th- and 14th-century records simply as Timberhithe, or as the street or lane called Timberhithe, this feature still exists as High Timber Street and is virtually unique as a thoroughfare south of, and parallel with, Thames Street, from which until recent years it was 17m distant. Its original name strongly implies that the lane marks the line of an early and well-established hithe which at the date of the rentals of *c*.1200 had already long been superseded by the advancing waterfront, leaving room for properties on its south side. The strip of land between Thames Street and High Timber Street, extending from Queenhithe to Broken Wharf along the foot of the archbishop's former plot, may therefore represent a portion of Alfred's 'trading shore' and 'ship station', probably in the form in which it had evolved by the 11th century.

The term 'hithe' ('landing place'), which features in the names Queenhithe (or 'Ethelred's hithe') and Timberhithe, follows an established pattern in Thames place-names of the mid and late Saxon periods outside London, now somewhat disguised in such modern forms as Chelsea, Putney, Lambeth, Stepney and Erith (Ekwall 1960, 99, 375, 284, 441, 168); while 'London hithe' also occurs in Ethelbald's charters of the 740s (above, p.15). However only two other specific locations in London were named as hithes, Fishhithe and Garlickhithe, and it is notable that both lay in the close vicinity of Queenhithe and Timberhithe. Fishhithe was allegedly confirmed

to Chertsey abbey by Ethelred II in 1006-12 (Sawyer 1968, no. 940) and, like Alfred's grants at Queenhithe, included the right of mooring as well as rights in market and toll. Known by the late 13th century as 'Fishwharf' (HR 21/44, 34/99), it lay at the foot of Trig Lane not far from Broken Wharf, where the abbots of Chertsey had abandoned their quay by the early years of the century (*Cal Charter Rolls*, 16; *Cal Misc Inq*, no. 246) and which itself adjoined Timberhithe and the Canterbury rents. A short distance downstream from Queenhithe lay 'Garlickhithe', a somewhat problematic name which first occurs as late as the 1270s and was applied to the local church of St James rather than to any individual feature on the waterfront. It is nevertheless of interest in the present context in that the waterfront of St James's parish was directly linked with Cheapside by Bow Lane, whose contemporary counterpart of *c*.900, Bread Street, served Queenhithe in exactly the same way: the name Garlickhithe may therefore preserve the memory of a harbour initially perhaps of equal importance with Queenhithe, just as it is comparable in location. The restriction of hithe names to this particular sector of the waterfront opposite Cheapside is certainly suggestive of an early concentration of commercial activity stemming more or less directly from Alfred's innovations at Queenhithe, and perhaps significantly predating the foreshore locations named as 'wharf', a term which was common in London after *c*.1100 but not recorded earlier (below, p.125).

Closely comparable with Bread Street Hill and Garlick Hill/Bow Lane in date and general function is Botolph Lane, which lies downstream of London Bridge, well to the east of the Queenhithe area. In several respects Botolph Lane seems to conform to the archetypal Alfredian street. It had no Roman predecessor, its early levels were cobbled in the manner of contemporary streets at Winchester (Biddle 1976b, 450), and in the late 9th or during the 10th century was occupied on its western side by a series of adjoining premises of uniform plan and semi-industrial character which were clearly part of a single, purpose-built development within a short distance of the waterfront (Horsman, Milne & Milne 1988, 13-16). In the early medieval period it also linked the waterfront to the south with the major thoroughfares of Eastcheap and Fenchurch Street to the north, just as Bread Street and Garlick Hill linked Queenhithe with Cheapside. In this case however there is no evidence from the intensively excavated waterfront at its foot for any activity comparable with that of Queenhithe until towards the mid 11th century. At present the best explanation is that Botolph Lane was laid out in or very soon after Alfred's reign, presumably to serve an intended second centre of activity on the eastern part of the waterfront, a scheme that in the event was to be deferred for a century. Consistent with this is the general impression of a cessation in the continued redevelopment of London in the first half of the 10th century, suggested by a contrast between the rare instances of streets shown to have been established c.900 (Bow and Botolph Lanes) and the great majority, where a late 10th-century date is indicated (Vince 1991, 424-7). Alfred may have provided the initial impetus for the resettlement of the intramural city and established its basic pattern, but the completion of the process does not appear to have been taken in hand until after the middle of the 10th century. The sites here reported show what form the developments of that period took on the foreshore around the Bridgehead.

3. THE SITES: ARCHAEOLOGICAL AND DOCUMENTARY SUMMARIES

In the previous part of this report, the history of the London waterfront in the years 400-1000 was outlined, essentially as an introduction to the more detailed treatment of the 11th and 12th centuries which follows. In this third part, the discoveries of 1974-82 on the four study sites are given in detail, covering the period 400-1200.

The four sites are grouped in two pairs, reflecting their positions: New Fresh Wharf and Billingsgate Lorry Park below the Roman and medieval bridges, and Swan Lane and Seal House above the bridges. After each pair of sites the documentary evidence up to 1200 is also presented.

NEW FRESH WHARF

(Figs 5-19)

The initial excavation at New Fresh Wharf took place over three months in 1974, in two trenches 15m by 9m and 9.5m by 6.5m (Areas I and II, site code NFW74; Fig 5). Lack of time led to inadequate recording of the Saxon occupation, and the description of this part of the sequence was compiled from photographs and sections rather than from written records and plans. The sequence was however confirmed by the excavation of a further trench about 6m to the west in 1975 (Area III; site code SM75).

In 1978 redevelopment of the site led to an eight-month watching brief (site code FRE78) as the site was levelled to the north of the former New Fresh Wharf warehouse (built in 1953 and demolished in 1973). The structures first observed in 1974 and 1975 could be traced in Area V (south of Areas I, II and III) in trenches excavated for the pile caps of the new building, and in the stripping of Area IV, north of the original excavations. In addition, Area I was excavated below the 1974 limit of excavation, and further evidence of Saxon

5. *New Fresh Wharf: areas of excavation I-V, with their site-codes, and the line of the ward boundary between Bridge and Billingsgate Wards. Scale 1:1250.*

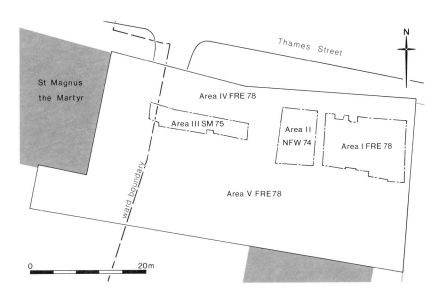

occupation was found. The excavations were supervised by Louise Miller (Areas I, IV, V), Gerald Clewley (Area II) and John Schofield (Area III); this summary is based upon the archive report by Louise Miller (1985).

The Roman strata on this site, which included two major stages of Roman land reclamation ending in an early 3rd-century timber waterfront and traces of the late 3rd-century Roman riverside wall, have already been published (Miller, Schofield & Rhodes 1986). The present report is concerned with the post-Roman strata reported in archive as Period 2 and Period 3 (Phases 1-4), and covering the period up to c.1200.

Period 2.1: the post-Roman riverbank
(3rd to 11th centuries)

(summarised in Fig 56 below)

A black silty gravel deposit in the north-east corner of Area I probably represented post-Roman silting. Its top was levelled at 1.7m OD and it sloped down to the south and west to 1.04m OD. This layer was seen to overlie a dark silt deposit which may have been dumped but which clearly overlay the timber piles of the early 3rd-century Roman quay at a height of 1.21m OD, and was recorded in Area IV rising north against the lower ragstone courses of the late Roman riverside wall to a height of 2.18m OD. It formed the river bank prior to the Period 2.4 clay embankment (see below p.29), and thus probably spanned Phases 1 to 3. To the south of the quay layers of light brown silty gravel extended for about 15m, becoming progressively deeper in the south (in Area V). These gravels were probably river-laid.

The superstructure of the quay may have fallen into disrepair before its destruction by either natural or human agency. In Area II, five of the quayfront beams were still *in situ*, three on the west and two on the east. The upper beams had either collapsed or been removed deliberately for reuse. The silts, coarse gravels and organic material 0.6m deep that probably formed the last phase of dumping within the structure of the quay slumped southwards over the undisturbed Roman beams. These layers contained large quantities of Roman material, especially fine colour-coated wares, which are unlikely to have been river-laid but might have been affected by the river, and they were sealed by a thin layer of fine gravel with organic lenses. They formed the edge of the river bank in Phase 1.

North of Area II, in Area IV, layers of black to grey silty sand with a high humic content and lenses of oyster shell were found against the Roman riverside wall at a level of 1.33m OD. These joined up with the deposits in Area II, 3.4m to the south at 1m OD. They were presumably deposited in the Roman period and they formed the surface of the river bank at the beginning of Period 2, the Saxon period.

At the west end of Area III the upper beams of the early 3rd-century quay were absent. A number of random timbers found in the silts on either side of the quay had either collapsed from the decaying structure or been discarded by the robbers. The quayfront was robbed down to the massive sill-beam itself, which was absent at the extreme west end, but *in situ* cradling timbers and ground piles indicated its former presence. The beams must have been removed by human agency for their size would have prevented them being washed away by the river, and cuts in the tie-backs to the north of the quay suggest deliberate robbing of the structure, though the date of robbing is uncertain. The timbers from the quay which lay on the foreshore to the south were covered by mixed silty gravel and fine silt with some organic material. These deposits contained mostly Roman material. It seems likely that material once dumped inside the quay had been brought southwards by river action after the robbing, and formed the foreshore of Period 2 Phase 1. Two cuts were observed in the silts, creating a shallow east-west trench about 0.4m deep and backfilled with fine silt and gravel. These could be construction trenches for the Phase 2 posts which were found immediately south of the Roman quay, but the majority of the posts had no construction trench, so that the position of the posts in the trenches may be coincidental.

North of Area III the post-Roman foreshore or river bank consisted of a layer of grey sandy gravel and silt with small fragments of ragstone, with larger ragstone fragments scattered on its surface. It reached a maximum of 1.12m OD against the timber piles of the late Roman riverside wall, sloping to the west to reach 0.68m OD at the western limit of excavation. In Area V, to the south of Area III, similar material was recorded sloping down to −1.80m OD and containing a squared Roman timber with a cross-section of 390 × 330mm which had probably come from the quayfront.

Dating evidence from the silts which covered the dismantled quay contained a range of pottery with a latest date of CP3 (1020-1050), but as these silts were not sealed until Phase 4 with the construction of the clay embankments, they must have been susceptible to contamination.

Period 2.2: Rubble bank and grid of stakes
(late 10th/early 11th century)

(Figs 6-10)

In Area II, a bank of flint, chalk and ragstone rubble including Roman building material lay on the slope of the shelving strand south of the Roman quayfront (Fig 7). The northern edge of this bank covered the extant third beam of the Roman quay and was levelled at Ordnance Datum. The maximum depth recorded for the bank was 0.3m OD but it seemed to gain in depth as it spread southwards. Retaining the northern edge of the bank was the displaced fourth beam of the Roman quay, which measured over 4.4m long east-west and rested on the northern ends of

6. New Fresh Wharf: planking from a clinker-built boat reused as a surface at the east end of the rubble bank; looking north. Scale 10 × 100mm.

fourteen silver birch poles which lay horizontally in an east-west row at irregular intervals of between 70 and 510mm. Their sections ranged from 120 to 150mm in diameter with a maximum length of 1.30m, although none was excavated completely. The birch had been roughly shaped in each case but bark survived on some of them. The rubble bank appeared to continue south under the birch logs, and clayey silt and rubble was excavated between them but to no great depth.

Above the birch poles lay the strakes from a clinker-built boat (Fig 6). These were aligned east-west covering an area 4.1m × 1.7m. Some of them were still pegged together with wooden trenails and the seams caulked with moss. The maximum width of the strakes, which were of oak, was 310mm and most of them were 30mm thick or slightly more. No internal fittings of the boat were found and it was clearly taken to pieces before being laid on top of the birch poles to form a horizontal surface. South of the boat timbers, on the same level (−0.34m OD), were further planks with a maximum width of 290mm. There was also a single post, its top notched, just to the south of the displaced Roman beam.

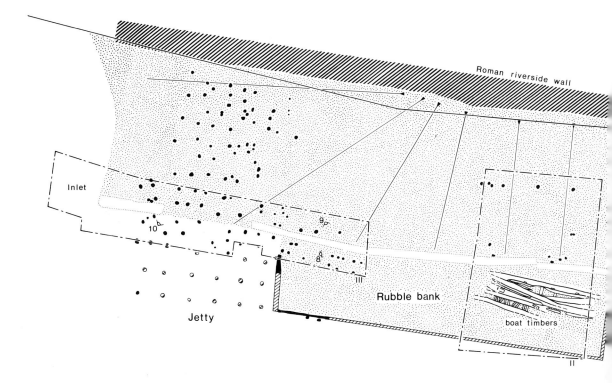

Roman riverside wall

Inlet

10

9

8

III

Jetty

Rubble bank

boat timbers

II

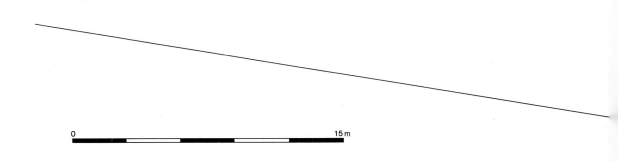

River Thames

0   15 m

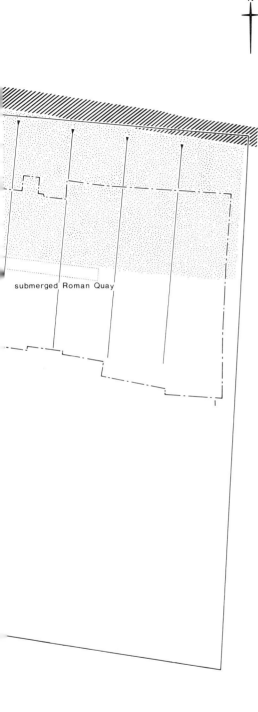

N

submerged Roman Quay

7. *New Fresh Wharf: the late 10th- or early 11th-century rubble bank and grid of driven stakes (Period 2.2) constructed over the post-Roman riverbank (Period 2.1). Scale 1:200.*

North of both the rubble bank and the former Roman quay front was a row of nine irregularly spaced vertical posts, with lengths ranging from 0.8 to 1.4m and diameters from 70 to 240mm. The greatest concentration of these posts was in the east where the third Roman quayfront beam had been removed. The maximum height recorded was 0.6m OD but if the posts were upright they would probably have reached a level of 1.4m OD. North of these posts the Roman piles had decayed to a level of 1.1m OD. Six further silver birch posts were added to the northernmost line of Roman piles lying about 3.6m north of the rubble bank and driven into the river bank/foreshore of Period 2.1. The diameters of the posts varied from 120 to 150mm, with a maximum height of 0.8m; some retained bark. At least two were inserted in post-pits which were then filled with rubble. The two rows of posts to the north of the rubble bank may have supported a superstructure, though they were perhaps too far apart (over 3m), and may instead have held an east-west revetment, or fence, in place.

In Area V and to the south of Area II, rubble and broken Roman tile (both *tegulae* and *imbrices*) at −0.34m OD continued the embankment southwards but appeared to end abruptly about 4m south of the Roman quay. This vertical edge must have been the southern limit of the rubble bank, any facing presumably having been later robbed. It also extended westwards for about 2.5m to within 3.6m of Area III. No boat timbers were observed but there were some planks on the surface of the bank and occasional horizontal timbers within. No posts projected from the surface of this rubble.

At the east end of Area III a second length of rubble bank of ragstone, chalk and occasional flint, Roman tiles, oyster shells and pebbles packed together with a little silty clay, was built against the front of the Roman quay, which was left standing three beams high (Fig 8). From its western end, which was clearly established, the bank extended at least 5m to the east, and was exposed for 1.5m north-south. The west end, revetted by a tree-trunk laid north-south which was pegged in position by oak stakes, coincided with the end of the third beam of the quay. The bank was solidly constructed with a timber lacing of oak branches about 2m long aligned east-west, with sections up to 190mm in diameter, roughly trimmed. There was also one large boulder about 1m square included in its make-up. This bank was in a similar stratigraphic position and level to that in Area II but differed in that it was built round

8. *New Fresh Wharf: the rubble bank in the eastern part of Area III, set around driven stakes and retained at its northern edge by remnants of the 3rd-century Roman quay (the Roman dumps having been partially excavated); looking north-east. Scale 5 × 100mm.*

9. *Part of the rubble bank at New Fresh Wharf Area III, looking south-east. The rubble has been laid against remaining elements of the late Roman quayfront, and around upright stakes which may have supported a planked walkway. Scale 2 × 100mm.*

two rows of stakes aligned east-west with a distance of about 0.35m between each row and irregular intervals of between 0.2 and 0.7m between the posts in each row. They were all of oak except one which was a soft wood, with diameters of 100 to 160mm, and their fully excavated height was up to 3.13m, of which just over 1m projected from the rubble bank, 1m was enclosed by the rubble bank (which was 1m high)

and 1m was driven into the Phase 1 foreshore below (Fig 9). The southern posts had collapsed forward and were broken but the northern ones reached 1.18m OD and their tops had tapered, probably as a result of decay.

10. New Fresh Wharf: the vertical posts of the jetty in Area III, driven into dumps north of the late Roman quayfront; the 5 × 100mm scale stands on the sillbeam of the quay. The direction of view is north-eastwards; in section behind are the dumps of timber and clay forming the overlying embankments.

In the silty deposits to the north of both the Roman quay front and the rubble bank stood a row of posts consisting of roughly shaped oak branches up to 160mm in diameter and 1.38m high, 0.6-2m apart. Smaller posts of triangular, semi-circular or circular section ran north from the western end of this row of posts, corresponding with the western limit of the rubble bank to the south. Some of these posts were almost completely covered by a layer of silting (Period 2.3) when found, and had possibly been shortened following disuse. They all leaned at an angle of as much as 75 degrees from the vertical, and some had several small stakes round their base to hold them in position. The maximum length was 1.51m.

In Area V, a further portion 2.27m (north-south) by 3m (east-west) of the rubble bank was excavated, in which chalk and ragstone rubble and smaller pebbles were packed around horizontal east-west timbers up to 2m long and 120mm in diameter. Towards the south these timbers were held in position by oak stakes, representing the vertical southern limit of the rubble bank about 3.8m south of the former Roman quay.

In Area III, about 1m west of the western boundary of the rubble bank, an irregular grid of posts covered an area approximately 3m north-south by 7.5m east-west, of which both eastern and western limits were clearly defined in the excavation (Figs 6, 10). There were five to seven posts in each east-west row, with two rows to the north of the line of the Roman quay and three to the south. Roughly 1m separated each row north-south and there was an interval of 0.7m to 1m between each post east-west. Where the posts were vertical and had not been crushed by later deposits or shortened, they survived to between 1.2 and 1.6m OD, with a maximum of 1.7m OD. This left at least 2m of post projecting from the foreshore (see Fig 10). As the foreshore sloped southwards the posts were longer; those to the north of the Roman quay were 2.6m-3m long and those to the south 3.4m-4m long. Most of the posts had circular sections of between 0.14 and 0.2m diameter, averaging 0.16m. They were chamfered at 1m above the base and were weathered above that point. One Roman pile, its top coming to a point at 0.44m OD, was included in this group of timbers. Three of the posts were found in shallow trenches filled with clay but it is uncertain whether these were construction trenches (see Period 2.1 above). All the posts were of oak. The western edge of the posts consisted of eleven posts in a rough north-south alignment, all of which were either shortened subsequently or pointed

towards the west. Those to the north of the Roman quay front were driven into a compact layer of mortar, rubble (including a large boulder) and Roman tile fragments packed with brown clay, revetted at its southern edge by the extant Roman sill beam; south of the quay a large amount of rubble lay around the base of the posts. The rubble may originally have been deposited in the Roman period within the quay structure, but some of it at least was found packed around the base of the Saxon posts.

In Area IV, the grid of posts found in Area III continued to the north to within 0.5-1m of the Roman riverside wall which at this point survived to a level of between 2m and 2.4m OD, over 0.5m lower than to the east. A total of 49 further posts were excavated and recorded in the same definitive area of 7.5m east to west. With the posts excavated in Area III in 1975 there were thirteen more east-west rows, the two northerly rows 0.2-0.4m apart and the others 0.5-0.9m apart north-south with 0.4-0.8m between each post east-west. There were some gaps in the grid, possibly because of truncation below the level of 0.75m OD which was the limit of the contractor's excavation. One Roman pile with a rounded top was reused *in situ* in this grid but there were few Roman piles in this area showing above 0.75m OD. These posts were up to 0.2m in diameter and only 1.91m long, with a chamfer of 0.6m at the base and 1.31m projecting from the river bank. Though they were about half the size of the southern posts found in Area III their tops survived to about the same level of 1.3 to 1.5m OD; where the ground rose to the north the posts were shorter, with the result that all their tops were at the same level. The easternmost north-south row of posts contained more posts than the others and these were closer together at 0.2-0.6m apart. However, some of these posts may have been later additions to the eastern boundary; during Period 2.4 more posts of a shorter length were added to the eastern boundary where seen in Area III, though this distinction was not apparent in Area IV.

One oak stake 0.14m in diameter was found in Area V. It is likely to have been part of the grid of stakes, extending it at least 13m south of the Roman riverside wall. Although there was no direct stratigraphic relationship between the bank and the stakes, they both overlay the same foreshore deposits and both were overlain by the Period 2.4 embankments, implying contemporaneity. The position of the solitary stake directly opposite the southern edge of the rubble bank, and the observation that the lines of vertical stakes set within the rubble bank appear to have continued lines of stakes to the west, may indicate that the two structures functioned together.

The dating evidence for this phase is sparse. The timber-laced rubble embankment found in Area II and the east end of Area III sealed the silts of Period 2.1; the grid of stakes to its west was an open structure, cut into the silts of 2.1. The ceramic evidence was slight and the dating relies on radio-carbon (c14) and dendrochronological analysis. A number of timbers from the rubble bank were sampled, birch logs from the eastern part yielding a c14 date of AD 760-980 (sigma = 100; University of Birmingham 548; all c14 dates calibrated according to tables in Stuiver & Becker 1988). One stake from the jetty structure to the west was sampled, giving a c14 date of 885-1019 (sigma = 80; HAR1422). Although several timbers from both the bank and the jetty were sampled for dendrochronological analysis, none provided a date. One of the boat timbers was dated by dendrochronology to 915-55, considerably earlier than its date of reuse on the bank. The mutually exclusive siting of the bank and the jetty provided no stratigraphic evidence that one was later than the other.

No evidence was found of Period 2.2 construction in Area I in 1974 or 1978.

Period 2.3: Foreshore deposits
(CP3, 1020-50)

Fine sandy gravel and silt south of the line of the Roman quay in Area I may belong to this phase but there were no structures of Period 2.2 against which the silt could have been deposited. The silt was levelled at −0.35m OD to −1.5m OD, 9m south of the quay. In Area II some silt overlay the boat timbers of the previous phase, whilst some 5m south of Area II thin deposits of fine grey silt interleaved with sands and coarser gravels, 0.33m thick in total, comprised river-laid deposits forming the foreshore prior to the Period 2.4 construction. In Area III, silts from inside the former Roman quay spilled outwards over the line of the sill-beam and mixed with water-laid deposits of fine gravel, and silting built up on the foreshore around the posts of Period 2.2 to a level of 0.2m OD. There was only a slight trace of sand and gravel in the east where the rubble bank stood, and none overlying the bank. In Area V, sands and gravels were recorded at −1.48m c.9m south of Area III.

Pottery recovered from the riverlaid silts which sealed the construction trenches of some of the stakes of Period 2.2, and also from those which accumulated around other posts, was assigned to CP3 (1020-50), whilst the silt which lay over the boat timbers contained a few sherds of Late Saxon Shelly ware (CP1 or later).

Period 2.4: Clay embankments based on timber and brushwood
(c.1020 to c.1090)

(Figs 11-16)

Three of the five adjacent embankments excavated were constructed in two stages, an initial timber and brushwood base, followed by a clay capping; in the phasing structure of the archive report these two stages have been split into two sub-phases, 2.4a and 2.4b. In the two remaining embankments no such distinction existed.

The five embankments (overall plan, Fig 11) can be seen to conform in the main to the boundaries of later medieval tenements (see Fig 19), whose numbering (2-6) has accordingly been adopted in the following description.

Areas III, IV and IV: embankments with timber bases to west and east

Tenement 2

On the west side of Area III, and to the north and south of it, was an embankment, based on clay and timber, and phased as Period 2.4a. Against the west side of the property boundary between this embankment and that on Tenement 3 (to the east), there was a layer of alder roots packed with organic material and blue-grey clay. This was 0.85-1.3m thick, extended 3.9-5m westwards, and was overlain to the west at 0.39m OD by layers of timber which consisted of branches, planks and reused worked fragments (Fig 12) forming a bank 0.7-1m thick. The western edge of the timbers was formed by five planks aligned north-south, piled between and over posts of Period 2.2. A number of post-holes to the west may be associated with this boundary, which lay on the edge of an adjacent inlet; they were overlain by sands and gravels (in Period 3.1) which also overlay the western edge of the timber group. North of the west part of Area III, no further

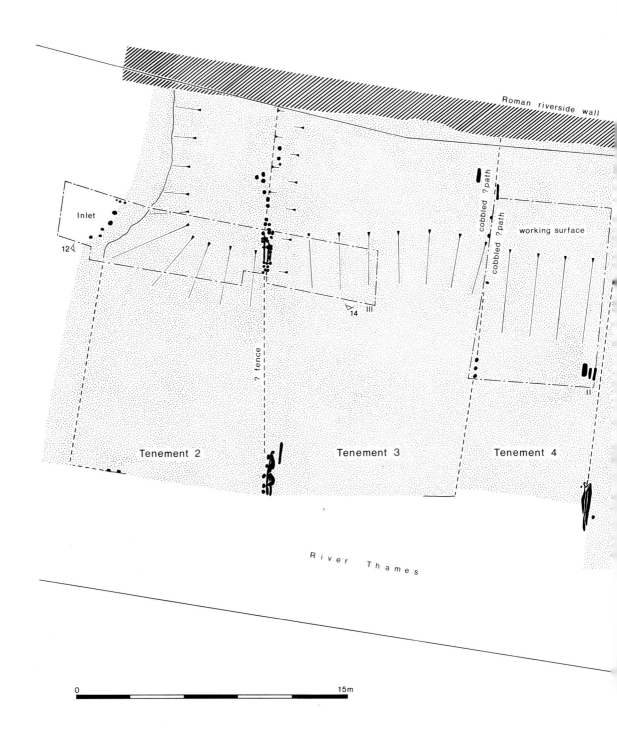

Roman riverside wall

Inlet

12

cobbled ?path

working surface

cobbled ?path

? fence

14 III

II

Tenement 2

Tenement 3

Tenement 4

River Thames

0   15m

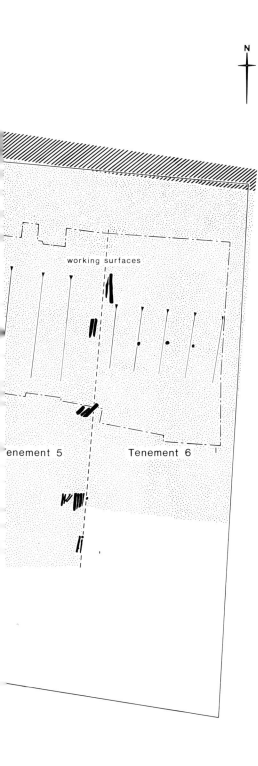

working surfaces

Tenement 5   Tenement 6

11. New Fresh Wharf: the Period 2.4 mid 11th-century clay embankments, with property divisions and tenement numbers indicated. Scale 1:200.

worked timbers were found at the base of the embankment, but alder roots and occasional branches formed a continuous layer westwards from the boundary fence (with Tenement **3**) to the limit of excavation, and continued north to the Roman riverside wall where they were packed against the exposed tops of the foundation piles, slightly underlying the masonry foundation and possibly filling an eroded area. The top of the layer was levelled at 1.46m OD. Further to the west the northern limit of the deposit lay about 0.8m south of the Roman riverside wall. South of Area III, the cut timbers and branches packed with clay were seen against the west side of the boundary fence about 20m south of the Roman riverside wall. The base of the timbers was levelled at −2m OD 20.7m south of the Roman riverside wall, and the full extent of the embankment was established with the southern limit against an east-west row of vertical posts, with rectangular cross-sections of 0.2m × 0.14m.

Further construction above the clay and timbers was phased as Period 2.4b. Above the layer of clay and alder roots on the west side of the property boundary there was a thin deposit of organic material and sedge which may represent debris collecting on the primary layer of timbers. This was covered by a relatively clean layer of blue-grey clay, 0.58m thick, revetted by occasional horizontal timbers. This was laid against the west side of the posts and planks of the fence (Fig 14) where it was levelled at about 1m OD, and was fairly level for 5.3m east-west. To the north it was packed against the foundations of the Roman riverside wall, levelled at 1.67m OD, but was not traced south of Area III. The length of this section of embankment was about 20.7m from north to south and its width was about 8m at Lower Thames Street and 11m towards the river.

Tenement 3

At the eastern end of Area III, the rubble bank of Period 2.2 and the gravelly foreshore of Period 2.3 were sealed by a 0.65m-thick layer of blue-grey clay (phased as Period 2.4a), containing cut branches, and extending to a north-south row of posts and planks at the point where the second beam of the Roman quayfront had been sawn through, about 2m west of the edge of the earlier rubble bank. The posts in this boundary were very closely spaced, about 100-200mm apart, possibly with one or two reused from Period 2.2. Eight of the posts lay north of the Roman quay

12. *New Fresh Wharf: unworked timbers comprising the base of the embankment on Tenement 2, laid around surviving posts of the earlier jetty (compare Fig 10). The clay capping to the timbers is visible in section behind. Looking north-east; scale 5 × 100mm.*

14. *New Fresh Wharf: the west side of the fence between the embankments on Tenements 2 and 3, in Area III, looking north-east. The 5 × 100mm scale stands on one of the piles of the Roman quay, in the silt beneath.*

13. *New Fresh Wharf: secondary stage of Period 2.4 embankment construction, Tenement 3, at the east end of Area III. Looking north-east; scale 2 × 100mm.*

front with maximum diameters of 200mm and lengths of 2.6m, reaching a level of 1.6m OD. The lower part of the post was chamfered at the level of the Period 2.3 foreshore and whereas the majority of the posts of Period 2.2 were driven

deep into the Roman levels down to a depth of −2.34m OD, these barely penetrated the latter and reached only −1.4m OD. The row of posts was continued by six others south of the Roman quay, having the same sections and heights but either bent over or broken with the upper part leaning south at an angle of approximately 30 degrees. Planks and branches were rammed in between the posts to form a rough hurdling aligned north-south (see Fig 14). The timber group which lay to the east of the hurdling contained semi-worked north-south timbers sloping down to the base of the hurdling and east-west timbers piled up against the hurdling, so that there was a marked hollow on the east side. To the north, the western limit of the embankment was marked by a rough revetment or fence comprising a concentration of planks and other worked timbers (including one with a mortice) laid around a north-south line of closely spaced posts (some of which may have been reused *in situ* from Period 2.2) and held in place by small pieces of ragstone rubble on the east side. The clay and timber sloped gradually from the west side of Area II, where it was levelled at 1.10m OD, to 0.5m OD at the east end of Area III, and to 0.18m OD against the boundary with Tenement **2**. Immediately west of Area II it was overlain by bands of organic material and large pieces of ragstone rubble based on north-south horizontal timbers, the same layers of rubble as were noted on the west side of Area II (below, p.34). They covered an area 2m east-west and 4m north-south and seemed to form the division between two properties (**3** and **4**), and may also have formed the base of a pathway leading to the river. South of Area III, deposits of clay, branches and worked timber overlay the foreshore layers, and were laid against a continuation of the western boundary fence, which consisted of posts 2.47-2.9m long with roughly rectangular or circular cross-sections of 140-250mm. The bases of the posts were either rounded or chamfered 0.6m from the base with axe-cut facets 70mm wide. These posts were dated by dendrochronological analysis to later than 1014. The timber and clay base of this embankment came to an end 19.75m south of the Roman riverside wall.

Over the primary clay and timber base was some further construction phased as Period 2.4b. At the east end of Area III a depression in the primary deposit of clay and timbers was filled with clay and covered with a compact mass of small branches (Fig 13). Additional timbers formed a rough box structure with north-south horizontal timbers about 2.8m apart and east-west timbers spanning the interval towards the south. None of the timbers was jointed to each other, although they were all worked. A further layer of blue-grey clay was packed around the timbers, overlying the matting of branches. A large amount of ragstone was found scattered on the primary clay and timber deposit to the west, and this may have been the remains of a small area of surfacing to the embankment at a level of about 0.59m OD. The division between the dumps constituting this embankment and those pertaining to Period 3.2 was not clear-cut in Area III, but the north-south hurdling was raised at some stage and it seems likely that the deposits against the upper parts of the hurdling were later. The clay first recorded in the western baulk of Area II (see below) continued northwards to the foundations of the Roman riverside wall where it was levelled at 1.68m OD, being fairly level for 7m north-south and 3m east-west, and it was seen to have continued uninterrupted for a distance of 10m from the west side of Area II, running up to a marked depression, 1.5m wide, on the east side of the boundary fence, where the timbers of the primary deposit were visible. This was presumably a continuation of the hollow seen further south, and which may have been a boundary ditch. This embankment, on the eastern side of Area III, and to the north and south of it, measured 19.75m north-south from the Roman riverside wall, and was 12m wide at both north and south.

Areas II, IV and V: clay embankment on brushwood base

Tenement 4

In Area II, a brushwood base (phased as Period 2.4a) of birch twigs, oak branches, fragments of planks and rough hewn logs sealed all previous deposits. These were laid in bundles north-south and east-west, giving the effect of matting (Fig 15). This was 0.6m deep towards the north where it was levelled at 1.1m OD. It sloped gradually towards the south, over the boat timbers of 2.2a, and here the twigs became finer and were aligned mainly east-west, being levelled at Ordnance Datum on the east side and slightly higher to the west. The bank became noticeably less thick at the southern extremity of the trench where there was an east-west line of rubble surrounding stakes and short planks, possibly the remains of a revetment. The brushwood base continued north into

Area IV, where it consisted of twigs and branches 20-40mm in diameter, and was found against the foundation raft of the Roman riverside wall at 1.32m OD, and south into Area V, where oak branches and clay packing extended to a southern edge where erosion seems to have taken place and where the face of the bank had slumped southwards. Black silt and sand represented silting against the southern edge of the embankment (phased in 3.1). At its southern limit, the eastern edge of the bank was marked by a group of horizontal timbers, including a sapling with the roots still attached, which had been rammed between vertical stakes to form the eastern boundary.

Over the brushwood base was some further construction, phased as Period 2.4b. In Area II, horizontal logs and edge-set planks rested on broken Roman tiles scattered on the surface of the brushwood. These formed a rough open-sided square about 2.3m across. The timbers were not jointed to one another but were held in position by small stakes. Against the south face of this feature, at about 2.5m from the southern limit of the excavation, there was a mass of ragstone and chalk blocks which extended east-west for 4.25m around a revetment of stakes (50-80mm in diameter) and wattle work of branches with larger horizontal east-west timbers levelled at 1.08m OD (Fig 16). North of the revetment the primary brushwood 'mat' was covered by blue-grey clay and rubble which was sealed by a thin spread of wood chips, thin planks, twigs and branches. Blue-grey clay and rubble with peat lenses and occasional twigs covered this and extended north and south of the east-west revetment described above. South of this revetment there was one further layer of blue-grey clay and rubble, whose top was 0.6m above the primary brushwood, levelled at 0.75m OD. The southern limit of this layer lay on the edge of the excavated area; in 1978, a section was obtained continuing south from Area II into the baulk which had been unexcavated in 1974, and this showed that the thin brushwood matting continued southwards but that the blue-grey clay above did not. A timber

15. New Fresh Wharf: Period 2.4 brushwood base to Tenement 4 embankment, looking north-west; scale 10 × 100mm.

16. New Fresh Wharf: internal revetment within Tenement 4 embankment, looking north. This revetment lay within the area of excavation shown on Tenement 4 in Fig 11; however, it is not shown in plan because the working surface marked on that figure would have covered it.

plate supported by five stakes was also found in the northern part of Area II, though the semi-circular mortice 65mm deep in its upper surface was empty, and while the plate bears some resemblance to one found to the south in a later phase, which possibly was part of a building, it seems likely that this was simply a random timber at the base of the clay bank.

North of the east-west revetment the clay was not uniform and lay in horizontal bands alternating with thin bands of organic matter, gravel, mortar or burnt clay. This dumped material reached a level of 2.06m OD, ie about 1m above the primary brushwood. The upper layer of clay, light green-grey rather than blue-grey in colour, was compacted, with gravel on its surface. This was also recorded to the north, where against the ragstone base of the Roman riverside wall at a height of 1.85m OD was a layer of blue-grey clay 0.38-1.25m thick growing progressively deeper towards the south, with a fairly level grey-green surface sealed by coarse orange sand and medium gravel. This clay contained tip lines of organic material with reddened flint gravel, grey sandy silt, and organic material with wood chips, small bones and tile fragments. Indications of the boundary between this embankment and that to the west were seen on the extreme west side of the trench, where a line of ragstone rubble running north-south for 2.5m was sealed by further layers of blue-grey clay and then by further ragstone rubble, based on horizontal timbers, which included a reused anchor stone contained within organic material. Tipping over this was a different deposit of clay only seen in section on the extreme west side of the trench, and this was probably clay from the adjacent embankment. This clay was 1m thick and, apart from the organic material at its base, was quite clean. Burnt wood, brown clay and mortar sealed the clay, possibly forming a surface at 1.99m OD. Further south this western boundary was not so clear. This unit of the embankment was 19m long (north-south) from the face of the Roman riverside wall, and at least 6.4m wide.

Areas I, IV and V: clay embankments to west and east

Tenement 5

A clay embankment was recorded on the west side of Area I, and to the north and south of it in Areas IV and V. The direct relationship of the clay with

the Roman riverside wall was not seen, as the foundations of the modern street frontage lay immediately south of the Roman wall, though at its northernmost point, about 1.1m south of the wall, the clay was 0.2m deep. Its surface was fairly level for about 6m southwards from the Roman wall though it increased in depth to 0.7m over the sloping river bank, and rose to a height of 2.05m OD. It was found to be a solid, clean deposit of blue-grey clay without organic traces and only occasional timbers, and there were no timbers at its base until it passed over the line of the old Roman quay. South of this line the base of the clay was at a lower level over the earlier foreshore and contained brushwood 20-50mm thick, Roman tile and flint rubble (possibly the remains of an internal revetment) and east-west worked timbers. A concentration of north-south worked timbers lay towards the east and probably marked a property boundary. Some of the timbers, including one with a chase mortice, were reused but others were semi-worked and seemed to be waste material. Two of the timbers were sampled for dendrochronological analysis (FRE 575A, 575B); only FRE 575A provided a date, having been felled sometime after 942. The clay continued for 8m south of Area I, and at its southern extremity, where truncated, it contained horizontal lenses of very peaty silt, decayed whelk shells, snail and oyster shells. Within the clay were oak branches 35-50mm in diameter, oak planks and other semi-worked timbers, which, like those further north, lay particularly towards the east where there was a later medieval and post-medieval property boundary; to the west the clay was also seen to lie against the fence incorporating the trimmed sapling (see above, Tenement 4) which formed the western property boundary. In the north-west corner of Area I, the clay was sealed by a layer of black clayey loam with yellow clay and charcoal lenses which contained Saxon pottery (of CP3, 1020-50) and was in turn sealed by a deposit of red clay at a level of about 2.25m OD. A similar sequence was found no more than half a metre to the north, where the clay was sealed by grey-brown and orange sands and grey silts and pebbles. South of these was a gravel metalling composed of pebbles and fragments of Roman tile set in a grey-green mortar, 120mm deep at 1.95m OD, and east of this the clay was either cut or sloped down to 1.3m OD. The organic deposit and the adjacent gravel metalling to the west probably represented activity on the surface of the clay bank, but this could not be defined in plan very clearly. The embankment on the west side of Area I was 21-22.5m long (north-south), and measured 9m in width at its northern end and 10m on the river frontage.

Tenement 6

On the east side of Area I, and to the north of it, organic material with oyster shells and wood chips sealed the river bank of Period 2.1 and 2.3, running up to 1.10m south of the riverside wall. On the surface of this layer, which varied from 150 to 900mm in depth, were timber planks of various sizes and large ragstone blocks. These formed the base for a dump of blue-grey clay which extended from a point 3.3m south of the wall, sloping gently south from about 2m OD for several metres, before dropping sharply to about 0.80m OD; the point where the level of the bank changed was found to coincide with the line of the Roman quay, and here there was an east-west row of posts about 1.3m apart. These posts were not completely excavated but are thought to be part of an internal revetment. South of the quay the clay bank was based on numerous horizontal timbers and abutted a further group of north-south horizontal timbers, axe-cut branches and worked fragments 1.5-1.81m long, which formed the boundary between the eastern and western clay banks in Area I. The clay, with occasional timbers within it, continued south of Area I into Area V for about 2.16m. The organic base to the clay also continued and while the clay could not be traced with certainty more than 16m south of the Roman riverside wall, organic material of a similar consistency was found a further 2m to the south. A deposit of sand and small pebbles and tile fragments overlay the organic material near the riverside wall, and this same surface was seen to the south in Area I, where a deposit of grey sand and mortar with gravel, 200mm thick, was recorded on the upper part of the clay bank, with an identical deposit at a lower level to the south. These fairly compact layers probably formed the surface of the embankment rather than make-up for any later building in the vicinity. The total length (north-south) of the raised embankment on the east side of Area I was c.18m and its width c.7m.

The two banks in Area I butted against the same group of timbers forming the property boundary and there is therefore little doubt that they were contemporary.

Dating and discussion

The division of the second Saxon embankment into Period 2 Phases 4a and 4b arose from the two stages of construction which were evident in three of the recorded sub-units: a base of brushwood or worked, but waste, timber, followed by an upper clay bank. The dating evidence suggests no great difference in date between the two stages and they are taken here as simply representing separate episodes in the construction of a single embankment. Differences in construction however indicate that the embankment was made up of several probably contemporary parts or units east-west. The continued use of some boundaries established in this phase into the medieval period suggests that the tenements which can be identified from documentary sources in the late 13th-early 14th centuries (below, p.73-4) were based on older divisions of the waterfront, thus justifying the introduction of the numbers assigned to the medieval tenements into the description of their 11th-century predecessors. The dating evidence comes from radiocarbon (C14), dendrochronology and pottery. The embankment is now summarised from west to east.

There were two embankment units in Area III, both based on branches and waste timbers. They were divided by a property boundary consisting of piles with planks and branches rammed between them; this division later became the boundary between Tenement 2 to the east and Tenement 3 to the west. Dendrochronology suggests a date of 942+ for a plank in Area III (SM 183) but the piles in this area cannot be dated. The timber base of both units continued south into Area V, where one large but weathered timber (FRE 3005) from the eastern unit is dated by dendrochronology to 978+. The boundary was also sampled; a pile from the fence (FRE 3008) was felled after 1014. There was no sapwood but the piles were apparently not re-used timbers. The boundary between 2 and 3, then, dates from after 1014; this would date the construction of Tenement 3, though not necessarily Tenement 2. It is possible that the embankments on these properties were not constructed at the same time; the small amount of pottery associated with the construction of the embankment on Tenement 3 is assigned to CP2 (1000-20) or later, while the strata comprising construction on Tenement 2 produced a single sherd of CP4 (1050-1100) among a CP3 (1020-50) assemblage.

The next property, in Area II, was based on

Roman riverside wall

Inlet

? path

? path

III

building

internal revetment

cobbled surface

2

II

3

4

cobbled su

? platform

River Thames

0   15 m

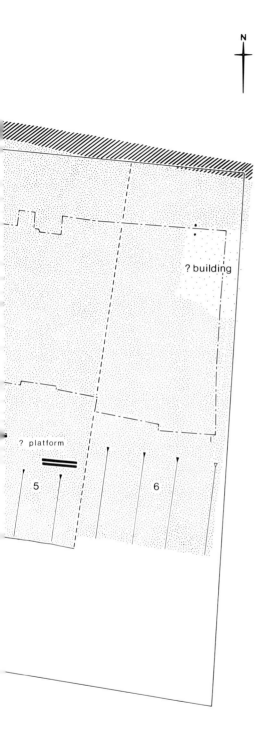

brushwood. A sample of this (NFW [II] 94) is dated by C14 equally possibly to the ranges 981-1004 or 1089-1123 (sigma = 80; HAR-2542). The upper bank consisted of bands of clay and organic matter containing late Saxon pottery, not conclusively later than that contained in the brushwood base. This embankment corresponded with Tenement **4** of the medieval period.

There were two units in Area I, corresponding to Tenements **5** and **6** in the medieval period, and divided by a property boundary with a timber dated to 942+ (NFW 575A). There was no sapwood and the timbers were probably re-used. Pottery of CP3 (1020-50) was recovered from the material dumped in the construction of these embankments.

Although two boundaries are dated, the vagueness of the dates and the lack of datable timbers for the third boundary means that any suggestion of piecemeal building, either from the east or from the west, cannot be made with any confidence. On the contrary, the nearly common southern boundary of the embankments, and similarities in construction, argue for a broadly common date of building. The ceramic dating indicates that the embankments on Tenements **3** to **6**, at least, were built during CP3 (1020-50). The embankment on Tenement **2**, built over the area of the previous stakes of Period 2.2, may have been slightly later, extending west from the stout boundary of Tenement **3**. The silts of Period 2.3 in the area of the stakes and beneath the Tenement **2** embankment contained CP3 pottery; although this could be the result of contamination from the overlying embankment, it may be that it represents silting contemporary with the Tenement **3** embankment, predating that on Tenement **2**.

Period 3.1: Waterlain accumulation against the embankments
(CP4, 1050-1100)

The western edge of the embankment on Tenement **2** was overlain by grey sandy gravel and silt, which extended into the adjacent inlet, where it was between 0.4m and 0.45m thick, and sealed the post-holes which marked an earlier boundary. On the lower slopes of the Tenement **4** embankment a layer of grey coarse gravel was recorded between the clay and timber base of the embankment and the subsequent organic dumping of Period 3.2, whilst at its southern edge the bank material had slumped over a 0.50m-thick layer

17. New Fresh Wharf: the late 11th- or early 12th-century structures of Period 3.2, with property divisions marked and tenement numbers indicated. Scale 1:200.

of black sand and silt. These three isolated observations represent evidence of what must have been a more widespread accumulation of riverlain silts and foreshore material over and against the embankments during their use.

The material from within the inlet produced pottery of CP4.

Period 3.2: Timber revetments, associated dumping and waterfront structures

(early 12th century)

(Figs 17-18)

This phase consisted of a fairly consistent heightening of the existing embankment, accompanied in several cases by new revetments. On Tenement 4 were structural remains possibly of a wooden building, with a cobbled surface to the south on the river side. There may have been a structure or building on Tenement 5.

The construction of the embankments of Period 2.4 demonstrated the likely origin of five adjacent properties identified with medieval tenements, numbered as Tenements 2 to 6 (Fig 17). The continued existence of these properties makes it possible to discuss the activities of the period by reference to them.

Tenement 2 (Areas III, IV and V)

At the west end of Area III, the Period 3.1 silting over the edge of the earlier embankment was overlain by further timbers, planks and cut branches. These included two planks set at right angles and retained by stakes, around which was packed clay at 1.04m OD. Immediately west of the boundary fence with Tenement 3 were several east-west horizontal planks, up to 2.4m long, with cross-sections of 220 by 100mm, which may have formed the base of a causeway down to the river's edge. These were partially covered by black humic silt with gravel at 1.5m OD, containing lenses of mortar, plaster, ash and sedge, and including some timbers. It covered the clay packing and timbers to the west. Similar organic dumping was recorded both to the north of Area III, running up to the face of the Roman riverside wall, and to the south, where there were indications of its southern limit. North-south horizontal timbers 0.60m to 0.75m apart, resting on diagonal struts, served to support east-west planks up to 1.7m long, with cross-sections of 300mm by 100mm.

The upper surface of this platform was at around 0.85m OD, and it is assumed that if there was a revetment along the southern edge of this new dumped embankment, then it lay a short distance further south. The dumped material itself did not seem to extend as far south as the clay and timber embankment below it. Along its western edge, a later robbing cut (in Period 3.4) indicated that there was probably some sort of revetment lining the inlet at this time.

Tenement 3 (Areas III, IV and V)

The upper brushwood of the earlier embankment was sealed by organic silt about 0.4m thick. Over this deposit were various stakes and posts, with plank fragments and spreads of clay, presumably acting as consolidation of the area, over which were arrangements of ragstone, tile and chalk fragments at 1.3m OD, with tips of organic silt sloping to the west. One of these timbers (SM 130) was felled after 910. The area adjacent to the boundary fence was levelled with thin layers of clay and gravel, through which were driven posts between 0.58m and 1.51m in length and with cross-sections of up to 230mm by 90mm. These posts were additions to the boundary of Period 2.4, about 1m to the east. Random timbers consolidated further tips of organic material, overlain by a more extensive layer at around 1.45m OD. East of the boundary fence there were eight planks up to 0.7m long, which could have been part of a path leading to the river, and there were traces of what may have been a cobbled surface nearby. The lowest organic deposits were recorded between Area III and Area II, and a more extensive upper layer was levelled at 2.67m OD near the Roman riverside wall. South of Area III, the organic dumps ran for a further 2.7m to a rough east-west revetment of timbers, south of which the dumping extended for another 7m, to a point where organic silt was sealed by a 0.2m-thick clay layer with patches of oyster shells. These deposits lay to the north of a vertical cut line, 1.6m high with traces of timber at its base, which must represent the position of a robbed revetment. This sequence of dumped deposits, with the clay layer uppermost, was observed across most of the southern end of the tenement, though alongside the western boundary was an additional layer of fine sand. The embankment created by this dumping had a gradual slope down from a relatively level upper surface, and extended no further into the river than its clay

18. New Fresh Wharf: the structural features of the possible building on the Tenement 4 embankment surface, looking north. Scale in 500mm units.

and timber-based predecessor. A piece of waste timber reused as a chopping block and subsequently incorporated in the boundary fence had a felling date of after 1055.

Tenement 4 (Areas II and V)

In Area II, overlying the south face of the clay embankment of Period 2.4, were organic deposits consolidated at their lowest point on the west side by substantial planks and other timbers, lying along the boundary with 3. Black gravelly silts and a thick layer of clay sealed these layers, incorporating various stakes, larger posts, and random planks. These organic and clay layers continued to the south, further consolidated with numerous horizontal timbers and several long posts, up to 120mm square, driven at angles down into the base of the dumping. Near its southern limit in the east the clay contained many horizontal timbers lying north-south at about 1.5m OD, the eastern boundary being marked by a rough fence of planks. Undulating spreads of

brown organic material with wood chips and oyster shells lay over the uppermost dumps in Area II, and were seen to extend several metres further south. Over these were various structural features which suggest the truncated remains of a building (Fig 18); an edge-set plank lay perpendicular to an east-west aligned log, alongside which was a line of large ragstone blocks and flint rubble with a further north-south line of rubble at right angles to it. Within the area defined by this rubble were two timber plates, one of which (0.6 × 0.4 × 0.1m) rested on small silver birch posts, and two rectangular posts. One post was within the north-south line of rubble, and the other projected above two horizontal plank fragments, 0.68m and 0.74m long, which may have been all that remained of a timber floor; the lines of rubble could have served as the bases for timber walls. North of the building, either the surface of the earlier embankment remained in use or the same truncation which removed much of the building had also removed any additional signs of activity there. South of the structural remains, and over the spreads of organic material, were two layers of flint cobbles and ragstone pebbles in a peaty silt forming a cobbled surface at 1.7m OD. This was traced south into Area V for about 3m, by which point it had sloped down to 1.45m OD. The cobbles seemed to have an eastern limit about half way across the property, and the underlying clay layer had its eastern edge marked by horizontal timbers and posts 150mm in diameter, while a line of posts, at 1.5m intervals, ran from there to the eastern boundary. Traces of cobbled surfaces were also found further south on the east side. The southern edge of this embankment lay over the foreshore of Period 3.3 (which must have originally accumulated against it), the dumped material having slumped southwards after the removal of the revetment which had retained it. The revetment face would have been at about the same distance south of the Roman riverside wall as its predecessor.

Tenement 5 (Areas I, IV and V)

In Area IV, a layer of dark grey silt with charcoal flecks, bone and oyster shells was recorded at 2.4m OD, cut by a later foundation a metre away from the Roman riverside wall. It lay over the earlier clay embankment, and was probably an extension of deposits with a greater organic content to the south. Here, organic silt and sand were consolidated by random east-west and north-south horizontal timbers packed with grey clay. The organic deposits were sealed by lenses of clay which separated them from less organic deposits overlying them at 1.35m OD; a cobbled surface was observed over these upper dumps near their southern limit. A change in the consistency between these dumps and less organic material further south might indicate the position of the southern frontage, which had presumably been robbed prior to dumping behind a subsequent revetment. About 4m to the north of this possible southern limit, the uppermost dumped material contained an east-west timber, 1.81m long and 300mm by 140mm in cross-section, with a continuous 100mm-wide slot along its upper surface. Large stones and edge-set planks supported this timber, and further west more edge-set planks supported horizontal planks up to 0.7m long. A rough line of small stakes running east-west and a larger post, 2.08m long, were further structural features in this area; although these features may have comprised parts of a building, their position on the slope of the embankment, and their level of c.0.75m OD, make this unlikely, and it is probable that they comprised parts of a platform or walkway associated with the waterfront.

Tenement **6** (Areas I and V)

On the gravel surface of the earlier embankment was a possible internal surface of compact mortar mixed with burnt red clay at 2.1m OD, over an area of at least 3.95m by 3.52m; it may not have extended much more to the north, while to the east it presumably ran up to the tenement boundary. Two post-holes probably marked the position of the north wall of the building which had enclosed the floor. South of this, organic dumps with stones, pebbles and charcoal flecks lay over the slope of the earlier embankment, whilst in the south-west corner of Area I organic silt at a maximum surviving level of 1.27m OD sloped south, and was seen continuing south (in Area V) to a point 19.7m south of the Roman wall. In the south-east of the trench, clayey organic dumps surviving as high as 2m OD may have been equivalents. No evidence was recorded for a vertical revetment frontage, though much of this area of the site remained unobserved during the watching brief.

In addition to the dendrochronological date of 1055+ for the re-used timber incorporated in the boundary between Tenements **2** and **3**, a timber within the dumping behind the subsequent revetment on **3** (which may have come from the rob-

bed revetment of Period 3.2) has a felling date of 1084+. This probably indicates a late 11th- or early 12th-century date for the revetment. The ceramic dating evidence was variable, only Tenement **4** producing any significant amounts, of CP5 (1100-50).

Period 3.3: Riverlain accumulation against the revetments or embankment edges
(CP5, 1100-50)

In Area III, black sand and gravel, containing several stray timbers, had accumulated in the inlet against the edge of the Tenement **2** embankment, and a linear robbing trench (phased as 3.4) cutting through this is assumed to mark the position of a revetment along the western edge of that property. Against the cut line which indicated the robbing of the vertical revetment frontage of **3**, black coarse sand and oyster shells presumably represented foreshore deposits which had accumulated against the frontage prior to its removal, reaching a level of Ordnance Datum. The collapsed southern edge of the embankment on **4** lay over a fine light grey-brown sand at −0.25m OD, also interpreted as foreshore accumulations, and a similar deposit was observed at about Ordnance Datum, beneath the Period 3.4 riverwall between **5** and **6**. All these accumulations were at least 0.7m deep.

The material within the inlet contained pottery of CP4 (1050-1100) or later; it is assigned to CP5 (1100-50) as being stratigraphically later than Period 3.2 above.

Period 3.4: Timber revetments, associated dumping, masonry buildings, Thames Street and Rederesgate
(12th century, possibly mid-late 12th century on Tenement **3**)

(Fig 19)

This phase consisted of the establishment (or re-establishment on the existing boundary) of a paved alley down the west side of the embankment to the water, and an associated river-stair; new revetments and, for the first time, stone buildings on Tenements **3**, **4**, **5** and **6** (overall plan, Fig 19).

Inlet (Area III)

The robbing trench, which cut into the riverlaid

accumulations of Period 3.3, was backfilled with black silty gravel. West of it was a timber structure which may have been the base of a river-stair; an east-west horizontal timber at 0.25m OD, 1.84m long and with a cross-section of 180mm by 100mm, had two mortices which fitted onto square tenons on the tops of two driven vertical piles, with cross-sections of 155mm by 100mm. Vertical stakes on either side of the beam may also have been parts of the same structure. It is not clear quite how the stairs would have engaged with these timbers, though they probably led down from Tenement **2**.

Tenement **2** (Areas III, IV and V)

A 3.06m-long edge-set plank was set to the north of seven upright timbers, three of which were surviving posts from the Period 2.2 jetty structure, and several more stakes lay south of it, having been driven into the organic dumps of Period 3.2. A tree-trunk, complete with roots, also lay over the earlier dumps, and this and the other timbers were sealed by a layer of clean grey gravel south of the plank. North of it was a dump of clay with chalk fragments, at 1.35m OD, extending 2.6m west of the tenement boundary, and this was in turn overlain by gravel which spread south of the plank, to be overlain by a layer of grey clay, at 1.6m OD. This clay layer contained more east-west planks, 120 by 100mm in cross-section, retained by stakes and running slightly south of the other plank, extending its line to the west and forming a low revetment about half-way down the length of the embankment. The clay was recorded to the south in Area V, 0.55m thick at the north and 0.20m at the south, varying in level from 1.58m to 1.75m OD, and it did not appear to extend any further south than the organic dumps of Period 3.2.

To the north, in Area IV, the remains of the Roman riverside wall were sealed beneath a levelling dump of silt with sand, gravel and ragstone, flint and chalk fragments at between 2.6m OD to the east and 2.1m OD to the west. In Area IV were also recorded two dumped layers of mortar based on several beech piles; the lowest layer was 0.19m thick, overlain by another 0.42m thick, with an upper level of 2.25m OD. Although changing in composition this dumping appeared to have continued further south, where there were deposits of burnt and unburnt clay with a chalk rubble surface. Similar deposits at 1.96m OD were also recorded in section on the northern edge of Area III, extending for 1.9m west of the tenement

boundary fence; the clay with chalk which extended 2.6m west of the boundary fence (see p.74 above) was probably a lower element of the same series of dumps, whilst immediately north of the plank revetment the clay was seen to have been paved with ragstone beside the boundary with **3**. These dumps and surfaces were all confined to a strip a few metres wide alongside the eastern boundary of **2** and are presumed to represent the alley of *Rederesgate*, recorded in documentary sources between 1147 and 1167 (below, pp.74-5).

Tenement **3** (Areas III, IV and V)

One metre south of the robbing cut marking the line of the vertical revetment on Tenement **3**, a new revetment was constructed; edge-set horizontal planks running east-west were recorded, 2.1m long with cross-sections of 420mm by 100mm. They would have originally been retained by uprights, but these were not seen over the short length of revetment recorded. Behind this revetment were dumped organic silts, and the uppermost layer was of oyster shells in fine grey sand. These deposits sloped up to the north from 0.75m OD by the frontage, which was at least 2m high (unlikely to be surviving to its original height), to over 1.5m OD a few metres further north. The dumps were consolidated by random timbers, four of which may well have been parts of the previous revetment; two planks up to 3.1m long could have come from the earlier frontage, whilst the remaining two may have been fragments of a back-bracing arrangement. One of the possible brace fragments, that with a 150mm-square mortice cut through it, was sampled for dendrochronology, and provided a date of 1084+. Two buildings were constructed to the north of this newly reclaimed land, though the reclamation and the construction of the buildings were stratigraphically distinct; the buildings definitely post-dated the dumping of Period 3.2, but could have predated the reclamation dumping.

Only the west wall of Building A was observed, running down the line of the boundary with Tenement **2**. In Area IV, a length of chalk-built foundation 0.88m or more wide was recorded at various points, surviving to between 2.5m and 3m OD at its highest. The foundation, of chalk rubble with layers of mortar, silt and gravel, had its base at 1.5m OD, cutting directly into Period 3.2 dumps, whilst just south of the Roman riverside wall, a raft of north-south timbers (either squared planks or roughly trimmed timbers) lay between layers of chalk rubble, 0.5m above the base. Fur-

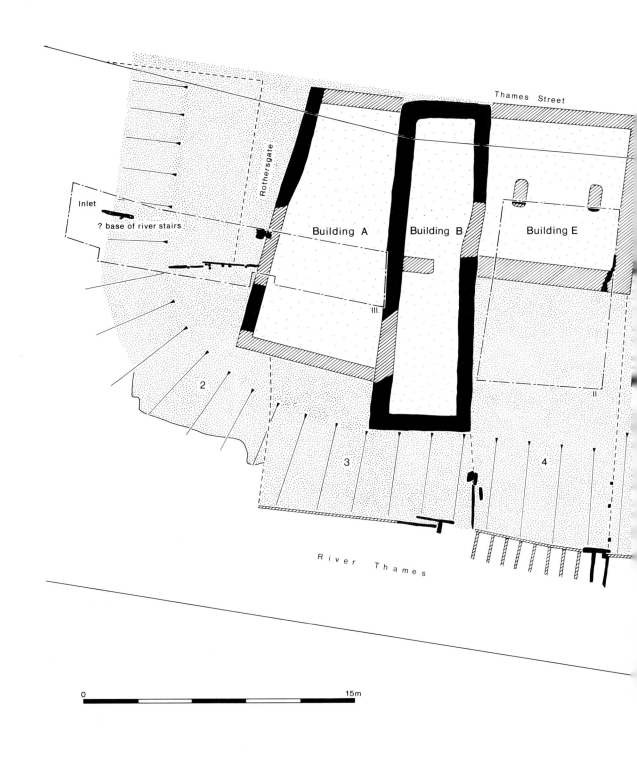

Thames Street

Rothersgate

Inlet

? base of river stairs

Building A

Building B

Building E

III

II

2

3

4

River Thames

0   15m

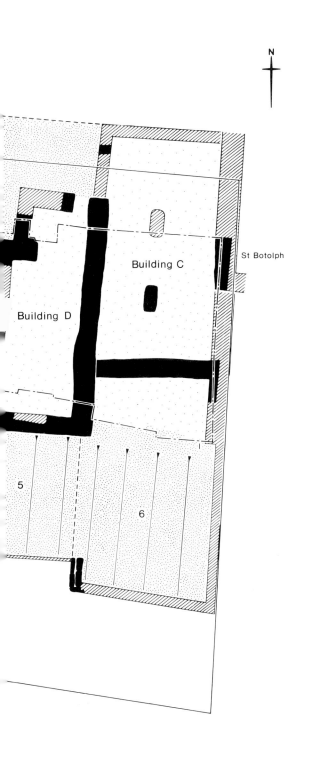

Building D

Building C

St Botolph

5

6

N

19. New Fresh Wharf: the late 12th-century buildings and revetments of Period 3.4, with property divisions marked and tenement numbers indicated. Scale 1:200.

ther north, over the Roman wall, the foundation of chalk and gravel ended at 2.68m OD with a 200mm offset on the east side, above which was a ragstone, chalk and flint rubble wall. This change in construction, and the offset, presumably marked the level of the internal surfaces. None were excavated, but a dump of sandy silt and gravel, recorded at 2.12m OD (the level of machine truncation) against the east side of the foundation to the south, presumably formed the make-up for floors. In Area III the continuation of the foundation, though lying slightly too far to the west, was also of chalk rubble and overlay part of the Period 3.2 plank pathway on **2**. It only survived to one course, having been later robbed, whilst south of the trench another stretch of chalk foundation gave Building A a total recorded length of nearly 14m. Its northern return was probably over a metre north of the southern edge of the Roman wall, on the same frontage line as Building B, but there is no real indication as to its full southern extent. Building A shared the west wall of Building B, giving it a width of 4.5-5.5m. It is also possible that, given its polygonal shape (wider at its south end than at its north), Building A may not have been roofed, and could have been an enclosed yard.

Building B survived to a greater extent, being 17.6m long north-south and between 5m and 5.6m wide, with its eastern wall lying along the boundary with Tenement **4**. The construction trench for the 0.9m-wide west wall was found just to the east of Area III, and at this point there was a 1.7m length of east-west wall tied into the north-south wall, forming the division between the two rooms of the building. The east-west aligned planks which lay beneath the north-south wall were both bedded on, and sealed by, layers of gravel, above which was chalk rubble up to 280mm deep covered by further gravel and chalk. This was overlain by a layer of mortar at 1.5m OD, presumably marking the top of the foundation, and this was also the level of a possible floor make-up in the south-east corner of the southern room. The north wall lay on the remnants of the Roman riverside wall, over a silty sand and gravel levelling dump. Here, only the lowest course of chalk rubble survived, 0.95m wide, over which was a half-metre-wide layer of mortar at 3.09m OD, perhaps an indication of the width of the wall above. A small area of mortar floor at 2.89m OD survived next to the northern foundation. The foundation of the east wall, at a depth of 2.34m OD at its northern end, dropped to 1.5m OD more than 3m to the south, and was at 0.75m OD at its southern end. At intervals along its length it was based on horizontal timbers, with chalk rubble or gravel layers over them. At the south-eastern corner of the building, the chalk foundations of both the eastern and the southern walls were sealed by layers of squared timbers, at around 1.5m OD, running in the direction of the wall, with a hammer-dressed ragstone wall built on them; it survived to 1.95m OD, with a brown mortar rendering on its southern face. At this corner, the wall had been cut from a level of 1.8m OD into the Period 3.2 dumping on the adjacent Tenement **4**, and the trench had been backfilled with sand, gravel and timber fragments. To the south, the ground sloped down towards the river.

North of Building B, layers of compacted sand and gravel overlay the same levelling deposit into which the north wall had been cut. The surface of these layers was at 3.54m OD, and they are assumed to represent part of medieval Thames Street.

Tenement **4** (Areas II, IV and V)

About 2m south of the presumed line of the Period 3.2 revetment on this tenement, a new revetment was constructed. A 3.66m-long oak timber, 350mm square, was set in the ground on the boundary between this property and **5**. It presumably engaged with edge-set planks to the west, one of which, of oak and 510 by 230mm in cross-section, was recorded behind it, but not in direct association. Two mortices cut in the west face of the upright may have engaged with tenons on the end of the planks, though this is not certain, and the joints may be evidence of re-use; if horizontal planks had engaged with the two mortices, they would presumably have retained vertical planks. Elm front braces, about 0.7m apart, braced the post and the plank. The east face of the upright contained a vertical groove 2.94m long, beginning 0.66m up from the foot. This must have contained the plank facing of the Tenement **5** revetment, for which there was no other evidence. The base of this slot was at -1.51m OD, and the damaged top of the corner post at 1.43m OD. The post was sampled for dendrochronology and produced a date of 1166-1211. A line of posts at intervals of 1.6m and 1.2m separated the organic dumps behind this revetment from those on **5**. The dumped material sloped up to the north from the revetment, reaching about 1.75m OD 6m north of it.

At the northern end of the tenement were the remains of Building E, which like Buildings A and B overlay the dumped material of Period 3.2 and could have predated the construction of the front-braced revetment and its associated reclamation dumping. At the northern end of Area II, and further north in Area IV, a mortar make-up overlay dumps of Period 3.2 and the earlier Period 2.4 embankment surface. The make-up was either set against, or cut by, a single course of chalk blocks set in mortar, 2m north-south, which represented the south-east corner of the building. North of this, and about 1.2m west of the projected line of the east wall, a 0.67m-wide foundation of chalk, one course high, seen in section on the north side of Area II, is presumed to have been a column base or post pad. A possible counterpart to this lay a few metres to the west, though all that remained was a charred plank about 0.70m long which may have been the base for another post-pad or column; it lay a similar distance away from the east wall of Building B. Nothing survived in the way of internal surfaces, as the area of the building was subject to truncation when a later building was constructed over it. The north wall is presumed to have been on the same line as the north wall of Building B, fronting onto Thames Street, giving an external length north-south of 9m, with the building occupying the full width of the tenement, namely 8.5 to 9m. To the south of the building, the ground was covered with layers of oyster shells, extending part of the way down the slope towards the revetment, at 2.06m OD by the building and 1.78m OD further south by the wall of Building B; this presumably acted as an external surface and for drainage.

Tenement **5** (Areas I, IV and V)

In Area V, the corner post of the revetment on Tenement **4** had a vertical groove on its east side (see above) indicating that a plank facing had formed part of the frontage on Tenement **5**. No other traces of the remaining structure of the revetment could be recorded, other than a difference in the consistency of the dumps to north and south of its projected line; the fact that the planks had been removed from the groove may indicate that the structure had been extensively robbed. The dumping north of the conjectured line was a silt with lenses of highly organic material, covering an area 3m to 4m north-south across the full width of the tenement, with a maximum surviving level of 1.34m OD. Further north, more dumping sealed the possible timber platform or walkway of Period 3.2, generally levelling the ground to a maximum of about 1.57m OD. Cutting into this made ground were the foundations of Building D, the only one of the buildings discussed so far which actually overlay reclamation dumping behind the new revetment.

Building D measured 6.1m east-west by 12.8m north-south, with two rooms, the smaller northern one measuring 2m by 3m internally, and the southern 4.2m by 12.8m internally. It did not extend over the full width of the tenement, being built against the eastern boundary, leaving a gap of 2.5m between it and the western boundary. This area was occupied by a cobbled surface at about 1.7m OD near the building's southern end. Nor did the building extend to the Thames Street frontage, there being an intervening area apparently filled by dumped clay and pebbles, which sloped down from the street (recorded north of Building B at 3.54m OD) to the internal surfaces of the building at around 1.75m OD. The foundations were, for the most part, 1m wide, with layers of chalk blocks alternating with layers of gravel, based in part on horizontal timbers and at one point on surviving timbers of the Roman quay. The foundations were deeper to the south, reaching a depth of about Ordnance Datum. Above the foundations the walls were of ragstone and some Roman tile, with 0.25m-wide offsets on the west sides of both east and west walls, ie internal to the east wall and external to the west wall. The east wall was rendered internally. The two rooms had internal make-up layers of clay at 1.75m OD, and the southern room had a compact layer of cobbles and pebbles over this at 1.77m OD.

Tenement 6 (Areas I, IV and V)

Projecting over a metre south of the presumed line of the Tenement 5 frontage was a north-south length of limestone ashlar walling surviving to 0.8m OD. Two courses were recorded, based on an oak plate 230mm thick and 820mm wide, and resting directly on riverlain deposits of Period 3.3. The oak plate (FRE 1001) was sampled and dated by dendrochronology to 1130+, at least 20-30 outer rings of the sample being unmeasurable. Three of the stones were chamfered along the southern edge of the wall, which is assumed to have turned to the east from here; a short pile stood at its furthest recorded point in that direction. Presumably this formed a river wall across Tenement 6, and dumped deposits of silt were recorded to north and east of it.

Building C shared the east wall of Building D. A ragstone wall built on chalk footings at 2.35m OD was recorded in section cutting into the Roman riverside wall, and this extended Building C beyond the north end of Building D up to the Thames Street frontage; thus the construction of Building C must have post-dated that of Building D. The eastern wall of Building C also made use of a pre-existing wall, the south-west corner of a building which lay on the adjacent property to the east, presumably the church of St Botolph. This wall survived up to 3.50m OD, being of hammer-dressed ragstone over a foundation of coursed ragstone and gravel with horizontal timbers. It had an offset to the west at 2.31m OD, and quoin stones indicated the south-west corner. An east-west foundation of chalk blocks alternating with layers of gravel abutted the east wall of Building D, and ran as a cross-wall to the eastern tenement boundary south of the existing adjacent building; a foundation joining the two is thought to be a later replacement. A foundation of ragstone and mortar which probably formed a pier base was recorded roughly in the centre of the area enclosed by these walls, and another may have lain further north, its southern edge partially visible in the north baulk; these bases may have supported piers for a vault of three by two bays. The construction of later buildings truncated much of the internal surfacing associated with this building, though several predominantly clay dumps, with scant remains of a burnt clay floor overlying them at 2.37m OD, may have been primary. South of the cross wall it was not even clear if the area was internal or external; several driven posts there, perhaps connected with a structure providing access to the waterfront, could equally well have been piling for a later building.

Dating of Period 3.4

The dating evidence for this phase is sparse. The corner post of the revetments on Tenements 4/5 produced a dendrochronological date of 1166-1211, and the baseplate of the river wall on Tenement 6 could be of similar date, indicating the late 12th century for these revetments. Few diagnostic 12th-century pottery types were recovered. Tenements 2 to 5 produced probably CP5 (1100-50) material in small quantities; deposits which may have been primary dumped rubbish behind revetments could not be properly searched for finds, since all lay within the area of the watching brief. Ceramic evidence does however indicate that Building C was constructed in the mid 13th century or later (Appendix 1 microfiche). There was certainly no dating evidence to determine whether, in those cases where there was no direct stratigraphic relationship, the buildings had been built before or after the construction of the Period 3.4 revetments. The only clear case is Building C, which contained mid 13th-century pottery in its floor make-ups and was therefore later than the river wall on the same tenement.

For this phase some early documentary evidence is relevant. During the priorate of the first prior Norman (1107-47), Holy Trinity Priory Aldgate leased two wharves with adjacent land in *Rederesgate* to a certain Brounlocus (see below, p.74), and the lease was renewed by the second prior Ralph some time in 1147-67 (PRO E340/7361); the wharves are identifiably the double-width tenement east of the lane, Tenement 3. Too much should not be made of the fact that the leases specify two wharves (*wervos*) and not buildings, but it is quite possible that Buildings A and B (of which, as suggested, Building A may in fact have been an open yard, surrounded by walls) were constructed in the years or decades after the lease of 1147-67; the revetment and its corner-post, dated to 1166-1211, could be part of this redevelopment.

The dating for Buildings A and B cannot be extended to the other new stone buildings, and hence a broad 12th-century date must be retained for the overall duration of the phase. From the stratigraphic relationships of their walls, Buildings A-B and D were first on the site, and Buildings C and E were later, infilling the intervening plots. Building C, with its stone wharf and possibly vaulted basement, was evidently the grandest in style, constructed in the mid 13th century or later. Its east wall appears to have been built out from the south-west corner of the adjacent St Botolph's church (Fig 19). Detailed presentation of these buildings will be made in the second volume on the post-Roman strata from these sites (Schofield & Dyson in prep).

Period 3.5: Silting later than the Period 3.4 revetments and features
(mid 12th to mid 13th century)

Riverlain deposits of silt and sand, 0.5m deep, which sealed the possible stair base of Period 3.4 in the inlet, contained pottery of early 13th-century date. Layers of sand, gravel and silt,

0.70m deep in total, reached a level of Ordnance Datum against the face of the Tenement 3 revetment, whilst against the stone river wall of Tenement 6 was silty sand and gravel containing 13th-century pottery. These deposits indicate that the Period 3.4 waterfront was in use for some time into the 13th century, before the revetments were replaced by others further south. The inlet was eventually filled in (Period 3.6) by dumps of material containing mid 13th-century pottery.

BILLINGSGATE LORRY PARK

(Figs 20-42)

Between March 1982 and February 1983 an area 20m east-west by 25m north-south was excavated in the north-west corner of the lorry park which had served the Billingsgate Fish Market (closed 1981) to the east. The excavation (site code BIG 82) was jointly funded by the Department of the Environment and the Corporation of the City of London, with additional grants from the Manpower Services Commission and the City of London Archaeological Trust. The supervision of the excavation and the compilation of the archive report were carried out by Steve Roskams.

The Billingsgate site record was divided into nineteen periods in the process of post-excavation analysis, running from the 2nd century AD to the 20th. These are labelled, as in the archive report, with capital Roman figures — Period I etc. Each period is further sub-divided into smaller groups relating to discrete phases of activity such as construction, occupation or destruction in various parts of the site. These are labelled below as IV.1 etc. In addition, the various waterfronts and buildings on the site have been labelled with arabic numbers, for example, Waterfront 2, Building 1. Only Periods III to VII are relevant to this publication. These are therefore described in detail below, together with a summary of the preceding periods as an introduction. Periods I-III, the Roman quay structures and their disuse, have been discussed by Brigham (1990). Period VIII and later will be the subject of future reports (Schofield & Dyson in prep).

Periods I and II: Foreshore and Waterfront 1
(2nd-3rd centuries)

Period I was represented by a series of gravel

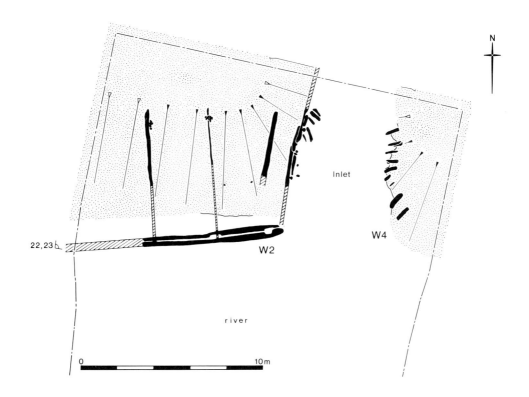

N

Inlet

W4

22,23

W2

river

0   10m

20. *Billingsgate Lorry Park: Waterfronts 2 and 4, both of 1039/1040, showing inlet linings on both embankments, and the base plate and tiebacks of Waterfront 2. Scale 1:200.*

accumulations which were only exposed at the northern end of the site. Their level surface might imply that they had formed against a waterfront which lay some distance to the north, and that they had been truncated when Waterfront 1 was inserted. This occurred in Period II: it comprised a substantial Roman quay of box construction, dated by dendrochronology to after 201-28, with a change in construction technique to the east where it may have incorporated a crane. It was modified substantially on at least one occasion but seems to have fallen out of use before the end of the Roman period (for dating and discussion, see Brigham 1990).

Period III: Silting above Waterfront 1
(late 3rd-11th centuries)

(summarised in Fig 56 below)

In Period III, deposits of variable character, ranging from coarse pebbly gravels to fine silts

and clays, accumulated above the Roman quay. Their southern edge displayed a distinct north-ward curve in the east, a line reflected in the position of the Period IV inlet but definitely ante-dating it. Random timbers and various amorphous intrusions within these silts may have derived from the robbing and disturbance of the underlying quay; several timbers which lay in front of it more definitely derived from the quay.

There is no reason to suggest anything other than ephemeral human activity during Period III; any more intensive activity is unlikely to have been eroded by the river. The accumulations do not constitute the single, undifferentiated horizon which might be expected of a natural agency, and they contained some cultural material. The inter-spersed cuts imply robbing of a quay which was accessible, even if not totally visible, over an extended period of time. The impression which emerges is of a partly dismembered and slowly decaying quay protruding above the silts, hardly conducive to organised exploitation of the water-front area. The distinctive northward curve of the silting in the east presumably relates to a feature off the site to the north, perhaps the mouth of a natural stream on or close to the line of Botolph Lane. This could also explain the changes in con-struction of the earlier Roman quay noted above, and the position of the later inlet described below (p.55). The Roman riverside wall, which must have been constructed in the period between the construction of the quay and the silt accumulations, must therefore have accommodated such a stream, perhaps by means of a culvert or wider opening.

Period III is dated by pottery, and by its stratigraphic position over the mid 2nd-century Period II, to *c.*270 or later (Brigham 1990, 106, 162 & 176, Table 5).

Period IV: Waterfronts 2 to 5
(11th century)

(Figs 20-6)

Waterfront 2

At the start of Period IV, a north-south trench was dug into the Period III silt covering the partially obscured remains of the Roman quay of Period II. Timber piles, some up to 2.6m in length, were set in this trench, forming a line at least 4m long (truncated to the south) immediately to the east of the northward curve of the pre-existing silts (IV.1). The tops of the piles, which protruded for 0.6m from the trench, were decayed

and had fallen over to the east from their original, vertical position (Fig 20).

Several horizontal planks and timber fragments consolidated the area to the west of these piles. Stone, clay and random timbers followed by pebbly clay were dumped on top as further consolidation. These elements thus formed a bank sloping from 0.35m OD in the north down to −0.4m OD where its southern limit coincided with the line of the earlier Roman quay. Layers of trample and organic refuse accumulating at the top of the bank were probably related to activities to the north outside the excavation.

Two parallel timbers 3.2m apart running roughly north to south were set above the bank. One was an unworked trunk at least 4.5m long and the other a plank set on edge at least 3.65m long. Both members were underpinned by three

21. Billingsgate Lorry Park: the hard-standing within the inlet (IV.3) looking south, with parts of the contemporary waterfronts seen in different stages of excavation to both east and west. To the west (right in the picture) the timbers (IV.1) which retained the Waterfront 2 embankment can be seen, with adjacent horizontal timbers representing consolidation of the underlying foreshore. To the east lie the clay and timber dumps (IV.2) of the Waterfront 4 embankment, with the collapsed retaining timbers of this and Waterfront 5. Timbers of the 3rd-century Roman quay can be seen to the south. Scale 10 × 100mm.

roughly worked timbers laid on the crest of the bank, and were retained at their northern ends by cross-pieces set in mortises and staked in place. A similar, unworked trunk further east, 4.75m long, had a mortise and traces of a cross-piece at its northern end but no stakes. It may have been a counterpart, disturbed subsequently, of the other timbers. All three sloped down to the south at a gradient of 1 in 12, to a point where the two remaining *in situ* were subsequently sawn through at an early date. This may have been the occasion when the third member was disturbed. All three would have acted originally as tiebacks for a revetment to the south.

Large, angular limestone blocks, some up to 0.5m across, and clay containing random timbers (including fragments of a clinker-built boat) were dumped around the tiebacks and across the entire bank (Fig 21). In the north further dumps of organic material and limestone rubble, some of the latter with mortar adhering to it, completed the process of consolidation. It raised the level there to 1.5m OD and formed a base for a layer of closely packed timbers and decayed wood fragments set in a matrix of mixed clays and organic silts, raising the level further to 2m OD in the north and to 0.5m OD in the south (Fig 22). The lowest of these timbers were laid regularly north-south

22. *Billingsgate Lorry Park: the rubble core of the 1039/1040 Waterfront 2 embankment (IV.1) seen in section and partially in plan, with the overlying clay and timber layer in section behind. In the foreground the remains of the 3rd-century Roman quay are visible protruding through the pre-embankment foreshore, whilst the southern edge of the rubble is retained by two driven timbers, part of consolidation prior to construction. Looking north-east; scales 10 × 100mm (vertical) and 5 × 100mm (horizontal).*

or east-west and were retained by driven piles. They underpinned mostly unworked branches, including however a significant minority of plank fragments, one a reused tieback brace.

The material dumped before the insertion of the main tiebacks was very similar to that dumped afterwards. There is therefore good reason to see all of these elements as part of a single process of construction, namely Waterfront 2. Deterioration of the timbers in the uppermost dump and the decay of a cross-piece of one of the main tiebacks suggests their exposure over an extended period of time, though exactly how long is difficult to gauge. An organic deposit was trampled into the surface of the bank during this period of use.

To the south of the bank, a substantial squared timber 11.45m long and 0.5m in diameter was set on the pre-bank foreshore, with its upper surface at c.-1.4m OD. Its eastern end, retained by two stakes, lay directly opposite the line of piles forming the east end of Waterfront 2 and it lay perpendicular to the line of the two *in situ* tiebacks incorporated within that bank, suggesting a relationship with them (Fig 23). The baulk was obviously reused, probably from the Roman quay in view of its dimensions, though a longitudinal groove in its uppermost surface was part of a later, secondary use, and was presumably intended to receive upright staves. Although later truncation had removed any evidence of direct relationship between this base plate and the elements of Waterfront 2 to the north, it seems likely that the tiebacks there originally related to staves inserted into the secondary groove in the plate. Projection of the slope of the tiebacks south to this line implies a low stave revetment between 1m and 1.5m high. The manner of articulation between tiebacks and postulated staves is unknown.

23. The clay and timber bank on Tenement 7 (Billingsgate Lorry Park Waterfront 2), seen partially in plan and in section. One of the north-south tieback braces lies along the top of the section face. The rubble core of the bank is visible in section, overlying the post-Roman foreshore, from which protrude elements of the 3rd-century Roman quay. Scale 5 × 100mm.

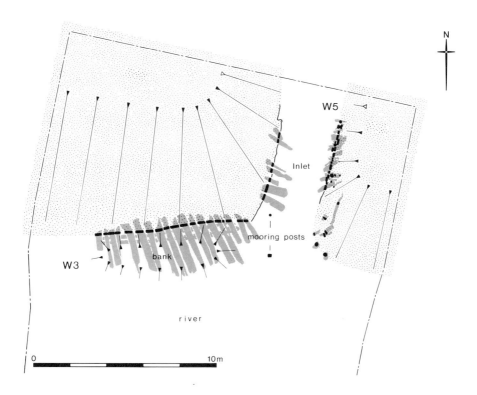

N

W5

Inlet

mooring posts

bank

W3

river

0   10m

24. Billingsgate Lorry Park: Waterfronts 3 and 5, both of around 1054/1055. The stave frontages are shown in their collapsed state (as excavated; in grey), but with their positions reconstructed as vertical (in black). Scale 1 :200.

Waterfront 3

After an interval, a north-south trench was dug along the east side of Waterfront 2 whose facing was now replaced by a series of staves and piles up to 2.5m long, packed with mixed pebbly silts and clays with rubble at their base (IV.4; Fig 24). These timbers may originally have been set either vertically in front of, or at an angle against, the bank to their west, with their tops resting on, and protruding above, the first facing. The south side of the bank was also refaced, with substantial earth-fast staves up to 3.5m long inserted against the north face of the base plate of Waterfront 2. These also could have been either raked back at an angle to revet the original bank, or set vertically; their subsequent collapse (Figs 25, 26) precludes any certainty about this, or about the depth to which they intruded into the pre-existing foreshore.

Whether sloping or vertical, however, their height before collapse was too great to have

allowed the sloping tiebacks which formed part of Waterfront 2 to pass above them, and there was no sign that the tiebacks could have passed through the staves at a lower level. It is thus quite clear that, while the base plate of Waterfront 2 was reused in order to stabilise the foot of each stave, they did not reuse its tiebacks. In fact their insertion was presumably the occasion on which the latter were sawn through. The staves themselves must therefore represent a new waterfront (Waterfront 3), of a substantially different character from its predecessor (Fig 24).

It is unclear how Waterfront 3 was supported if it was a vertical feature. There was no sign of a second set of tiebacks to the north, nor of braces on the foreshore in front. However, the area behind the staves was extensively truncated during later rebuilding, which could have removed any trace of supports. Equally unclear, and for similar reasons of later intrusion, is whether the staves stood on the foreshore to be surrounded by water at high tide, or whether they revetted a horizontal or sloping ground surface behind them; the lengths of the staves make it unlikely that any such surface was at the level of the top of the Waterfront 2 bank. Any material dumped to provide the surface could have fallen away when the staves collapsed, and been swept away by the river. A shallow clay bank, reinforced with

wattle panels and cut branches was set in front of the staves to form a raised beach, presumably for landing ships. Sandy foreshores and organic debris then accumulated on the bank (IV.6), eventually being sealed when the staves collapsed.

To the north, occupation debris accumulated on the primary bank behind the waterfront (IV.7), with gravel and disturbed timbers dumped above to form a new bank at 2m OD (V.2; see p.58 below for a discussion of the relationship between this and the Period V base plate to the south). Clay was then dumped on top, laced with variously-sized timbers along the lower parts of the bank to the south and along its eastern edge (V.3). Most of this timber comprised unworked

25. Billingsgate Lorry Park: the collapsed staves and posts of the inlet lining of Waterfront 3 (IV.4), with three of the staves of the southern frontage visible behind. Reclamation deposits of Waterfront 3 have already been excavated; the upright timbers are part of a later waterfront. Looking south; scale 5 × 100mm.

26. The collapsed staves of the late 11th-century frontage on Tenement 7 (Billingsgate Lorry Park Waterfront 3), looking south. The staves have collapsed southwards and lie over the wattle-reinforced bank and the foreshore which accumulated over it. In the foreground the clay and timber bank has been partially excavated, revealing timbers of the 3rd-century Roman quay. Scale 10 × 100mm.

branches and offcuts from trees, though some reused boat and house timbers may have formed a cribbaging, with several north-south notched timbers retaining east-west members along the frontage. Sand lenses at the surface of this dump suggest water action on the slope of the bank. Further timbers were found along this break of slope (V.4), thus lying at the junction of dry land and tidal zones and possibly disturbed from the main dump below.

Waterfront 4

A north-south line of piles comprising circular timbers up to 2.5m long (Figs 22 and 23) was inserted into the Period III silting 5m east of Waterfronts 2 and 3 (IV.2). These had collapsed to the south-west but, in their original, upright position, would have retained clay dumps further to the east which contained random timbers in a similar fashion to Waterfront 2, thus creating a bank at a level of 0.3m OD in the north dropping to -0.5m OD in the south. These elements constitute an easterly counterpart (Waterfront 4) to those features to the west described above.

Waterfront 5

A second line of timbers was added just west of those of Waterfront 4, presumably due to their collapse (Fig 24). It comprised planks and staves up to 2.1m long holding a rough cladding of planks set on edge, including some reused boat timbers. Clay laced with timbers, including occasional piles and wattling, was dumped as consolidation behind the second line. On excavation and even during post-excavation analysis these features did not appear sufficiently dissimilar from the features of Waterfront 4 to indicate that they were secondary to it. However, there were obvious variations within the group as a whole and the dendrochronological evidence makes it clear that there were two phases of construction. The second has therefore been labelled Waterfront 5. The nature of the southern frontage of Waterfronts 4 and 5 is unclear because of later disturbance. Organic dumping behind Waterfront 5 brought its level in the north to 1m OD. It may have been movement of this material which caused its eventual collapse to the west.

The Inlet

The 5m-wide gap between the two pairs of waterfronts (2/3 and 4/5) formed an inlet (Fig 24) in which a hard-standing was created by compacting pebbly deposits of clay and silt into the remains of the robbed Roman quay (IV.3). Organic debris concentrated at the northern end of the inlet was accompanied by gravels to the south nearer the river, and both were sealed by water-laid sands which accumulated over the whole of the access, perhaps the result of slower moving water. The north-south trench for the staves and piles of Waterfront 3 was dug into these accumulations.

Two timber uprights set a short distance south-east of Waterfront 3 may have been mooring posts or part of a groyne to prevent silting. A variety of foreshores later accumulated in front of both Waterfront 3 and Waterfront 5 (IV.5).

Dating of Period IV (Waterfronts 2-5)

The relationships between Waterfronts 2-5 can be deduced on both stratigraphic grounds and from dendrochronological evidence. Waterfronts 2 and 4 both postdated Period III silting in the west and east of the site respectively. Waterfront 3 was inserted after 2 and, most critically, after some material had accumulated in the inlet to the east, implying a substantial interval. Waterfront 5, though probably later than 4, cannot be related to such accumulations because it was only later positively distinguished from 4 on dendrochronological grounds, rather than at the time of excavation. The small amount of pottery associated with the construction of Waterfront 2 has been assigned to CP3, while the silting and foreshore within the inlet contained pottery of CP4 (1050-1100). Later Waterfronts 3 and 5 had CP4 pottery within the dumps, while the silting in the inlet, contemporary with their use, contained CP5/6 (1100-80) types.

From the dendrochronological study, one pile of Waterfront 2 in the inlet yielded a date of 1014+ and a stake related to a tieback in the bank a date of 1015+. Though these dates support the broad contemporaneity of inlet lining and tiebacks, neither timber contained sapwood, so they can only give a *terminus post quem*. The latest date from the timber dumped to form the bank proper behind the pile line is 1039/40. The spring of 1040 might be the best time of the year for such construction activities.

The staves which formed the south front of Waterfront 3 have a general felling date of 1049-70, though the corresponding staves lining the inlet are undated. At the time of excavation, the material dumped behind Waterfront 3 appeared to postdate the base plate marking the start of Period V (see below — V.1). However, the timbers from this dump form a tightly dated group derived from trees felled in 1054/5 and 1055, and are thus much earlier than even the earliest timbers of Period V elsewhere. It therefore seems reasonable to suppose that the stratigraphic relationship recorded on site was due to Period IV material slipping forward some time after the Period V base plate was inserted, perhaps when its superstructure was robbed. Hence it is most likely that Waterfront 3 was erected in 1055, the fifteen-year interval between it and Waterfront 2 marking the period during which the initial foreshore intervening stratigraphically between them accumulated in the inlet.

To the east, one of the piles associated with Waterfront 4 was felled later than 1008. The latest felling date for timbers from Waterfront 5 comes from two piles felled in 1045-90. The material dumped behind these features was interpreted originally as a single phase of dumping but as mentioned previously dendrochronological analysis of the associated timbers indicates at least two felling dates. A large proportion belong to a group felled in 983-90, whilst most of the remainder could have been felled in 1047-70. The deposit also included one timber with a felling date of 1039/40 and two more which may have been contemporary with this. Given that the dumps are proven stratigraphically to postdate a pile of 1008+, the group 983-90 must originate from an earlier feature, perhaps one nearby since they are unlikely to have been stockpiled. Of the remainder, the timber related to 1039/40, even if disturbed and redeposited in a later bank, implies that the initial bank behind Waterfront 4 was constructed at exactly the same time as that behind Waterfront 2. Hence the date of 1008+ for the related pile would be merely a *terminus post quem* for the inlet lining, in the same way as a pile associated with Waterfront 2 gives a date of 1015+. The later date of 1047-70 accords well with the pile of Waterfront 5 of 1045-90, and allows the possibility that this was constructed in 1054/5, at the same time as Waterfront 3 to the west.

In conclusion, it can be suggested that Waterfronts 2 and 4 were constructed to west and east in 1039/40, in an integrated development to either side of a pre-existing access point. The latter waterfront incorporated timbers from an earlier feature, perhaps nearby, which dated to the very end of the 10th century. Foreshores then accumulated within the intervening inlet for fifteen years, after which Waterfront 3 was installed in the west. Waterfront 5 may have been inserted at about the same time, though whether in an integrated response similar to that of the initial development is unclear. Dating of the following periods suggests that this second phase of activity lasted until at least 1080 (ie for 25 years), though almost certainly no later than the end of the 11th century.

Period V: Waterfronts 6 and 7
(late 11th to early 12th century)

(Figs 27-30)

Waterfront 6

In the west of the site three horizontal timbers up to 2.40m long, reused domestic base plates (discussed with other reused timbers in Milne in prep), were laid to form a frontage at least 6m long (V.1; Figs 27, 28), directly above the line of the collapsed staves of Waterfront 3. They were held in place by posts inserted through mortises. The superstructure set above them had been removed subsequently, as had any relining of the western side of the inlet which may have taken place at this time. At 2.5m to the south lay a parallel timber, another reused, probably domestic, base plate set in a cut then packed with gravel and overlain by organic silts flowing around both edges of the feature below foreshores and outwash (V.5). Similarly, in the inlet, silty gravels were interleaved with organic material, the latter possibly occupation debris dumped into that area. The structural elements here formed a new feature, Waterfront 6. The timber to the south was either part of a bracing arrangement or, more likely, a platform in front of the new frontage.

To the north, behind Waterfront 6, clayey and silty gravels were dumped to consolidate the dry land, and were cut by a series of irregular features for the insertion of timber (V.6). Planks were set in the base of these intrusions, held in place by stakes which were sometimes robbed, elsewhere left to rot *in situ*, then covered by a further consolidation of pebbly clay containing wood offcuts and trampled debris at its surface flecked with

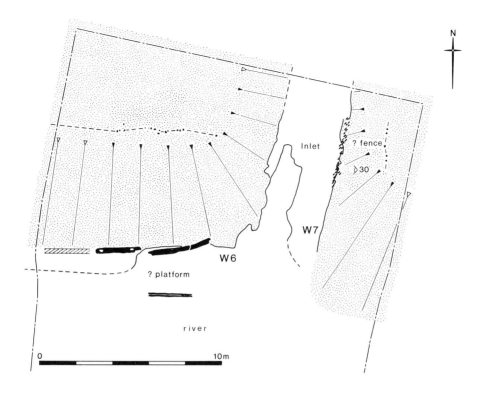

27. Billingsgate Lorry Park: Waterfronts 6 (to west) and 7 (to east), both of around 1080+, with the bank on the upper parts of Waterfront 6. Staves of Waterfront 5 were retained in the structure of Waterfront 7. Scale 1:200.

mortar and chalk. The trample formed an east-west band across the northern fringe of the site, and was cut by a second set of intrusions on its south side to create a timber frontage retained by north-south timbers with cross-pieces at their northern ends. Piles forming this southern face clustered around the positions of these tiebacks.

The successive cuts within this sequence of dumping and timber construction were inserted in very similar positions. This, and the fact that the intervening dumps formed no proper surface but were merely subject to trampling, implies a single phase of construction, thus creating a bank consolidated by the timber framework on the dry land north of Waterfront 6 (Fig 28). Clay was later packed in the gaps between the timber frames, perhaps because they had moved slightly, and a mortar skim was spread on top as a base for a formal gravel and cobble surface at 2.4m OD in the north, sloping down to 2m OD as it approached the break in slope of the bank below. A post-hole inserted into this surface is the only sign of structural activity in what was presumably

an external working area. It seems to have continued in use throughout Period VI and for much of Period VII.

Waterfront 7

To the east, a north-south cut above the line of the collapsed timbers of Waterfront 5 suggests a new lining for the east side of the inlet (V.7) and thus a new feature, Waterfront 7 (Fig 27). The exact form of this replacement is unclear from the few elements which survived later robbing. Behind it, the bank was reconstructed, with dumping of grey pebbly clay (V.8). This contained mostly north-south timbers sloping down to the south and laid from north to south, but also some east-west elements (Fig 30). Organic silts on top brought the level of the eastern bank to 1.7m OD. They also incorporated stakes for a possible fence line running approximately north-south. Charcoal and sand spreads above the silts and disturbed timbers represent the use of the new bank, followed by clay repairs to the surface and then by further organic dumps (V.9). Post-holes related to these secondary activities may have been an attempt to reinforce the original fence line and mark the end of Period V in this area.

28. *An intermediate stage in the construction of the late 11th-century bank on Tenement 7 (Billingsgate Lorry Park Water-front 6), looking north-east. Scale 5 × 100mm.*

29. *Billingsgate Lorry Park: the reused timbers (V.1) which comprised the frontage of Waterfront 6, laid directly over the collapsed staves of Waterfront 4. Scale 5 × 100mm.*

Dating of Period V (Waterfronts 6 and 7)

Stratigraphically, Waterfront 6 and its associated cribbaging to the north cannot be related to the construction of Waterfront 7 to the east, though both postdate all Period IV features. From dendrochronology, timbers from the consolidated bank behind Waterfront 6 can be shown to have been felled between 1059 and 1064. More importantly, one of the posts driven through the reused base plate of the waterfront to the south, which should predate the bank timbers, was felled some time after 1080. As there is no reason to question the order of construction, the consolidation appears to have utilised reused timbers. To the east, timbers dumped behind Waterfront 7 included one member felled between 1056 and

30. *Billingsgate Lorry Park: the clay and timbers (V.8) of the reconstructed embankment of Waterfront 7, partly retained by the collapsed timbers of Waterfront 5. Scale 10 × 100mm.*

1101, which establishes a *terminus post quem* for that feature and shows that it could have been built at the same time as its western counterpart. However, other timbers dumped here show an earlier phase of felling, dated to between 1011 and 1056. This group may have derived from disturbance of the Period IV material below. In view of the dating for Period VI, Waterfronts 6 and 7 were probably constructed after 1080 and continued in use until at least 1108, and probably into the following decades. Pottery associated with the con-

struction of both these waterfronts is assigned to CP5/6 (1100-80), and material from the foreshores in the inlet to CP5/6 or later.

Period VI: Waterfronts 8 and 9
(early 12th century)

(Figs 31-3)

Waterfront 8

In the west of the site, a set of three base plates was inserted in an east-west cut (VI.1), directly above the line of Waterfront 6. The longest was

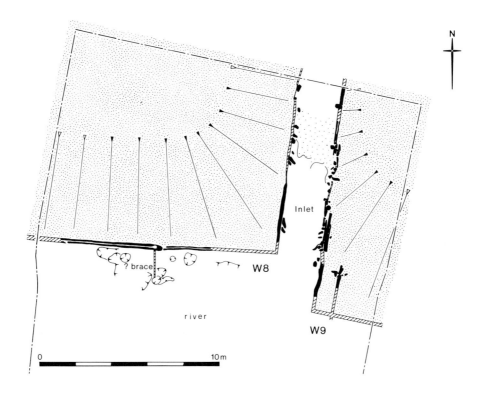

river

W8

Inlet

W9

N

0   10m

31. *Billingsgate Lorry Park: Waterfronts 8 (to west) and 9 (to east), with the inlet narrowed and all frontages replaced. The Period V bank was retained behind the frontage of Waterfront 8. Scale 1:200.*

5.2m, though the easternmost had been truncated near the inlet. Each had a groove in its uppermost surface to accommodate vertical staves. Piles set on the south side of the plates prevented slippage in that direction and the cut was then packed with pebbly silt and clay. This feature thus constitutes a replacement of the sixth waterfront, and is designated Waterfront 8 (Fig 31). Timbers packed in grey clay were placed behind it, comprising branches and some worked fragments including planks and domestic base plates (Fig 32). Shell-flecked peat overlay the dump, possibly a build-up in a tidal zone, sloping from a level of 0.9m OD down to −0.3m OD beside the river. Further clayey organic dumps brought the upper level to 1.1m OD in the north, petering out against the Period V cribbaging. These dumps were capped with a gravel foreshore beside the revetment in the south.

Extensive, though shallow, cuts were inserted into the foreshore in front of Waterfront 8. Some were direct replacements of others but all would originally have contained substantial timbers, although only the stakes and wedges associated with them survived later robbing. They suggest the position of open-work platforms, landing stages or mooring posts, and a possible front-bracing timber opposite the junction of two of the

baseplates. Sand and gravel foreshores accumulated around these successively replaced features throughout the rest of the period.

At the same time, the western side of the inlet was reconstructed, with a new north-south cut 6.8m long dug 1.2m east of its predecessor (VI.2). Eleven piles up to 2.6m in length with tapered heads and square bases were then placed within, rather than driven into, the sandy silt and gravel which lay in the cut. They lay in two groups but probably represented one phase of construction, amounting to a lining 7.4m long. Some uprights were charred at their tops, suggesting the reuse of timbers originally set the other way up. Cuts for the insertion of cladding were evident to the west of the pile line, though little survived later disturbance. That which did was of very low quality given the substantial size of the pile line, and it may have been a repair or poor quality replacement. Piles and cladding together made up the east side of Waterfront 8 (Fig 33). A compaction of clay containing charcoal or coal (VI.3) formed a possible surface in the inlet beside it,

32. *Billingsgate Lorry Park : the clay and timber deposit behind the frontage of Waterfront 8 (VI.1), the grooved base plate of which can be seen in the left foreground. Note the reused domestic base plates. Looking north-west ; scale 5 × 100mm.*

with brown streaky clay then compact sand and silt as a further concretion on top. The fibrous clay above this was dumped during the use of the inlet.

Waterfront 9

To the east, intruding into the material representing the use of the inlet beside Waterfront 8, was a north-south cut (VI.4). It contained four upright timbers, three thin boards and one larger squared pile, packed with clayey silt and further dumps, into which a further 26 piles were then inserted (Fig 33). Light grey sticky clay was packed between these members in the south to hold in place wattles woven around the uprights, creating a continuous panel 2.5m long. Planks, including a high proportion of reused house and boat timbers, were set to the north and south of

this panel to complete the cladding. The diversity of timbers used, and their interspersing with phases of dumping, may mean that several phases of construction and/or repair were involved, though this is by no means certain. As a whole they formed a new revetment, Waterfront 9 (Fig 31).

The southern limit of the new feature was unclear but a north-south tieback was inserted towards the river just east of the new inlet lining, retained by a cross-member set in a mortise in its northern end and staked in place (VI.5). Though cut away, its projected southern end may correspond with the line of an east-west cut seen in section to the south. If so, given the angle of the tieback and the position of the cut, Waterfront 9 must have had a low frontage. Whether of one or more phases, the insertion of Waterfront 9 must have been later than the construction and use of Waterfront 8 to the west, given the intervening accumulations and resurfacing within the inlet. This suggests that the integrated development seen on either side at the start of Period IV had now become a more piecemeal process, as also

33. *Billingsgate Lorry Park: the renewed inlet linings of Waterfronts 8 (right) and 9 (left) (VI.2 and VI.4 respectively), looking south, showing how narrow the inlet had become. The 10 × 100mm scale rests on the compacted clay resurfacing of the inlet (VI.3).*

does the greater southward extent of Waterfront 9 compared with that of Waterfront 8. At the same time the actual revetments, at least in terms of their surviving elements, were becoming more variable, being constructed in a less systematic and less regular fashion. As a result of the creation of Waterfronts 8 and 9, the width of the inlet was reduced to 2.2m, too small for ships of any size.

In a secondary phase, silt and pebbles were dumped behind Waterfront 8, after which structured peat and other clay and pebbles accumulated here and in the inlet against Waterfront 9

(VI.6). The corresponding foreshores to the south in front of Waterfront 8 were noticeably more sandy and more obviously derived from running water. This area was covered by water most of the time, that to the rear only at high tide. A series of slots dug along the line of the eastern side of the inlet (VI.7) represent a final change at the end of Period VI. They were filled with a concreted silty clay containing lumps of slag which had discoloured the adjacent stratigraphy by exposure to heat, suggesting a nearby source of industrial residues still hot when deposited here. Black silt containing further slag spread above these features, which were either pits and channels to dispose of the slags or, since they directly overlay the line of Waterfront 9, a modification of its western limit.

Dating of Period VI (Waterfronts 8 and 9)

Stratigraphically, Waterfront 8 was created at the start of Period VI and Waterfront 9 was then inserted after it had been in use for some time. From dendrochronology, the base plate for Waterfront 8 was dated to 971 or later and thus

34. Billingsgate Lorry Park: the mid 12th-century stave revetment which blocked the inlet (Waterfront 10), looking northeast; scale 5 × 100mm. Behind can be seen various posts which retained tiebacks related to a later repair of Waterfront 10 (see Fig 37), and parts of the earlier lining of the east side of the inlet (Waterfront 9).

was clearly reused. The timbers from the consolidation behind it included one member felled after 1060. More importantly, three piles from the new lining of the western side of the inlet, which can be argued on structural and stratigraphic grounds to be an integral construction, were all of a similar date — 1108 or later. They did not appear to have been reused timbers and therefore provide the best *terminus post quem* for Waterfront 8. Samples from piles associated with Waterfront 9 gave a definite date of 1108+, but might extend as far as 1125 on the evidence of another pile dated 1080-1125. This would make better sense of the foreshore deposits accumulating between the insertion of the two waterfronts and, given the dating of the following period, allows for their continued use to the middle of the 12th century. Both waterfronts had CP6 (1150-80) pottery associated with their construction, and dumping and silting in the inlet contained pottery of a similar date.

Period VII: Waterfronts 10 and 11, Building 1
(later 12th century)

(Figs 34-42)

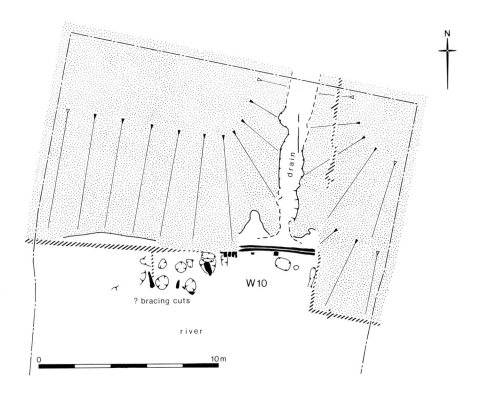

? bracing cuts

W 10

river

drain

N

0   10 m

Waterfront 10

An east-west trench was cut into the latest
accumulations of Period VI across the mouth of
the inlet, and a timber 4.2m long, with a groove
in its uppermost surface, was laid in the cut as
a base plate to hold 22 vertical staves up to 1.25m
long (VII.1; Fig 34). Seven further staves were
driven directly into the earlier foreshore just to
the west, although marks on them showed that
these also had been set originally in a base plate.
Several piles to the north may have been part of
a tieback arrangement related to the low stave
wall thus formed in the mouth of the inlet, Waterfront 10 (Fig 35). The cut was backfilled with
organic clay and silt containing gravel lenses, suggesting that water continued to flow into the inlet
after the waterfront was inserted. The east-west
section of the earlier Waterfront 8 to the west
remained in use, and in fact the Waterfront 10
base plate may have been obtained by cutting
away the eastern element of that revetment,
which was found to be missing, and sliding it to
the east. The gap thus formed was filled with
reused staves driven directly into the foreshore.

The blocking of the inlet carries the narrowing
seen during Period VI to its logical conclusion,
since its site was absorbed by the western prop-

*35. Billingsgate Lorry Park: the blocking of the inlet by the
construction of Waterfront 10 (VII.1), some time between 1144
and 1183, with a drain (VII.4) built in the partially infilled
inlet area. Most of the Period VI revetments, Waterfronts 8
and 9, remained in use, though the western inlet lining was robbed and the eastern remained only as a property division for
most of its length. Scale 1:200.*

erty. The line of its eastern side thus became a
property boundary dividing the eastern quarter
of the site from the western three-quarters.
Organic material and gravel were dumped within
the inlet and behind the retained Waterfront 8
to the west (VII.2). The timbers which this
material contained may have been disturbed from
the bank of the earlier feature. The organic element suggests rubbish accumulating in a marshy
area but the gravels show that it was still subject
to water action.

To the south, pebbly sands and clay patches
accumulated on the foreshore, cut by a variety
of slots and circular intrusions packed with gravel
or clay (VII.3). Some of these features contained
stakes and several held larger members such as
driven planks. They were sealed by mixed pebbly
sands and silts interleaved with clay patches.
Purer sand towards the surface suggests water
sorting. The cuts were not all of one phase but
did form two east-west lines to the south of the

revetment, offset by 0.4m and 0.8m, which terminated in the west opposite the remaining portion of the base plate of Waterfront 8. This suggests that they represent successive attempts to shore up that part of Waterfront 8 which had been weakened when its base plate was removed. Silt and further sand behind this frontage suggest water action to the rear of the revetment line, with organic refuse on the top. The frontage must have been low enough for the front slope of the bank to its rear to be flooded at high tide.

Within the inlet, a north-south trench was dug (VII.4). It may have removed those elements of the inlet lining which were no longer needed when the access was blocked. A drain was then inserted, running for 3m from the northern limit of excavation and leading down at a gentle gradient to the south. Its eastern side was formed by reused planks staked in place but the nature of the western side is unclear. It was back-filled with orange sand containing pebbles and chalk to form an apparently open, timber-lined channel. It seems to have been quickly choked with sands and organic silt, two boat timbers found above this material presumably having been later disturbed

36. Billingsgate Lorry Park: the base plate (at top of picture) and probable back-bracing elements of Waterfront 11 (VII.5), looking west; scale 5 × 100mm.

from its lining. Further stakes by its outflow to the south, surrounded by sand and pebble and clay lenses, suggest that the feature may have extended almost to the line of the revetment. However, the staves of Waterfront 10 did not provide for drainage across its line, so the feature must have disgorged around its edges, probably the reason for its speedy demise. The placing of the waterfront across the mouth of the inlet shows that it was no longer an access point to the foreshore. But the insertion of the drain demonstrates that its secondary role in waste disposal persisted, presumably because of the continuing activities off the site to the north.

Waterfront 11

To the east, a layer of mainly pebbly mortar with other building material and shells was dumped over the southern parts of Waterfront 9, forming a rubble raft on the eastern bank (VII.5). It was bounded in the west by a base plate running south from the eastern end of Waterfront 10 (Fig 36). This reused timber was 3.6m long, with a groove in its uppermost surface to hold staves originally wedged in place; these had been robbed subsequently and some wedges displaced. Reused timbers to the east may have braced an eastern

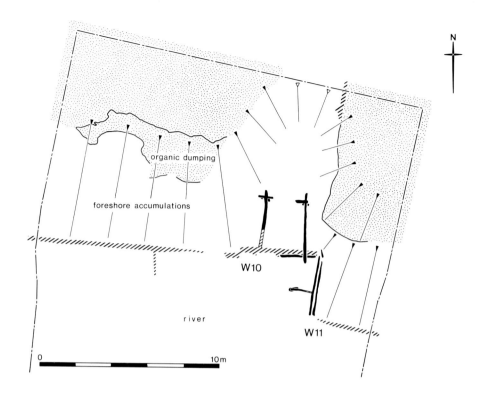

N

organic dumping

foreshore accumulations

W10

river

W11

0   10m

return for the feature at its southern end. A post and further wedges reinforced this apparent junction. Unusually, posts and piles retained the east side of the base plate, but not the west side. Together these elements constituted a new feature, Waterfront 11 (Fig 37), inserted when the drain in the inlet had been in use for some time. This drain was itself only added behind Waterfront 10 after the latter had been in use for a while. Once again, therefore, there are clear differences in the process of development to either side of the site.

Pebbly silt formed a foreshore against the east side of Waterfront 11, whilst later foreshores lapped Waterfront 11, Waterfront 10 and the retained part of Waterfront 8, demonstrating that all three were in use together. Compact clayey silt covered with a spread of marine shells formed a surface to the north of Waterfront 11 at a level of about 1.6m OD, capped with brickearth at 1.8m OD in the extreme north. Silt and orange clay on top were the result of treading during occupation. The character of the brickearth, and a post-hole inserted at its north-eastern limit, might suggest an internal clay surface belonging to a building mainly lying off the site. If so, it would constitute the first sign within the excavation of structural development on the eastern property. The case

37. Billingsgate Lorry Park: Waterfront 11 added south from Waterfront 10, with front-bracing elements to the west. Waterfront 10 now had tiebacks to its north. This plan omits the back braces for Waterfront 11 shown in Fig 36. Scale 1:200.

for it being an internal surface is not, however, sufficiently certain to allocate a building number.

Modifications to Waterfronts 10 and 11

To the west, two north-south tiebacks were inserted behind Waterfront 10 (VII.6; Fig 37). They were retained in the inlet by cross-members set in mortises and staked in place. The staves of the waterfront had been cut away to accommodate the south end of the eastern tieback, and a cross-member 1.9m long set in a mortise at this end ran across half the width of the waterfront. The western tieback was cut off in the south, so that the nature of its articulation with the staves is unknown. However, if it had a southern cross-member of the same length as its eastern counterpart, it would have held in place the western half of the waterfront. Furthermore the staves opposite the line of this western member had a notch cut in their tops which would have accommodated such an arrangement. Thus it is likely

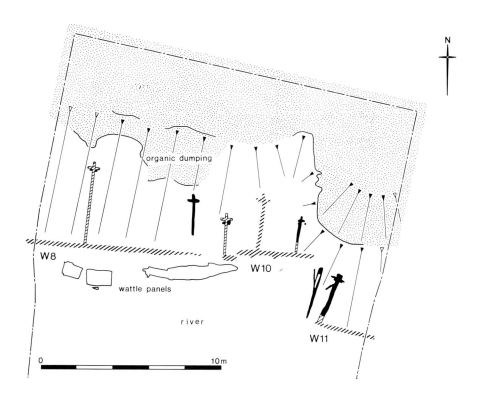

N

W8

organic dumping

W 10

wattle panels

river

W 11

0   10 m

38. Billingsgate Lorry Park: replacement tieback and cladding on Waterfront 11, with additional tiebacks and wattle panels along Waterfront 8/10 frontage. Scale 1 :200.

that the tiebacks together supported Waterfront 10 across its full width.

Organic silty clay was dumped over the north ends of the tiebacks, marking the demise of the short-lived drain inserted at the start of the period. This dump consolidated the area but did not create completely level ground in the inlet, which now existed as a low depression towards the centre of the site. In that depression, black sandy gravel accumulated, containing yellow sandy gravel lenses and, near Waterfront 10 in particular, water-sorted clay lenses (VII.7). This deposit was more mixed in the east beside the junction with Waterfront 11. It shows that the land within the southern part of the inlet was flooded at high tide.

Further south, a raking brace was set up on the foreshore for Waterfront 11 (Fig 37). It is surprising that such a support was not in evidence from the start, though one may have existed originally and been completely robbed away. Further foreshores accumulated around the brace, presumably protected here from excessive scouring

because of the angle between Waterfronts 10 and 11. To the west, the corresponding accumulations had a higher organic content initially, containing straw, but became more gravelly at the surface and more sandy further out into the river. At the same time, pebbly foreshores mixed with organic material and some large cobbles accumulated on the banks behind the waterfronts, showing continued exposure to water here. Dumps of organic material then sealed these secondary deposits.

Further north-south tiebacks were inserted behind the line of Waterfronts 10 and 8 (VII.8; Fig 38). One, reusing a base plate, lay within the inlet and was held in place by a cross-piece set in a mortise at its north end and staked in place. It replaced a similar earlier feature (see VII.6), but was set at a higher level, presumably as material continued to accumulate within the inlet from natural and human agencies. It had been truncated to the south so that its form of articulation with the staves is unknown. A second tieback, similarly located with stakes and also truncated, originally supported the retained element of Waterfront 8 to the west. Between these features, and to the west of the second tieback, stakes and padstones mark the positions of two further tiebacks, later completely robbed. One would have supported the junction between Waterfronts 8 and 10. In the west, on the foreshore, a section of wattle panel (Figs 38 and 40) formed a consolidation in front of Waterfront 8, associated with timbers of a platform or mooring posts.

To the north, organic layers and building material were dumped behind the revetment, the latter material matched by chalk-flecked silt containing building debris deposited in the inlet. This profusion of building material would suggest a nearby source, although no masonry foundations were found within the excavation. Its deposition brought the level in the inlet almost up to that of the adjacent banks. However, pebbly silts on top show that it was still occasionally riverine, even if only a marshy hollow. The uppermost gravels started to spill out over the top of Waterfront 10. Indeed, it may have been their combined weight which required the insertion of successive tiebacks behind the feature. Other dumps in the area contained inclusions of charcoal and daub, probably from nearby hearths. They suggest that the marshy hollow was also a convenient place to dispose of such residues. This completed the process of evolution of the inlet: first a major

access, later reduced in width; then blocked off and incorporated within the western property as a drainage feature; and finally a convenient hollow for rubbish disposal.

To the south-east, a new tieback was set behind Waterfront 11 (VII.9; Fig 38). At least 2.4m long (south end truncated), it had a 0.7m-long crosspiece wedged in a mortise at its north end and retained by a pile. It formed a more substantial tieback than those behind Waterfronts 10 and 8 to the west. A series of planks set horizontally above the base plate formed the west limit of Waterfront 11. Some were articulated boat timbers, others either single boat timbers or of domestic origin (Fig 39). A reused house stud supported this new cladding on its west side. The level of the top of the cladding, at 1.7m OD, suggests that the vertical front of Waterfront 11 was heightened in these modifications, in contrast

39. Billingsgate Lorry Park: reused boat timbers and other planks forming a replacement cladding (VII.9) for Waterfront 11, with (in foreground) a new tieback. Looking west; scale 5 × 100mm.

40. Billingsgate Lorry Park: wattle panels (VII.8) laid to consolidate the foreshore south of the frontage of Waterfronts 8 and 10. Looking north; scale 2 × 100mm.

41. Billingsgate Lorry Park: late in Period VII, towards the end of the 12th century, with much of Waterfront 11 obscured by foreshore accumulations. An enlarged area of external surfacing has been laid out on the west side of the former inlet, and Building 1 constructed to the east. Scale 1 :200.

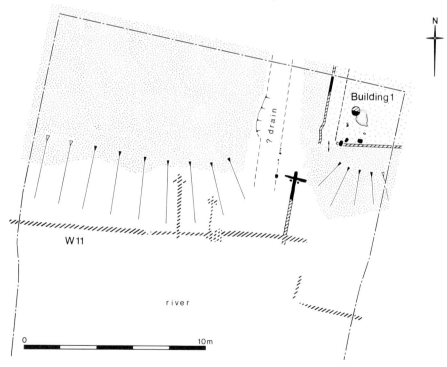

Building 1

? drain

W 11

river

0   10m

N

with the lower frontages retained by Waterfronts 8 and 10 to the west.

In the north-west of the site, yellow pebbly mortar was set above the Period V cribbaging to give a good quality surface (VII.10). A drain was inserted at its eastern edge, thus reinstating the drainage function of the now mainly disused inlet (Fig 41). Sand from the drain outflow spread across the east side of the mortar surface. Further west, the surface had been discoloured by exposure to heat, suggesting an open hearth. On this, organic dumps alternated with layers of ash, whilst further amounts of charcoal, ash and burnt daub accumulated to the south and west of the surface proper, probably swept there. Hence there is some suggestion of industrial processes in what was presumably an external area. To the south a gravel metalling surfaced the area beside the waterfront proper and the former inlet to the east (VII.11). Pebbly repairs to areas of underlying subsidence or slippage overlay the new metalling. Its irregular, sloping profile to the south, where it approached Waterfront 8, was later redressed by alternating dumps of organic debris, gravel and building material.

Later a new gravel metalling was laid over this southern area (VII.12). It incorporated cobbles and, at its surface, a trodden sandy layer below local repairs which included a mortar skim. Irregular intrusions could represent beam slots for an overlying building, especially as some of the spreads containing wood, charcoal and slag, which accumulated on the surface, appeared to sweep up against their line. However, other accumulations crossed this line, so that they are unlikely to have been divisions of lasting significance and could equally well have been cracks caused by underlying subsidence.

Final additions to Waterfront 10 and construction of Building 1

A final north-south tieback, at least 1.5m long (truncated in the south) and located in the usual way, was set within the former inlet (VII.13; Fig 41), directly replacing one described above (see VII.8). Further west, others inserted in Period VII.8 were probably retained. Just to the west of the new tieback, a north-south line of piles 1.6m long formed the east side of a drain or fence. If the former, it must represent a replacement or modification of the previous feature (see VII.10; Fig 41) in use with the main mortar surface. Pebbly sandy silt interleaved with grey sand and clay

accumulated to the south of this feature, around and in front of Waterfront 10, thus creating a slope here from 1.3m OD down to −0.1m OD in the south.

To the north-east, an area of brickearth was laid at a level of around 2m OD (VII.14; Fig 42). It was exposed to heat in one area and the trodden occupation layer on top incorporated flecking, suggesting associated burning, perhaps the result of industrial activity. A shallow post-hole was inserted at the edge of the surface in the north, and to its south was an east-west line of three shallow cuts which appeared to bound the brickearth. These features and the character of the layer suggest an internal clay floor, part of a structure, Building 1 (Fig 41). The shallowness of the cuts implies a framed superstructure rather than free-standing earth-fast posts, the remainder of the

42. Billingsgate Lorry Park: the brickearth floor of Building 1 (VII.14), looking west, with shallow post positions along the southern edge and to the north, and with an area of scorching implying a hearth. The 0.5m scale rests on a strip of a trampled occupation layer, indicating the narrow western room or corridor, with access to the waterfront to the south. Much of this western area has slumped down adjacent to a retained section of the Waterfront 9 inlet lining (visible behind), which was probably incorporated into the western wall of the building (for plan, see Fig 41). Scale 5 × 100mm.

building presumably lying off the site to the north and east. It may have had an access point at its south-west corner, either an entrance into the building or into an alleyway along its west side. Driven stakes inserted into the floor suggest internal divisions.

The position of layers above this suggests that Building 1 was dismantled. The fence line to its west was then modified, organic material being dumped on its site (VII.15; not illustrated). However, further yellow brickearth above suggests the insertion of another floor, petering out to the south, where it appeared to be bounded by a large post-hole. The replacement structure, though constructed after the apparent dismantling of Building 1, followed its lines closely and was probably a second phase of the same building. The more substantial element to the north with which both are assumed to have been associated may have remained unaltered. It has not, therefore, been allocated a separate building number. Like its predecessor, the floor was exposed to heat at one point on its surface, the trample above corresponding with a mixed deposit of silt and brickearth spreading to the south, which probably derived from the floor's disturbance. It may be that the replacement building was open to the river on this side. Above this tread was pebbly silt, the pebbles especially concentrated in the east, which may have formed a rough external metalling, flanking the building. To the west organic dumps followed by charcoal and sand spreads accumulated in the inlet and against the eastern property boundary, presumably the result of activities off site to the north.

Robbing of Waterfront 8

An east-west trench was cut in the western part of the site directly above the line of Waterfront 8 (VII.16; not illustrated). It terminated in a butt end opposite the western limit of Waterfront 10 and was filled with grey sandy silt containing sandy clay lenses. Its purpose must have been the robbing of the superstructure of Waterfront 8, whose base plates were however left *in situ*. The timbers of Waterfronts 10 and 11 were intact, though the former had been largely sealed in and obscured by sands and silts disgorging from the now disused inlet. The robbing of that element of Waterfront 8 which had been retained when Waterfronts 10 and 11 were constructed brought Period VII to a close and prepared the site for the changes of the following period.

Dating of Period VII (Waterfronts 10 and 11)

Stratigraphically, Waterfront 11 was inserted some time after Waterfront 10, because the drain installed to the north of the latter remained in use for some time and then became choked with sands and silts before the eastern area was extended. Both waterfronts were modified in various ways on two occasions, all of which implies that Period VII was of considerable length.

Dendrochronology dates the timbers incorporated into Waterfront 10 to between 1144 and 1183. Its base plate appears to have been reused, a conclusion already implied by the structural evidence and supporting further the suggestion that it was removed from Waterfront 8 to the west. It would therefore seem reasonable to suggest that Period VII started some time early in the second half of the 12th century. No diagnostic material was included among the initial timbers of Waterfront 11, of which several were reused, one possibly a two-hundred-year-old relic. However, a fragmentary plank from a tieback later added behind Waterfront 11 was dated to 1172-1216. Since further modifications followed this, and since Building 1 was constructed in the north-east corner of the site at a similarly late stage and was then rebuilt in a second phase, Period VII seems certain to have stretched to the end of the 12th century and quite probably into the early 13th.

St Botolph's Church

The south wall of St Botolph's Church was recorded in the north-west of the excavation trench (Period XIII.2); this is not illustrated here. The date of Period XIII.2 is late 14th century, but it is possible that the wall of this period sits on earlier foundations. It is known from documentary sources (see below, p.77) that St Botolph's Church was in existence by the 1140s. The south-west corner of a rebuilding on the same alignment was recorded on the adjacent site of New Fresh Wharf (Fig 19; above, p.47) and dated to the 12th or 13th centuries; it preceded Building C, of mid 13th-century date. It is therefore likely that the south and east walls of St Botolph, as excavated, represent a late 14th-century rebuilding of the south wall of the church, which was originally built in stone in the mid 13th century. Because the end-date of the present report is around 1200, this phase is considered in detail in the forthcoming volume (Schofield & Dyson in prep; the only major 13th-century development illustrated here is New Fresh Wharf Building C, to complete the sequence on that site).

As St Botolph's was in existence by the 1140s, it must however have been contemporary with much of the sequence on the Billingsgate site just described. The dendrochronological dates imply that the church was probably there prior to Period VII (1144+), whilst Period VI (1108+) involved no structural activity in the north-west corner of the site, Waterfront 8 being constructed south of the retained gravel bank of Period V (1080+). It is therefore possible that the very deliberate consolidation of the area at the top of the bank in Period V, namely the dumping of gravel over a timber framework, was connected in some way with erection of the church or protection of an existing south wall; the (approximately) north-south timbers in the bank ran perpendicular to the later Period XIII (late 14th-century) wall, implying that it perhaps shared the alignment of the earlier church. This must have been smaller than its successor; if it had been coterminous with the 14th-century structure then, until the blocking of the inlet (Period VII, above p.64) and the expansion eastwards of the high-grade external surfacing over the bank (in VII.10), there would have been insufficient space for access past its eastern end to the external area which lay to its south.

The evidence of Periods V-VI therefore suggests that St Botolph's Church lay immediately north of the Billingsgate excavation area by the late 11th or early 12th century. The earliest recorded remains, those of the south wall and of the return of the east wall, were of late 14th-century date but probably lay on foundations of mid 13th-century date.

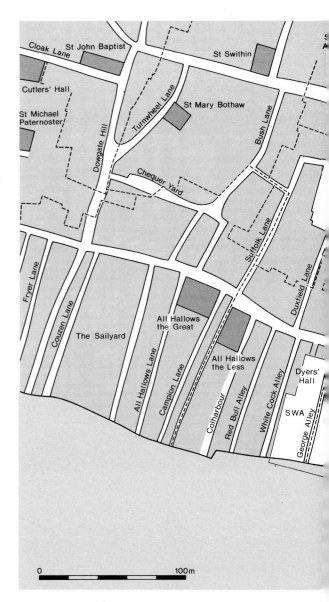

DOCUMENTARY EVIDENCE FOR NEW FRESH WHARF AND BILLINGSGATE LORRY PARK

The excavations at New Fresh Wharf and Billingsgate Lorry Park spanned the Thames frontages of the eastern end of the parish of St Magnus the Martyr and of all but the eastern extremity of the parish of St Botolph Billingsgate (Fig 43). The New Fresh Wharf site corresponded with the position of six medieval tenements, each extending from Thames Street to the Thames. Two of them (**1-2**) lay between the church of St Magnus to the west and a lane to the east which marked

43. Plan of the bridgehead area based on the street outline of Leake's map of 1666, simplified south of Thames Street. It shows, to the east of the bridge and Fish Street Hill, the pattern of streets in the district bounded by the 11th-century embankments and Billingsgate to the south, and by the length of Eastcheap to the north. Excavation site outlines superimposed, and parish boundaries shown as dashed lines. (Based on the 1980 Ordnance Survey 1:1250 map, and reproduced with the permission of the Controller of Her Majesty's Stationery Office: Crown Copyright.) Scale 1:2500. For location, see Fig 65.

the parish boundary; the other four (**3-6**) between the lane and the church of St Botolph. The church itself, together with St Botolph's Wharf to its south and east (**7**) and part of a further tenement beyond them (**8**), lay beneath the lorry park site.

Tenements 1-6; 8

None of the private tenements is continuously documented before the late 13th century, in common with most of their counterparts elsewhere on the waterfront and in the City generally, and thereafter measurements are only rarely recorded. However the late 16th- and 17th-century evidence for **3-5** shows that the number of tenements was still the same, suggesting that the basic medieval pattern remained largely unchanged up to the Great Fire and had probably been established long before the date of most of the written records. Indeed, that kind of continuity might itself help to account for the scarcity of recorded measurements, which tended to be used only where a tenement was partitioned, as between co-heirs, or when it was important for other reasons to differentiate one particular part of a property from another. The available measurements for Tenements **1-6** and **8** broadly correspond with the archaeology (Figs 11, 17, 19) and may be summarised as follows:

1-2 In the period up to *c*.1200 covered by this report the site of **1** comprised an inlet which was subsequently infilled to create additional space for occupation. In 1326 the width of **2** between *Rethereslane* to the east and **1** to the west was 18 feet 2 inches along the quay next to the Thames, and, at a distance of 79 feet 10 inches to the north, 19 feet 6 inches (HR 54/102). In 1405, however, the width of the quay from east to west was given as 13 feet 11 inches (Chew & Kellaway 1973, no. 645). No comparable measurements have so far been traced for **1**, which between 1333 and 1348 was described as abutting west on a lane leading from Thames Street to Fishwharf (HR 61/65, 63/165, 75/157), the latter being situated to the south of the church of St Magnus. The lane presumably led along the east end of the church, which in 1403 itself appears as the western abutment of **1** (HR 131/75). The Ogilby & Morgan map of 1677 shows the distance between the contemporary east end of the church and the apparent former position of *Redereslane* (marked here by the parish boundary between St Magnus and St Botolph) as 25 feet.

3 The width of the eastern part only along the Thames was 21 feet 9 inches in 1544 (GL MS 14004), and 21 feet 'or thereabouts' in 1684 (*ibid*, 14014).

4 At least 18 feet from east to west, half-way down the length of the tenement, in 1466 (GL MS 59, ff. 26v-28v); an encroachment on the Thames in 1612 measured 26 feet 'or near thereabouts' (GL MS 14003). Deeds of 1622 specify an east to west measurement (exact location unspecified) of 21 feet 3 inches, but also refer to a parcel of ground before the western part of the messuage, to be used for access between wharf and street (GL MS 14003). In 1684 the Thames frontage was defined as 39 feet wide 'or thereabouts' (GL MS 14014).

5 A plan of the tenement, probably dating from 18 March, 1684, or soon after, shows the Thames frontage as 39 feet 6 inches; at other points successively further north the width is shown as 35 feet 11 inches, 36 feet 6 inches and 30 feet 10 inches (GL MS 14008).

6 No measurements available.

7 St Botolph's Wharf and church (see pp.75-6). From the late 13th century the Wharf was extended to the east by the incorporation (p.75) of **8**.

8 No measurements available.

In the later 13th and early 14th centuries, closest to the date of the structures described in the present report, each property was usually defined simply as a 'tenement', with or without reference to quays. In 1278, however, **2** was described as comprising a house, solar, kitchen and cellar, together with two further houses and another cellar (HR 9/10), and in 1290 as a tenement with houses built thereon and quay (19/79). In 1294, **1** comprised a newly built house 'from the entrance of the royal street (*vicus regalis*) as far as the Thames' (23/10); 20 years earlier a shop also existed at the corner of the street and an access-way to Fishwharf (6/39) to the south-west. Tenement **5**, described in 1291-3 as 'land with houses', (22/10), was defined from 1294-5 onwards as 'a tenement with quay, houses and shops' (25/19, 40/17, 45/83); a deed of 1283 (14/14) also refers to a solar next to the Thames. There is no reason for supposing that these tenements were exceptional, or for attaching particular significance to the absence of such detail in deeds relating to the other tenements. The occupants of the tenements in the late 13th and early 14th centuries included, where their trades are specified, fishmongers (much the most common category; **1, 2, 4, 5**), vintners (**2, 6**), a currier (**5**), a woolman (**5**) and a merchant (**3**).

The immediate context of the tenements was provided by *Rederesgate* between Tenements **2** and **3**, by the wharf and church of St Botolph (**7**) and by Thames Street to the north.

Rederesgate

Between Tenements **2** and **3** in the medieval period lay a lane which led from Thames Street to the river (*cf* Figs 17, 19) and also marked the boundary between the parishes of St Magnus Martyr and St Botolph and the wards of Bridge and Billingsgate. *Rederesgate*, the name given to this lane, first occurs between 1107/8 and 1147 in connection with the lease of two wharves by Holy Trinity priory, Aldgate (PRO E40/7309). At least one, and possibly both, of these wharves was later represented by Tenement **3**, whose common name of 'Fresh Wharf' was subsequently added to the dorse of the original lease. The excavations at New Fresh Wharf showed that the lane of *Rederesgate* had originated in the late 10th or early 11th century when its position was marked by the eastern edge of a timber jetty, and by traces of a path or alleyway of the later 11th and 12th centuries (above, p.28-9, 40, 42-3). *Rederesgate* continued north of Thames Street, where it was known as *Retherlane* (Ekwall 1954, 102-3) or *Retheresgatelane* (HR 51/90, 65/114, 87/8 etc) until the mid 14th century, when the more familiar name of Pudding Lane first appears. The early use of the same name to either side of Thames Street is paralleled by Botolph Lane and St Botolph's Wharf, and strongly suggests that the two parts were regarded essentially as a continuous, integral thoroughfare. Archaeological evidence indicates that while Pudding Lane was only fully developed as part of the street system proper in the 12th century, it is likely to have been preceded by a back lane (Horsman, Milne & Milne 1988, 19-21), and the presence of the *Rederesgate* jetty at its foot would certainly suggest that some kind of access was available from the north by the early 11th century.

St Botolph's Wharf (Tenement 7)

St Botolph's Wharf, which lay to the south and east of the church of St Botolph, occupied the whole of the Lorry Park site. In 1283 it measured at least 54 feet from east to west along the south side of the church (below, p.77), at that date probably extending only sufficiently further to the east to allow for access from Thames Street and Botolph Lane past that end of the church. Within a few years however the mayor and aldermen acquired Tenement **8** to the east of the existing wharf (p.74), whose width was thus increased by an estimated 10 to 20 feet to a total of perhaps 80 feet. Some 50m upstream of the better known harbour of Billingsgate, St Botolph's Wharf is in some respects the better documented of the two. By 1368 all corn, lambs and small victual 'from the east' were to be unloaded there unless the Bridge was to be passed, or the victual was not for sale (*Cal Lbk G*, 225): the role and scope of Billingsgate at this period is much less clearly defined. The wharf is first recorded in 1200-1 in connection with the receipt of royal customs at *Botuluesgat'*, or 'Botolph's gate' (Pipe Roll 2 John, 150), but there is also an indirect allusion to it in the mention of Alfwold *de porta Sancti Botulfi* in a spurious charter of William I confirming to Westminster Abbey numerous donations including Alfwold's property and wharf at the head of London Bridge (*Cal Charter Rolls* iv, 330-6). Since the document is in all probability a forgery of the 1140s (Chaplais 1961, 89-110) it provides no evidence for the existence of St Botolph's Wharf much earlier than the middle of the 12th century. Though at all periods the documentary sources leave unclear the exact relationship of the wharf to Billingsgate, the excavations have revealed that the earliest activity on this part of the foreshore in the late Saxon period must have occurred at much the same time as the establishment of Billingsgate. Billingsgate itself is first mentioned in a law code of Ethelred II (Thorpe 1840, 127-9) which is usually dated to *c*.1000, though some of its contents may date from towards the middle of the 11th century (Richardson & Sayles 1966, 24-5) and so possibly relate to Dowgate. According to this text, Billingsgate was capable of accommodating a full range of shipping from small ships (*navicula*), which paid a half-penny toll, to the larger ships with sails (*si maior et haberet siglas*), which paid a penny, and the barge (*ceol*) or merchantman (*hulcus*), which both paid fourpence. There can be little doubt that the late 10th- or early 11th-century embankments at the sites described above formed part of this context, and cannot be considered in isolation from Billingsgate.

The Eastcheap street grid

There are other reasons for regarding the present sites and Billingsgate as belonging to the same, integral development. Following the crest of the hill above and behind all three is the street called Eastcheap, which now merges almost imperceptibly with Cannon Street to the west and (Great) Tower Street to the east. On Leake's plan of 1666 (Fig 43) and Ogilby & Morgan's map of 1677, however, Eastcheap is shown as an altogether more distinctive and individual entity, its meandering and shapeless conformation sharply contrasting with the straight, regular courses of Cannon and Tower Streets, and on a different alignment from both. Cannon Street closely follows the course of a major Roman thoroughfare which may or may not underlie Eastcheap as well. Tower Street, as depicted by Leake, is less obviously a feature earlier than Eastcheap, or of similar date to it, than one tacked on subsequently. In fact it is shown not so much as a deliberate continuation of Eastcheap as such, as an accidental offshoot from Idle Lane, which itself linked the eastern termination of Eastcheap with the waterfront some 60m downstream of Billingsgate. Since Tower Street led directly to the original entrance to the Tower of London, built in the 1080s, it may well not have been laid out before the late 11th century. The distinctive conformation of Eastcheap, still apparent in the 17th century, thus raises the possibility that it owes its origin to the planned development of the area to the south, between Bridge Street and Idle Lane, in response to new activity along the corresponding sector of the waterfront represented on the present sites by the 11th-century embankments, and doubtless also including Billingsgate. With the evolution of the ward system, which also appears to have occurred in the 11th century (Brooke & Keir 1975, 168-70), the whole of this area, including both sides of Eastcheap, was contained within the single ward of Billingsgate.

The name Eastcheap itself points in the same direction: first occurring in *c*.1108 (Ekwall 1954, 185), the earliest date at which any London street is mentioned by name, it means 'eastern market'; contrasting with (West) Cheap, or Cheapside, it emphasises the existence of a separate commercial centre in the eastern half of the City, which bore much the same relationship to the local waterfront as Cheapside bore to Queenhithe. The comparison with Queenhithe is further underlined by the presence of streets leading south from Eastcheap to the waterfront as the local equivalents of Bread Street and Garlick Hill (above, p.17-18). Of these Botolph Lane, leading to Botolph Wharf, was already in existence at the turn of the 9th and 10th centuries, as shown above (p.19-20); and Idle Lane seems likely to share the same date as Eastcheap, of which it is in effect the southward continuation. So presumably does St Mary's Hill, which must certainly have followed the establishment of Billingsgate, to which it led directly; like Botolph Lane, and in contrast with Pudding and Lovat Lanes, it continued northwards beyond Eastcheap to Fenchurch Street.

The Eastcheap area would have depended for access to the western part of the city on the line of Cannon Street and, beyond that, of Knightrider Street, the *publica strata* which formed the northern boundary of the Alfredian plots at Queenhithe (above, p.16-17). Until the appearance of Thames Street, probably in the second half of the 11th century (see below, p.130), this would have been the readiest means of east-west communication between various points on the waterfront. Still more important to Eastcheap, and almost certainly the main reason for its development and that of the waterfront to the south, was

London Bridge which, like Billingsgate, is first mentioned in a text dating from the first half of the 11th century (see above, p.75). Whenever it was built, whether in the reigns of Alfred or Edward the Elder or closer to the date of the embankments, the bridge would have greatly increased the potential of the immediate area around its head as a point of interchange between road and river traffic. It may also have restricted the passage of shipping further upstream: Earl Godwine's fleet, on its return from exile in 1052, was obliged to await a suitable tide before it could pass beneath (*ASC*). With some important exceptions (see below, p.129-30) it would doubtless have been simpler and more convenient for most ships from downstream or overseas to berth in the Botolph Wharf – Billingsgate area just below the bridge.

St Botolph's Wharf in the 13th and 14th centuries

After 1200-1, when customs were paid on the goods it handled, there is little evidence of St Botolph's Wharf during the 13th century, except as a location. In 1270 it was referred to in a deed relating to Tenement **6**, on its western side, as a *kayum commune* (common quay) of the City of London (HR 4/57); a term frequently used thereafter to denote its public ownership, vested in the Commonalty, and also applied to Billingsgate and Queenhithe. In 1297 however the wharf, in a ruinous condition, had to be 'restored' to the City (*Cal Lbk B*, 243), and in 1325 it was decided that since the houses and wharf of St Botolph were in such a delapidated state that they brought no profit to the City, the current wardens of the bridge should be charged with repairing it from the profits of the bridge as a repayable loan (*Cal Lbk E*, 149). These repairs were still in progress in 1332 (*ibid*, 271), and the following year the wharf was leased out for varying terms by the City Chamber (*ibid*, 282-3; *Cal Lbk F*, 53). At some date between 1275 and 1284, presumably in anticipation of repair and restoration, the City also acquired Tenement **8** to the east from Thomas de Grascherche, his brother Robert quitclaiming the mayor and commonalty in 1305 (HR 33/74). Subsequently the deeds of the next tenement to the east refer to the common quay as its western neighbour (eg HR 46/24, 50/147, 62/52). Its acquisition by the City would have enlarged the overall area of St Botolph's Wharf, and in particular could have allowed for improved access from Thames Street past the east end of St Botolph's Church: though this access must, as the southern extremity of St Botolph's Lane, have existed from the period of the earliest embankments, little clear trace of it up to the end of the 12th century was found during the excavations (above, p.72).

St Botolph's Church

The church of St Botolph adjoined Thames Street to the north and St Botolph's Wharf to the south. In 1282 the mayor and commonalty granted to Richard de Kingston a portion of the common quay which extended along the south side of the church from Richard's property to the west (Tenement **6**) to the 'head' of the church and to the common way leading to the Thames to the east (GL MS 15364, p. 7). The length of this plot, and therefore of the church to the north, was 54 feet 9 inches; deeds of 1409 and 1443 concerning the same plot give its length as 53 feet 4 inches (GL MS 59, f.11^v-12^r; HR 172/1). Leake's survey of 1666, made immediately after the Great Fire and before the demolition of the church, shows that at that date its plan was roughly square. The church, like St Botolph's Wharf, is first indirectly alluded to in the name of Alfwold *de porta Sancti Botulfi*, who appears in the Westminster abbey charter probably forged in the 1140s (above, p.72). It has been suggested that the dedication to St Botolph, which was shared by several other churches situated by the City's gates, reflects a fashion set at St Botolph's Aldgate in the early 12th century by the first prior of Holy Trinity Aldgate who was formerly a canon of the first Augustinian house in England, the priory of St Julian and St Botolph outside the south gate of Colchester (Brooke & Keir 1975, 146). Even if so, dedications are no necessary indication of the dates of churches themselves, but the archaeological evidence from the lorry park site would suggest that St Botolph's Billingsgate was in existence by *c*.1100 (above, p.72). This conclusion is indirectly supported by its unusual location on the south side of Thames Street, for the churches of only three other waterfront parishes share this characteristic: St Magnus the Martyr immediately to the west and the two churches of All Hallows, the Great and the Less, in the Dowgate area (Fig 43). The remainder all favoured a location to the north of the street. The correspondence between untypical setting and centres of exceptional waterfront activity in the 11th century is unlikely to be coincidental and must have some common and specific explanation. One obvious possibility is that the provision of churches to cater for rapidly developing local communities in these areas occurred only after land subsequently on the north side of Thames Street was already fully occupied, leaving the reclaimed area on the waterfront to the south as the sole alternative site. At Dowgate, where the gently shelving terrain was particularly favourable to reclamation, this would have been a natural expedient which may also have set a precedent for the two churches immediately downstream of the bridge. St Magnus's Church, closest to St Botolph's, was described in 1108-16 as a stone chapel (Johnson & Cronne 1956, no. 1177).

SWAN LANE

(Figs 44-7)

The archaeological investigation of this site initially comprised a single narrow trench, 22m by 3m, running north-south within the basement of an existing multi-storey car park. Excavation took place over four months prior to the demolition and redevelopment, and was assisted by a grant from Edger Investments. Following demolition, a seven-month watching brief was carried out on the whole redevelopment area during ground reduction and foundation works, with financial support from the City of London Archaeological Trust and the Museum of London Trust Funds.

Within the narrow trench, full recording in both plan and section was possible to a considerable depth before the water-table was reached. In the watching brief, the timber structures were recorded in plan where possible, the associated deposits being recorded either in sketched or measured sections; in addition many finds groups were collected, frequently by metal detection, from material machined out of pile clearance holes and other machine excavations.

The excavation and subsequent watching brief were supervised by Geoff Egan, who also carried out the initial post-excavation analysis and preliminary phasing. Revised phasing and further integration was carried out by Ron Harris and Liz Shepherd in the course of producing an archive report for the whole sequence, and it is on that report that this summary is based. The

44. *Swan Lane: the first embankment, Waterfront 6, of mid 11th-century date, showing its presumed relationship to surviving Roman quay structures (shown dotted) along its southern edge. In Figs 44-7 the outline of the area excavated by hand is shown by the dash and dot line. Scale 1 :200.*

W6

River Tha

contexts recorded on site have been phased in Groups, sub-divided in accordance with discrete stratigraphic sequences, such as sections. The present summary refers to this phasing structure, and also uses the same numbered sequence of waterfronts.

Roman occupation on this site has been summarised elsewhere (Brigham 1990). Successive waterfronts (numbered 1 to 5; Groups 1-19) were recorded, dating from the mid 2nd to the mid 3rd century, with several revetments, associated drains and possibly a quayside building.

Groups 20 and 21: Robbing and post-Roman erosion and accumulation

(late 3rd to early 11th centuries)

(summarised in Fig 54 below)

Robbing of various structural elements and dumping of deposits indicated disuse of the Roman waterfront (Group 20). Several deep cuts appeared to have been dug to rob timbers from the revetments or associated structures; some cuts had been backfilled, and others contained water-laid accumulations. Roman drains were infilled after partial robbing, and a possible waterfront building was sealed by dumping marking its disuse.

These robbing cuts were only part of a more widespread and piecemeal dismantling of the revetments which left some surviving almost to their full original height, whilst only the base plates remained of others. The removal of parts of these structures would have destabilised the deposits originally retained behind them, leading to the erosion and spreading of that material. The post-Roman rise in river levels was clearly seen on this site, in the form of erosion and deposition of material in several places (Group 21); the extent of survival of the revetments, particularly their height, was an obvious indication of the degree to which this had occurred. Fresh

W7

River Tha

0   15 r

45. *Swan Lane: the second embankment, Waterfront 7, of late 11th-century date. The limit of stippling indicates the probable northern limit of the accumulation of foreshore material. Scale 1 :200.*

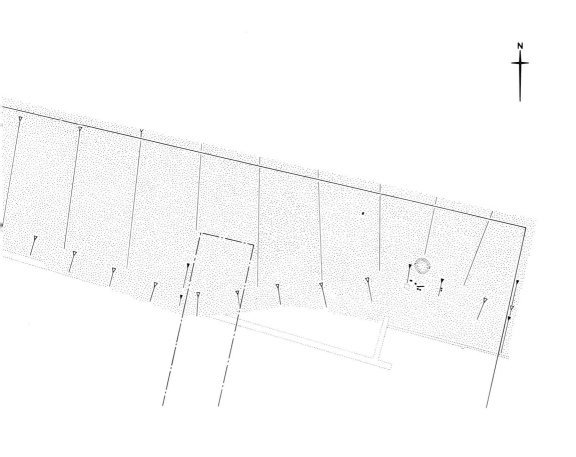

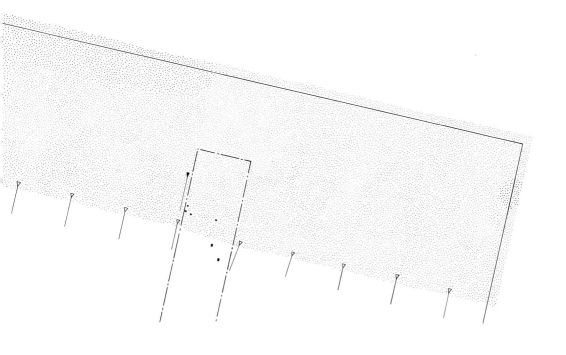

accumulation of silts and sands overlay the earlier deposits which marked the disuse of a large north-south drain, and its planking and supporting timbers. On the east side of the site the dumps associated with Waterfront 2 were eroded into a step-like profile rising from the south at between *c*.0.2m and 0.5m OD, the level at which the revetment to the south had been robbed, to a level of *c*.0.7m OD, with a further rise to *c*.1.om OD at the northern limit of excavation. The varying composition and compaction of the existing deposits (the upper layer had a high mortar content) seems to have led to this unusual profile (see Fig 54). Over this erosion horizon various silts and foreshore-like deposits accumulated on the different 'steps'. Other riverlain sands and silts were recorded at *c*.1.1m OD, immediately behind a part of Waterfront 2 which had survived to a higher level.

Datable material from Groups 20 and 21 was entirely Roman pottery, presumably disturbed during the robbing and erosion, but an 11th-century *terminus ante quem* is provided by the date of the embankments which followed.

Groups 22-24: Waterfront 6; the first embankment

(CP3, 1020-50)

(Fig 44)

In one area of the site, several dumps of organic material containing residual Roman pottery (Group 22) overlay some of the riverlain deposits of Group 21 and, although they differed generally in their composition, are likely to represent the earliest stage of the extensive phase of dumping which followed. Over the erosion and deposition horizon and the surviving elements of Roman revetments were dumped mixed deposits of clay and silt, with inclusions of stones, gravel and Roman building material (Group 23). Although virtually all these deposits were recorded in sections, some very widely spaced, enough was recorded to enable their extent to be reconstructed. The dumps formed an embankment which extended across the full width of the site and was highest in the centre of the site at the northern limit of excavation, where it appeared to have a fairly level surface at around 2.5m OD. From that point it sloped gently down (at about 1 in 6) to both west and south for several metres to a level of between 1.3m OD and 1.5m OD, before dropping more steeply (at about 1 in 4) to a level of about 0.2m OD at its southern edge. On the basis of the

levels of the dumps and of the surviving Roman quays it is proposed that in places the southern limit of the embankment would have been formed by the upper timbers of those earlier structures. The resultant frontage extended further to the south at the western end, though the slope there indicates that it may have been turning more to the north, if not actually terminating, a short distance further west. The eastern end also showed signs of returning to the north a short distance further east and there were also signs of an indentation close to the line of the underlying Roman drain, perhaps due to a lower degree of consolidation of the dumped material there. Much of the extent and level of the south-western part of the bank has been conjectured from nearby sections, though its conformation is confirmed by dumps, the upper surfaces of which were unfortunately truncated.

Foreshore deposits which had accumulated over the southern part of the embankment were recorded in two places: within the excavation trench, sands and gravels overlay the lowest recorded part of the bank, whilst at the bottom of a borehole two deposits of sandy gravels were observed on the line of its projected southern edge.

Various signs of occupation were recorded on the surface of the embankment (Group 24). On its eastern half several stakes lay in a rough east-west line along the edge of the steep slope at its southern edge. Their tops had broken off, and they survived to various heights between 0.1m OD and 1.5m OD. Their purpose can only be guessed at; the assumed river levels at the time, to judge by the height to which the riverlain material had accumulated prior to construction of the embankment, would have meant that these stakes, and the material into which they had been driven, would have lain below water during some part of the tidal cycle, and this could imply that they functioned as mooring-posts for boats which berthed on the lower slopes of the bank. A hearth was seen in section a short distance to the north, set within a hollow in the surface of the bank; a shallow cut contained three halved logs laid north-south, with a layer of fire-cracked flint pebbles overlying them at a level of about 0.9m OD. At this level it, like the stakes, would have been beneath water during part of the tidal cycle. The care taken to construct the hearth, however, implies that it might have been connected with some specific, perhaps industrial, use. Some, or all, of the stakes to the south may have formed a windbreak used with the hearth, which could have been used, between tides, for repairs to boats berthed on the surface of the embankment. Further stakes on the western part of the bank were less clearly attributable to any structural function, and may have been mooring posts. A possible trampled occupation layer of clay and charcoal was recorded on the surface of one part of the embankment, spread between it and subsequent dumping (part of Group 25).

The length of time which elapsed between the construction of this embankment and its successor (Group 25) is unknown, and it is possible that the Group 23 dumps may have been merely the first phase in the creation of a single embankment; the few traces of recorded occupation possibly occurred during a temporary halt in the dumping. However, the presence of the foreshore accumulations between the two embankments does imply that the break was more than temporary and only a very small proportion of the surface of the embankment was actually seen. The dating evidence is very sparse, comprising a few pottery sherds; most of the dumps which have been assigned to the earlier embankment (Group 23) contained pottery of CP3 (1020-10), and those of the later one (Group 25), and the occupation on it (Group 26), contained sherds which were of CP4 (1050-80).

Groups 25 and 26: Waterfront 7; the second embankment
(CP4, 1050-80)

(Fig 45)

The surface of the second embankment lay at about the same height as its predecessor on the northern edge of the site, at around 2.5m OD, but extended this higher surface several metres to the south, as well as to east and west. The newly created surface sloped only very gently down to the southern edge, where it dropped steeply (about 1 in 1) from about 2m OD onto the foreshore. The dumped material consisted of predominantly dark clayey silts though, where seen, the steeply sloping southern edge was consolidated with a layer of pure compacted clay. The southern edge thus formed described a straighter, more east-west, course, the whole embankment evening out the irregularities of the earlier one and extending up to 2.5m further south. Most of the area of the embankment would have been dry land, whilst the southern edge was clearly too steep for boats to have been berthed on it, though they could have been moored alongside.

Within the excavation trench, the upper surface and the steep southern edge of the embankment were recorded. The dumps there included four thin stakes of uncertain purpose, whilst two less securely stratified deposits have been attributed to this embankment, both because they lay south of the presumed line of the first, and because they were of similar composition to the others in Group 25. A compacted pebble surface was also recorded on the dumps in one area.

Group 26 comprised the only signs of activities which are directly attributable to the use of the second embankment; subsequent reclamation to the south does not appear to have significantly raised the ground level to the north and seems only to have extended the area south of the embankment edge, with the result that it is impossible to tell if evidence of occupation directly overlying the embankment surface, particularly when only seen in section, was not contemporary with these later phases. For this reason, Group 26 describes only evidence recorded within the excavation trench rather than during the watching brief. Other traces of occupation are described in Group 45.

A single oak plank had been set vertically into the sloping embankment edge, protruding above the clay surface by about 0.7m. Too insubstantial to have been a revetment, it may have functioned as a mooring post. This is the probable interpretation of another reused timber, a post inclined at about 45 degrees, but probably originally vertical. A foreshore of sands and pebbles with some clay had accumulated against the face of the bank, around the plank and probably the post also (though the post may have been driven through it), reaching a level of 1.1m OD and sloping down (at around 1 in 5) to the south. The accumulation was about 50mm deep, and was probably consolidated with a layer of deliberately placed large stones. A post-hole showed the position of a vertical timber at the top of the southern slope, which could have been a mooring post or part of a fence along the edge of the embankment.

Group 27: Waterfronts 8 and 9
(?early 12th century)

(Fig 46)

The first evidence of further reclamation was recorded some six or seven metres south of the second embankment, near the eastern site limit. A 60mm-thick oak plank, seen in section and for a short distance in plan, ran east-west into the limit of excavation at Ordnance Datum beside three displaced posts and another plank fragment. These are assumed to have been parts of a partially robbed revetment, but the full depth of even the single plank was not reached, so that little can be said of the construction of the revetment and no material was recorded as being specifically retained by it. Though designated Waterfront 8 there was no evidence that the timbers continued across the site as a revetment, and so little was seen of them that they may only have been discarded fragments from within dumping behind a revetment further south, or parts of a temporary and intermediate revetment.

More convincing evidence exists for a revetment frontage which ran the full width of the site several metres further south (Waterfront 9). A 1m-wide trench dug within the excavation area uncovered timbers which comprised the remains of a cruciform back brace or tieback, and which would presumably have engaged with a revetment to the south. The south end of the tieback, which was a reused timber, had been broken, perhaps during the robbing of the revetment, which probably ran a short distance south of this broken end. The tieback was not horizontal, being at 0.56m OD at the north end and −0.11m OD at the south; projecting this inclination further south and assuming a length of about 3m (a fairly typical length recorded on several other sites), the tieback would have engaged with the frontage at c. −0.2m OD, though the manner in which it engaged is unknown. Its inclination could of course have resulted from the robbing of the revetment. Even if a slot near the southern end of the tieback supported an angled brace, it seems that the frontage would not have been high enough to retain land at the level of the upper embankment surface, and it is likely that, as at other sites (see New Fresh Wharf, p.21, and Billingsgate Lorry Park, p.48), the ground behind it sloped down from dry land to a low revetment. The material upon which the tieback lay was not recorded, though it is probable that it lay on top of or within the dumped material behind the revetment. The dumps behind this revetment are discussed in Groups 34 and 35 (below, p.85), which comprise all the dumps behind this frontage and its successor to the south, machine excavation having made it impossible to assign them to specific episodes of reclamation.

Over 9m west of the remains of this tieback were the more fragmentary remains of another. The brace timber itself was missing, presumably

46. Swan Lane: Waterfront 9, of 12th-century date, with potentially contemporary hearths, and extent of internal surfaces recorded in section (Buildings 1-3, Group 45; internal divisions in Building 2 shown by dashed lines). The position of its possible predecessor, Waterfront 8, is also indicated. Scale 1:200.

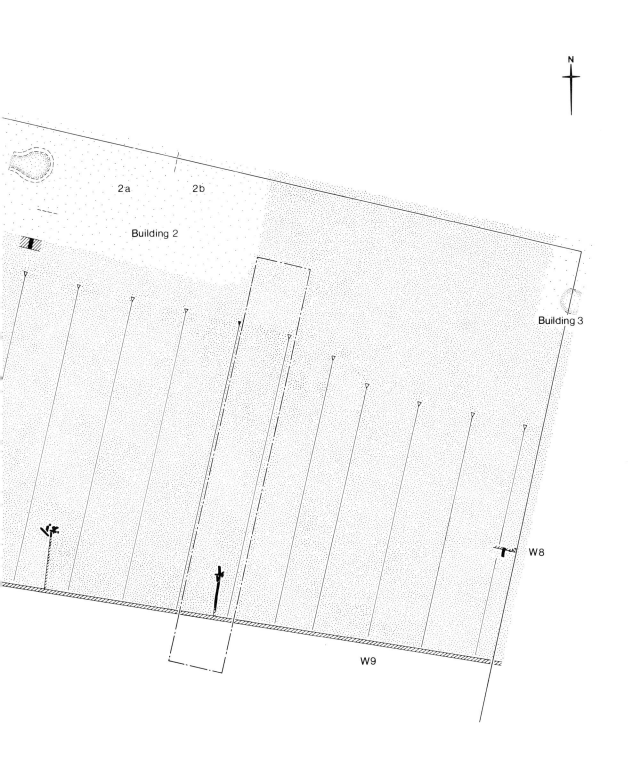

N

2a   2b

Building 2

Building 3

W8

W9

due to robbing, but elements of the cross-piece and the retaining stakes as well as probable underpinning timbers were recorded, though unfortunately without levels. In this case, the dumped material on and partially within which the timbers lay was recorded, as distinct from the material which overlay them (part of Group 35). A nearby upright post, over 1.9m in length and over 0.3m wide, may have been contemporary. Although to the north of the projected line of the frontage, it appears to have been either earlier than, or to have been positioned within, dumps which may have been retained by the revetment; it could have been part of another back-bracing arrangement, or a mooring post.

Several other timbers lay on the projected course of the revetment further west. An east-west row of vertically-set planks was noted during the excavation of overlying deposits of Group 35, though unfortunately no levels were recorded or details of how the timbers articulated; they probably represent further confirmation of the conjectured frontage, as do three posts further west. A squared upright timber, 0.3m by 0.1m in section, was recorded with a smaller 0.1m-square post set against its southern face. Both were at least 0.7m in length, and 3m to the east lay a third post, 0.15m square. They were about 0.5m to the north of the line of planks, and may have been supports for the planking of a revetment or have been associated with some kind of bracing. The bracing of this western section of the revetment is not clear, though it may well have been back-braced, like that to the east. Foreshore deposits which are likely to have been associated with Waterfront 9 were recorded in two places. The baseplate of a revetment (Group 29) used in the subsequent waterfront had been laid directly on a deposit of sand and gravel, presumably a foreshore contemporary with the waterfront previous to it. Unfortunately no levels were taken on this foreshore. A very coarse sand, horizontally banded, and including freshwater snails, was also seen south of the suggested line of Waterfront 9. Its surface, sealed beneath the dumping behind the subsequent waterfront, was levelled at −0.6m OD, making it fairly certain that at least its upper parts were contemporary with Waterfront 9, whilst its depth of over 0.8m makes it likely that the remainder represented successive foreshores from as early as the Roman period.

The dating of Waterfronts 8 and 9 depends almost entirely on the pottery recovered from the dumped material associated with them; the recording conditions made it difficult to dis-

tinguish between material retained by these waterfronts and those which followed, and all the dumps are discussed in Groups 34 and 35 (see below). A dendrochronological date of 1042+ was however obtained for a timber from Waterfront 8 (SWA 3018).

Groups 29-33: Waterfront 10
(?late 12th century)

(Fig 47)

Whilst Waterfront 9 seems to have described a fairly straight east-west line across the site, its successor, Waterfront 10, incorporated several north-south revetments as well as those running east-west. The westernmost revetment was a post and plank front-braced structure (Group 30), of which five upright posts were recorded. Two of them were jointed to angled front-braces with mortice and tenon joints, while two others included mortices from which the braces had been removed; the base of the structure was not seen so that the presence or absence of a base plate, and the manner in which the braces were footed, is unknown. A decayed timber fragment on the top of one upright may have been the remains of a top plate, suggesting that the original height of this revetment was about 1.05m OD, though the timber fragment could have been part of the base for another level of upright planks. Dumps directly associated with it (parts of Groups 30 and 34) consisted of redeposited foreshore material overlain by a clay deposit with silty deposits on its surface. These deposits were at too low a level, 1.4m OD, to have remained as dry land if, as seems likely, the river level was still as high as has been inferred from earlier erosion. It is possible that these deposits represented a formal working surface by the waterfront (the silty deposits representing trample), though clay can hardly be regarded as an ideal material for such a surface, and it seems more likely that it was tidal action, following the disuse of this revetment, which exposed a clay layer within the retained dumps. A sandy foreshore seen to the south at about −0.05m OD and sloping steeply south was probably contemporary with the revetment. Three metres to the north and east of this revetment was evidence for another (Group 28). It comprised a horizontal timber about 0.35m square and over 4m long which, although removed by machine and observed only from a distance, so that no joints or other features could be seen, is presumed to have been the base plate for an east-west revetment. A north-south revetment connecting these two east-west revetments is likely to have existed; that they were contemporary is implied by the presence of dumps containing 12th-century dating material to the north of the Group 30 revetment, and 13th-century material south of the Group 28 revetment.

A north-south revetment (Group 29) was recorded about 3.5m to the east of the Group 28 structure. A squared horizontal beam measuring about 0.2m by 0.3m and over 2m long, with a groove running along its upper surface, was found in association with at least two horizontal planks, the lowest of which was set in the groove and supported by several posts which may have been jointed into the base plate. It is assumed to have retained land to its east rather than the west, though no bracing was definitely found in either direction. Two reused upright timbers to the east may have been part of its back-bracing, or could have supported a drain. Both these squared timbers had tenons at their feet and grooves running down two adjacent sides, features which they shared with timbers from revetments further east but which were not apparently functioning in their recorded positions. A series of drains (Group 36) led down to this area from the north, and the squared timbers may well have been connected with them in some way.

Directly opposite the southward projection of the Group 29 revetment was the westernmost of an east-west line of at least five upright posts, elements of another revetment (Group 31). These squared timbers had grooves cut into their east and west faces which would have received horizontal planks, later robbed, and one of them still had the remains of a front-raking brace jointed to it. It is not known if this structure had a base plate, and although one of the timbers was at least 3m long, no levels could be recorded, so that its original height is unknown; one of these timbers (SWA 1579) produced a dendrochronological date of 1123+. Dumped organic material, horizontally banded, was recorded behind it, containing pottery of late 12th-century date. Around 1.5m to the south and 1m to the east of the line of this revetment were the remnants of another (Group 33). Two vertical posts had fragments of planks remaining against their northern faces, whilst a further post with grooves cut in its sides, though apparently reused here, was set between them with its northern edge on the line of the planks; no information about bracing or foundation was recorded. Dumps of organic material,

with bands of silt and more structured organic constituents, probably represented the reclamation dumps behind this structure and, like the dumps of Group 31, contained late 12th-century pottery. The easternmost revetment (Group 32) of Waterfront 7 lay about 3m to the east and 2.5m to the north, where three vertical squared posts, up to 0.36m in width, and at least 2.05m long, survived to above or around Ordnance Datum, but would originally have been much higher; no planks or bracing survived.

Groups 34 and 35: Reclamation dumping behind Waterfronts 9 and 10
(12th century)

(Figs 46-7)

It is possible that other revetments lay between Waterfront 9 and those described above, but remained undetected under watching brief conditions; similarly any of the east-west revetments could have extended further than conjectured above, where the simplest explanation is presented. It seems reasonable to conclude that the 'stepped' frontage reflected the existence by this date of several distinct properties across the site, establishing a pattern which became more obvious with subsequent reclamation. In only three cases, mentioned above, was it possible directly to relate dumps to specific revetments. The remainder of the dumps behind this waterfront have been discussed in two groups, Groups 34 and 35, material recorded in section and in plan respectively. There was apparently no difference in date between deposits in the north, which directly overlay the southern edge of the later embankment, and those in the south, which were retained by Waterfront 10. Although some stratigraphic relationships were observed, particularly in the excavation trench, there was not enough evidence in most cases, nor was there any clear division in the dating, to distinguish dumps which were specific to one waterfront; extensive robbing of Waterfront 9 would in any case have meant that much of the area behind it may have been covered by dumping related to subsequent reclamation. In the few places where it was recorded, the top of these dumps was at a level of 1.4m-1.7m OD, which implies that not only was there a step or slope down from the level of the embankment to the north, but that much of the reclaimed land would have been below water at high tide.

The dating material was virtually all of the 12th century, with some obviously residual material. A timber (SWA 523C) from within the dumping was felled after 1142.

Group 36: Drains

(Fig 47)

Group 36 consists of a series of drains which lay in the centre of the site, not far to the north of the line of Waterfront 10, and presumably served the reclaimed area behind it. Two ran north-south and one east-west.

No dating evidence was recovered from these features.

Groups 37-44 describe revetments of 13th-century or later date, and are not considered here.

Group 45: Occupation over second embankment

(? late 11th/late 12th century)

(Figs 46-7)

Group 45 comprises the evidence for activities (internal occupation surfaces and hearths) directly overlying Waterfront 7, the second embankment; all the features of this group were recorded in section. They could have been contemporary with Waterfronts 7-10 which spanned the late 11th to mid/late 12th centuries. When combined, the alignment of the mid to late 12th-century waterfront (Waterfront 10) and later documentary sources (below, pp.93-5) indicate the presence of five properties on the site.

Towards the north-west of the site was an isolated hearth with a brickearth kerb and tile burning surface, cut directly into the underlying dumps of the Saxon bank (Fig 46). No associated surface survived, but the hearth has been labelled Building 1. If similar in plan to hearths which followed, the hearth may have been keyhole-shaped and had its mouth to the west or south. It could have been either domestic or industrial in function.

Buildi

Building

W 10

River Thames

0   15m

47. Swan Lane: Waterfront 10, probably late 12th-century, comprising the revetments of (from left to right) Groups 30, 28, 29, 31, 33 and 32. Potentially contemporary features to the north (Building 4, Group 45) also shown, and the drains of Group 36. Scale 1:200.

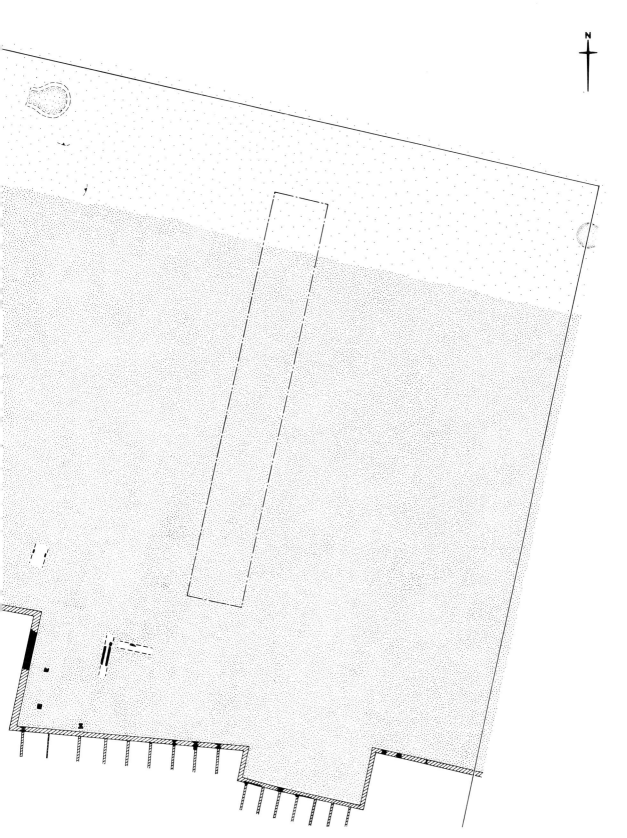

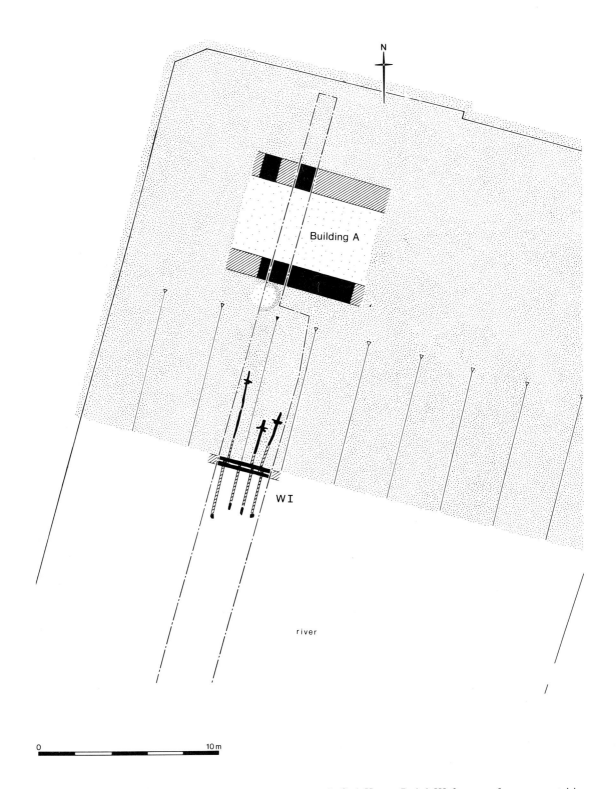

N

Building A

W I

river

0   10 m

48. Seal House: Period III features, of c.1140, comprising Waterfront I and Building A. On Figs 48 and 50 the outline of the area excavated by hand is shown by the dash and dot line. Scale 1 :200.

Further east was a stone and clay hearth, again possibly domestic and far enough away from Building 1 to have been part of a separate building (Building 2), divided into two rooms (A and B). The hearth lay within Room A and the stones incorporated in it had apparently been hewn or split along the grain to form flat pieces, then laid horizontally. A later hearth above this opened to the west, suggesting the orientation of the lower hearth. Associated with the hearth were occupation surfaces and the foundation of an east-west wall perhaps forming the southern boundary of the building, though as similar surfaces continued to the south it might have been an internal partition. Further clay floors lay within Room B and occupation surfaces extended to the north.

At the eastern edge of the site was another hearth with associated burnt floors to the north, assigned to Building 3. This hearth did not incorporate tiles in its surface and may have been domestic in character; but it had been truncated by later activity, and possibly only the base survived to be recorded.

Further activities above the Saxon embankment (Building 4) occurred about 2m south of the alignment of Waterfront 7, and it is possible that they were contemporary with Waterfront 10 to the south (Fig 47). The base of an internal building division, with floors to east and west, was at a level of around 1.7m OD, whilst further surfaces lay east at 2.2m OD. North and east of these were pits cutting into the embankment surface and parts of the first building described above; east of the pits was a possible hearth. Also recorded was a gravelled surface, perhaps a yard or a path leading to the river, with a possible gulley on its eastern side. The hearth from the first building was sealed by further occupation layers and burning, including another hearth, and these were in turn sealed by make-up dumps. To the south, further make-up dumps sealed other features. A clay floor and possible clay sill, with a stakehole within it, lay to the south, and may have been a continuation of the building with the clay sill mentioned earlier.

All of these features were recorded in section, and as such they produced virtually no dating evidence. Most probably range between the late 11th and late 12th centuries, assuming that they are contemporary with Waterfronts 7-10.

(Figs 48-52)

In 1974, over a six-month period, a trench measuring 26m north-south by 3m east-west, with a 1m-wide extension for a further 14m to the north, was excavated at 105-6 Upper Thames Street (SH74). The site was an open basement, adjacent to Seal House to the east. In 1976 redevelopment by the Fishmongers' Company of the area around the original trench presented the opportunity for a watching brief over a wider area (SH76). The supervision of the excavation and watching brief and compilation of the archive report were undertaken by John Schofield (1978).

Boreholes indicated that the site lay immediately south of the pre-Roman north bank of the Thames. London Clay lay at about -7m OD, overlain by gravels at between -2.4m OD and -3.1m OD.

The sequence was phased into *Periods*, sometimes further subdivided into *Phases*, cited here as III.1 etc. Eleven Periods were identified. Period I covered the Roman waterfronts, discussed in more detail elsewhere (Brigham 1990). Periods II-IV, discussed here, cover the period up to the early 13th century.

Period II: Erosion and deposition
(3rd-12th century)

Sand and gravel layers were deposited in front of and over the remnants of the latest Roman waterfront structure, which must have been partly visible as a hump in the foreshore. Some early medieval pottery sherds were recovered from these foreshore deposits, but most of the finds were rolled Roman sherds, shoe fragments and stray timbers of oak.

Period III: Silting, Waterfront I and Building A
(*c.*1140-70)

(Figs 48-9)

The silting-up over the disused Roman quay continued with the deposition of more gravel interleaved with layers of organic material (III.1). Within these layers, but imperfectly recorded because of restricted access, were many cut oak

twigs which may have been the remains of hurdles, perhaps originally involved in the consolidation of the foreshore; finds included a German coin of c.1080-1100 (Stott in Vince 1991, 320, no. 165). A timber structure was laid on the foreshore (III.2), consisting of large planks running east-west with squared timbers driven vertically between and on either side of them. During excavation this was thought to be part of Waterfront I to the south, but it is equally likely that it represents an earlier structure on the foreshore; its extent is unknown, and it was not observed in the watching brief. It was covered by further deposits of clay and gravel (III.3).

About 5m south of the plank-and-post structure, the base plate of Waterfront I (III.4) was placed directly on the foreshore, with its upper surface at between −1.04 and −1.13m OD (Figs 48, 49). This oak timber, running east-west, was at least 2.7m long, 0.5m wide and 0.36m deep. A longitudinal notch of a slight V-shape had been cut along its upper surface, presumably designed to hold vertically set staves. There was evidence of both front- and back-bracing associated with this revetment (Fig 48). Four cruciform tiebacks, retained by stakes driven into the sloping surface of the earlier foreshore, would have helped to brace the upright stave frontage; they were retained at distances of between 2m and 5m north

49. Seal House: the base plate of Waterfront I, looking north, with the angled bracing pads set in the foreshore to the south. Scale 2 × 100mm.

of the base plate, the longest reusing stakes from the earlier structure. Between 2m and 2.5m south of the base plate, four pads, each made of two plank fragments, were set into the foreshore at an angle to serve as the base for diagonal front-braces. While the tiebacks were buried within the dumped material retained by the revetment, and were undoubtedly primary to the construction, the front-braces may well have been added at a later date as extra support. The cruciform braces were covered by a thick layer of organic dumping which extended from the line of the revetment to the extreme northern end of the trench, having risen from a level of around 1m OD at the edge of the cut resulting from the later robbing of the revetment face, to a relatively level surface of around 2m OD, 7.5m to the north. This change in level could have been due to river erosion following the disuse of the revetment, though if the revetment had originally supported a level surface it would have been over 3m high; alternatively it may have been designed to protect only the lower parts of a sloping embankment, as was the case with Waterfront 8 (1108+) at Billingsgate Lorry Park (above, p.60).

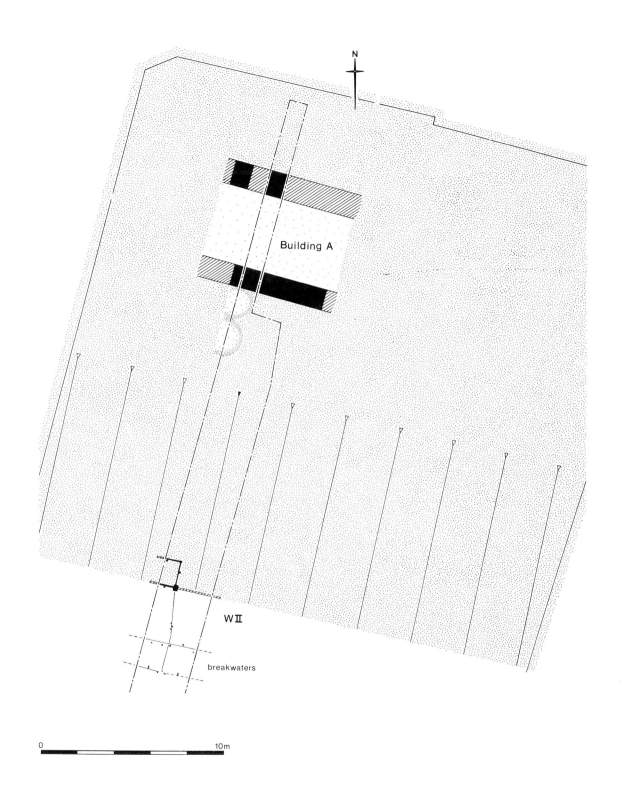

Building A

WII

breakwaters

0   10m

50. Seal House: Period IV features, of c.1170, comprising
Waterfront II with Building A remaining in use. Scale 1:200.

On top of the dumping lay two parallel east-west foundations, each 1.2m wide and chalk-built, with shallow foundation trenches (Building A). They appear to have been the bases for narrower walls, later robbed, giving an internal width of over 4m; observations during the watching brief imply a length east-west of at least 6.5m. Internal surfaces of rammed, decomposed sandstone, charcoal and sands in thin bands were recorded. Just to the south, the external area also had several superimposed hearths at 1.92m OD, south of which the ground sloped, or had been eroded, to the revetment frontage. Light grey-brown and black silt and gravel formed a contemporary foreshore south of the base plate.

Dendrochronology has shown that timbers from Waterfront I were felled between 1133 and 1170, whilst the associated pottery was of CP5 (1080-1150).

Period IV: Robbing of Waterfront I, construction of Waterfront II
(1163-92)

(Figs 50-2)

Waterfront I was robbed (IV.1), all the superstructure except for the severed tiebacks being removed, and the shoreline was extended about 7m to a second structure of different design, Waterfront II (IV.2). A substantial vertical oak post, 0.34m square in section, tapering slightly towards the top and with grooves on all sides but

51. Seal House: the post and plank construction of Waterfront II, looking south-west, following removal of the retained dumps. The eastern part of the revetment (to left) was robbed during subsequent advancement of the waterfront. Scale 5 × 100mm.

52. *Landward side of the frontage of Waterfront II at Seal House, the retained dumping and associated post and planks having been removed. Looking south; scale 5 × 100mm.*

ing to the south of Waterfront II, beneath Waterfront III, was presumably of this period.

No directly associated stratigraphy could be identified to the north; presumably Building A continued in use with Waterfront II, and the hearths continued to build up to the south of it.

Timbers from Waterfront II were dated by dendrochronology to between 1163 and 1192. The ceramics comprised a coherent group of CP6 (1150-80) pottery with some residual material.

Following its partial robbing, Waterfront II was succeeded by Waterfront III, built 6m further south, in *c*.1210. This structure is not described here, but in the report dealing with subsequent periods (Schofield & Dyson, in prep). Appendix 1 below contains notes on the ceramic dating for Waterfront III, as it helps to define CP7 (1180-1240).

DOCUMENTARY EVIDENCE FOR SWAN LANE AND SEAL HOUSE

the south, was set in the foreshore. Horizontal planks fitted into these grooves to form the frontage, whilst a smaller grooved post behind would have engaged with planks running north from the large post, with further planks running from it westwards, presumably to form boxes (Figs 50-2). Later robbing associated with the construction of the subsequent revetment (Waterfront III) had removed most of the planking east of the large post, though there was no groove on the smaller post to suggest that the arrangement of boxes behind the frontage had continued in that direction. The design of Waterfront II presumably allowed for the creation of a vertical frontage, perhaps with its top at a level of around 1.20m OD, stabilised by infilled compartments behind. Organic material, silt and rubbish filled the area behind the revetment and the intervening space between it and the robbing cut of Waterfront I. Various timbers consolidated the dumped material, including a cruciform tieback perhaps robbed from the previous revetment. Two further compartments formed of smaller piles and timbers lay to the south of the main timber, with east-west lines of single planks on edge forming a breakwater or groin in front of the revetment wall. Silt-

These two sites lay on either side of Ebbgate (now known as Swan Lane) which in the medieval period and later formed the continuation, south of Thames Street, of St Martin's Lane, and was followed by the boundary between the parish of St Lawrence Pountney and the ward of Dowgate to the west, and the parish of St Martin Orgar and the ward of Bridge to the east (Figs 43, 53). Ebbgate, first recorded in 1147-67 (Hodgett 1971, no. 394), is comparable in name and no doubt in function and general date with *Rederesgate* at the foot of *Retheresgatelane* or Pudding Lane, 'Botolphsgate' at the foot of Botolph Lane, and Billingsgate at the foot of St Mary's Hill. The pattern suggests that the gates on the waterfront and the streets leading to them from the interior of the city were regarded as single entities in which both elements are likely to be of broadly 11th-century date (see Part 6), though the case of Pudding Lane (see above p.75) would indicate that the chronological correspondence between them was not always exact and sometimes was not complete until the 12th century.

Swan Lane (Tenements 1-5)

The excavations at Swan Lane coincided with a line of five medieval properties to the west of Ebb-

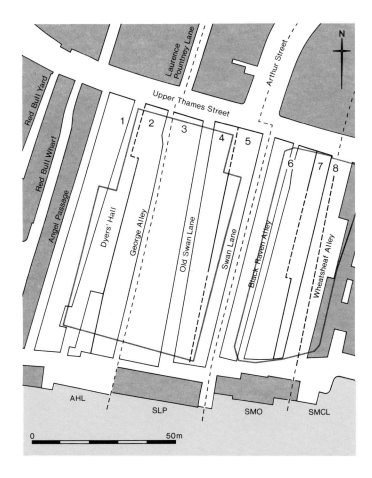

Upper Thames Street

Laurence Pountney Lane

Arthur Street

N

Red Bull Yard

Red Bull Wharf

Angel Passage

Dyers' Hall

George Alley

Old Swan Lane

Swan Lane

Black Raven Alley

Wheatsheaf Alley

1 2 3 4 5 6 7 8

AHL   SLP   SMO   SMCL

0   50m

53. Location of medieval tenements **1-8** *on the Swan Lane and Seal House sites, from documentary evidence (the modern site outlines shown in grey line). Based on the early 19th-century street plan, with parishes indicated as follows:* AHL = *All Hallows the Less;* SLP = *St Lawrence Pountney;* SMO = *St Martin Orgar;* SMCL = *St Michael Crooked Lane. For location compare Fig 65. Scale 1:1250.*

gate (Fig 53), two of them (**1-2**) at the eastern end of the parish of All Hallows the Less, and the other three (**3-5**) together comprising the narrow southern frontage of the parish of St Lawrence Pountney. In 1459 **2** measured 40 feet 6 inches along Thames Street and 31 feet along the Thames, street and river then being 305 feet apart (HR 188/6). Immediately to the east **3** measured 52 feet from east to west in 1402 (131/37). Measurements of this kind are not available for any of the other tenements in this group, so that the locations of none of them can be plotted out across the width of the site. Nevertheless the two measured tenements can be compared with two adjacent river frontages recorded on site with widths of 12m (39 feet 4 inches) and 13m (42 feet 8 inches) (Fig 64, below). Though the relative widths of the two tenements were not proportionate, as between the archaeology and the documents, the structures found on site were late 12th-century in date and lay well to the north of the frontages of the first half of the 15th century. There is ample evidence that the waterfront ten-

ements were not regular in width along their whole length, but often tapered both inwards and outwards, and it is possible that nearer to Thames Street their dimensions were closer to those observed. An identification of these two frontages with Tenements **2** and **3**, the Swan Lane trench lying within the eastern half of the latter, would mean that Tenements **4** and **5** would correspond to two further late 12th-century frontages, each on a different alignment (Fig 64). If correct, this interpretation of the evidence would place Tenements **1** (from soon after 1484 the site of Dyers' Hall) and **2** to the west of the later George Alley; **3** roughly between George Alley and Old Swan

Lane; and **4** and **5** between Old Swan Lane and Ebbgate. As on the waterfront below the bridge, the properties tended to be described simply as 'tenements' up to the mid 14th century, though **5** was defined in 1296 as a capital messuage with shops in front (HR 25/23). Tenement **3** was occupied by goldsmiths (as was **5** on one recorded occasion); the early 14th-century occupants of **4** included a former royal cook, a vintner, a wax-chandler, two drapers and a dyer; and those of **5** a grocer, a corndealer, a goldsmith, a dyer, a tanner and a stockfishmonger.

Seal House (Tenements 6-8)

Like that of St Lawrence Pountney on the west side of Ebbgate, the frontage of the parish of St Martin Orgar on the east side comprised three tenements only (**6-8**) (Fig 53). No measurements are available for any of them during the medieval period, or until after the Great Fire. A Fishmongers' Company plan of 1686 shows an area between Black Raven Alley to the west and a property to the east which can be identified with **8**; if, as seems most likely, Black Raven Alley is identical with the *Popys allye* which in 1541 bisected Tenement **6** (GL MS 25121/1394), the frontage of the latter property would have measured some 50 feet along Thames Street (comparable with Tenement **3** at Swan Lane), the Seal House trench falling within its eastern portion. Interpreted in that way, the plan of 1686 shows the length of the Tenement **7** frontage as 17 feet, leaving for Tenement **8** a frontage of only 9 feet within the 75-foot width of the parish as it was constituted from the 1670s. As elsewhere, the three properties are typically defined only as tenements

in the late 13th and early 14th centuries, though **6** was described as 'land' (*terra*) on one occasion between *c*.1225 and 1243 (GL MS 25121/1389), and **7** as a capital house (*capitalis domus*) in 1298 (HR 27/34). No early occupational details are available for **6**; **7** was held by ironmongers or smiths and stockfishmongers, and **8** by a dyer and fishmongers.

The early dumped deposits on the foreshore at the Swan Lane site were seen to taper away towards the north-east (above, p.80), in the direction of Ebbgate, and no sign of them was found at Seal House on the far side of Ebbgate (pp.89-90). The Swan Lane site evidently coincided with the eastern extremity of late Saxon embankments upstream of the bridge. In several respects this arrangement compares with that at New Fresh Wharf, downstream of the bridge, where the western termination of embankments of similar character and date was marked by a jetty and trackway (above, pp.28-9, 40, 42-3) coinciding with the location of *Rederesgate*. Ebbgate and *Rederesgate* therefore appear to have shared a similar relationship with the inner ends of embankments to either side of London Bridge, and they also defined the western and eastern limits respectively of Bridge ward. The wards themselves, as units of local administration and defence, are thought to have evolved during the course of the 11th century (Brooke & Keir 1975, 168-70); at or soon after the date of the second phase of embankments on the present sites and when *Rederesgate* and, apparently, Ebbgate were already conspicuous features on the foreshore. The two gates also served to mark parish boundaries when these came to be defined, probably towards the middle of the 12th century (*ibid*, 129-33).

4 : THE WATERFRONT *c*.400-1200

Any understanding of the topography of the area prior to the revival of the 10th and 11th centuries must include the extent to which it was affected by the disused Roman waterfront structures, including the riverside defensive wall.

The late Roman port

The extensive series of quays constructed along the waterfront during the Roman period involved the reclamation of large areas of the foreshore. The reclamation, particularly in the later Roman period, was not the result of any population pressure for more building land, but more a by-product of the need to advance further out into the river to maintain sufficient depth of water at the quayfront for the docking and unloading of vessels, as a consequence of the persistent drop in river levels which continued throughout the Roman period (Brigham 1990). By the latter half of the 3rd century, the Roman port was in decline, due probably to a combination of economic factors and the tidal regime of the Thames; the drop in the river level could have resulted in the movement east of the tidal head, rendering more and more of the waterfront unusable for the docking of boats (Milne 1985, 85). The construction of the Roman riverside wall, at some time between AD 250 and 270, effectively cut the City off from the quays.

The decline of the port, and the construction of the wall, led to the disuse of the waterfront structures, with various degrees of dismantling or abandonment reflected on the excavated sites. In some cases virtually all traces of the quay were removed, such as the length between the east side of Billingsgate Lorry Park and the present Custom House (Brigham 1990), though for the most part the dismantling was restricted to the superstructure and some of the tieback braces and upper quayfront timbers. The removal of such structural elements inevitably led to a destabilisation of the remainder of the quay, rendering it an inadequate defence against the river, and leading to the erosion and spreading of the relatively uncompacted, dumped material previously retained by the revetments.

The post-Roman riverbank: archaeological evidence

(Figs 1-2, 54-5)

The silting and erosion following the disuse of the Roman quays has been seen clearly on several sites, as has evidence that the dropping of the river levels experienced during the Roman period was now reversed; erosion by the river subsequently reached as far north as the Roman riverside wall. When the wall was built, the high tide level of the river was, for the most part, below that of its shallow foundations, and the adjacent quayfront, where still present, lay between 6m and 8m to the south, and must have been regarded as ample protection against river action.

The late 2nd- or early 3rd-century Roman waterfronts recorded during excavations at Custom House (Tatton-Brown 1974) had been either partially robbed or allowed to fall into disrepair, and dating evidence implies a 4th-century date for their disuse. Over the remains of these revetments and dumps was a clear erosion horizon, overlain by sands and gravels containing well-rolled late Roman pottery, as well as the occasional sherd of Saxo-Norman pottery and 12th-century imports. These deposits were found in all trenches where excavation was of sufficient depth, with their base describing a relatively gentle incline from −0.7m OD to the south of the disused Roman revetments to +0.5m OD at the

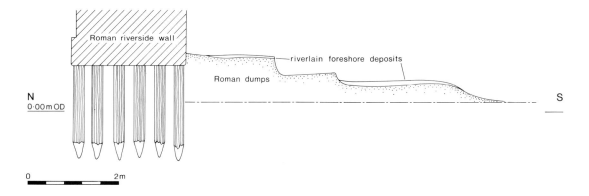

N
0·00m OD

S

0   2m

54. *Reconstructed section showing the stepped erosion profile of Roman dumps at Swan Lane. The position of the late Roman riverside wall is conjectured. Scale 1 :80.*

extreme north of the site, where the gravels over-lay the sparse remnants of what can now be recog-nised as the southern edge of the Roman riverside wall foundation. With the northern part of the wall foundation lying outside the excavated area, it is impossible to tell if part of the wall survived as a barrier to further erosion inland. Elsewhere erosion of the southern side of the riverside wall was recorded during observations along the east side of the old Billingsgate Market building (Brigham 1985), and at the opposite end of the City at Baynard's Castle (above, Fig 1, site BC75; Hill, Millett & Blagg 1980) and Peter's Hill (Fig 1, site PET81; Williams 1982). At Custom House to the east, and on these other sites at the western end of Thames Street, it was not until at least the late 12th century that the area south of the wall was reclaimed, and it remains unclear how far the erosion had progressed by the late 9th century.

At New Fresh Wharf, the Roman timber quay of AD 224-44 was dismantled to varying degrees along its length. It was almost totally removed at its western end, where an inlet appears to have formed as a result (see Fig 55), perhaps to allow access to the river from a gate in the riverside wall (Miller, Schofield & Rhodes 1986, 72). River action resulted in the deposition of silts over col-lapsed quay members, as well as erosion and dis-persal of material originally dumped behind the quayfront. In places, some waterlain gravel deposits overlay this dispersed material. Between the disused quay and the Roman riverside wall, some 8m to the north, there was deliberate dump-ing of silty gravels and some occupation debris, and these, combined with the silts and waterlain gravels to the south, comprised the shelving river-

bank prior to the late Saxon construction work, reaching a maximum level of 2.18m OD against the Roman riverside wall at the eastern end of the site, and dropping to 0.68m OD at the western side. The deposits contained late Roman and late Saxon pottery. There appears to have been some erosion of the wall, particularly at the western end where there were no dumped deposits to protect it, but this was restricted to the exposure of some of the piles at the edge of the foundation raft. The erosion and undermining of the wall was only a fraction of that recorded at Baynard's Castle, and this may indicate that the worst of the erosion occurred at some time after the stretch of wall at New Fresh Wharf had been protected from the river by the construction of the late Saxon embankments (*ibid*, 70).

At Billingsgate Lorry Park, immediately to the east of New Fresh Wharf, a similar sequence was excavated, though the excavation did not extend as far north as the Roman riverside wall. Follow-ing some dismantling, including its almost total removal in the eastern part of the site, the quay was allowed to silt up before the western part underwent a short-lived reconstruction. This reconstruction, incorporating what has been interpreted as a crane-base, occurred at around the same time as the construction of the riverside wall (AD 255-70). It may have been carried out purely for the unloading of building materials for that project, though it could equally well have been connected with a continuing, but reduced, level of trade. Whatever the case, this reconstruc-ted portion was not in use for long as it was partially robbed and sealed by dumped material of late 3rd- or early 4th-century date, reaching about 1m OD. This has been interpreted as an embankment for the protection of the 8m-wide strip of land between the river and the wall (Brigham 1990), and the curving to the north of its eastern end (see Fig 55), echoed by the position

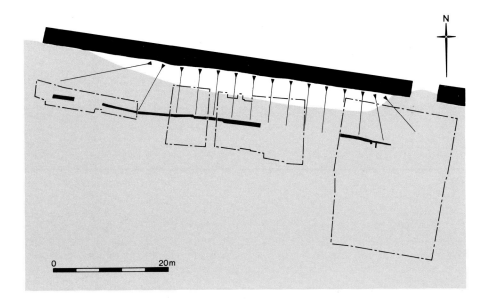

N

0   20m

55. Plan of the riverbank at New Fresh Wharf and Billingsgate in the late 10th century, with surviving elements of the late Roman quays protruding above the foreshore. Areas of controlled excavation shown; blue indicates probable extent of the river at proposed mean high tide of + 1m OD. Scale 1 : 1250.

of a Saxon revetted inlet, hints at the existence of a late Roman gate in the wall at this point. Whether or not there were gates here and at the western end of New Fresh Wharf, those areas on both sites where the Roman quay was most thoroughly robbed were maintained as inlets into the medieval period. On this site therefore, as at New Fresh Wharf, the mid Saxon riverbank was composed of late Roman dumped deposits and the silted-up remains of the partially robbed Roman quay, overlain in places by foreshore deposition.

The two sites above the bridge contained lengths of the late Roman waterfront (described fully in Brigham 1990), though neither excavation extended far enough to the north to encounter the riverside wall. At Seal House, about 80m upstream of the Roman bridge, the waterfront had been partially dismantled, or had been eroded, though several horizontal timbers, possibly parts of a quayside building, did survive at what must have been the original working level of around 0.41m OD. In front of and over the disused quay and its eroded dumps were deposited mixed clays and gravels which, like those at Custom House, represented the post-Roman erosion horizon. Some 10th- to 12th-century pottery came from these layers, but the bulk of the datable material was waterworn Roman sherds. At Swan Lane, just to the west of Seal House, extensive remains of several phases of Roman waterfronts were recorded. The latest of these were robbed following disuse, though some parts remained to virtually their full height and survived *in situ* to

be used as retaining elements for the initial late Saxon embankment. Subsequent erosion cut step-like profiles into the dumps behind, apparently corresponding to the degree of compaction of the eroded deposits, and silts and gravels accumulated above (Fig 54). The erosion reached at least 1.2m OD at the extreme northern site limit, beneath deposits associated with the construction of the embankment. The projected line of the riverside wall is not far to the north, and it may be that the erosion neither reached much further north nor a much higher level than recorded, before construction of the embankment halted it.

For gravels to have been deposited over the erosion horizons, as they were on several sites, the river not only must have continued to rise, but must have been flowing fairly fast to carry them. The growth of vegetation on the riverbanks would also have aided the deposition of silts when the river rose to cover them.

The influence of the riverside wall on development of the riverbank

The structural features of the late Roman waterfront were clearly an influence on the topography of the pre-Saxon shoreline. The degree to which the timber waterfronts were dismantled affected the subsequent level of erosion, and created topographical features which persisted into the medieval period. The riverside wall was one of the strongest determining features; it can be seen to have functioned as the southern kerb for Thames Street at various points along its length, as at the Baynard's Castle, Peter's Hill and New Fresh Wharf sites. Its survival as a landmark is highlighted by its mention in the two late 9th-century charters cited earlier (pp.16-17; below, pp.130-1), where it separated the properties concerned from the foreshore, a situation confirmed by the archaeological evidence from the sites discussed above. The continuity of the wall as a viable defensive work has been inferred from various historical references (Dyson in Hill, Millett & Blagg 1980, 9; Miller, Schofield & Rhodes 1986, 73), and it does seem likely that it had survived, in whatever condition, to virtually its full length at the time of the reoccupation of the City. The erosion of the southern face may only have begun by this date, with the river reaching a height of at least 1.4m OD, as shown by the slight erosion and exposure of the foundation piles at New Fresh Wharf and by the level of the riverlaid deposits at Swan Lane. Contrary to its original purpose, the wall now acted as a riverwall, sitting at the head of a gently sloping foreshore of gravels and eroded Roman reclamation dumps, out of which protruded, at intervals, the decaying timbers of the long disused Roman quays. The rising river levels must have returned the tidal head to a point west of the City, and this undoubtedly aided the development of international trade, as the late Saxon port began to develop.

At New Fresh Wharf and Billingsgate Lorry Park, the two inlets south of the wall may have corresponded to the site of gates, or other means of access through the wall. The presence of an opening to the north of the eastern of these two inlets, that at Billingsgate Lorry Park, is also suggested by the position of Botolph Lane, considered to have been laid out in the late 9th or early 10th centuries (Horsman, Milne & Milne 1988, 14), which would have led directly to the inlet. There was no corresponding north-south street leading to the western inlet, though there may instead have been a precursor of Thames Street running along the riverbank behind the surviving wall and linking the two access points to the water.

As the evidence becomes more detailed after about 1000, it is necessary to consider the two pairs of sites separately: New Fresh Wharf and Billingsgate Lorry Park below the site of the Roman and medieval bridge, Swan Lane and Seal House above it. The different degrees of reclamation on the four sites over the 11th and 12th centuries are shown in Fig 56.

New Fresh Wharf and Billingsgate Lorry Park

First structural activity: jetty and rubble bank c.1000

(Fig 57; *cf* Figs 6-11)

Large baulks of timber from the disused Roman quays protruded above the silts and gravels of the foreshore, and survived to such an extent that they served as the basis for the earliest post-Roman structures found on these sites. To the south of the line of the Roman quay, in the central area of the New Fresh Wharf site only, a rubble bank was created against the highest surviving quayfront timbers, incorporating others which had collapsed southwards onto the foreshore. It comprised ragstone, flint, chalk and reused Roman building material laid up to 1m thick, with a regular and gently sloping upper surface. In places it was interlaced with unworked branches, and was retained to west and south by horizontally laid timbers held in place with oak stakes, giving it near vertical edges; the western end was coincident with the end of the highest surviving tier of Roman quayfront beams. Although the eastern end of the bank was not actually seen it is assumed to have been retained in a similar fashion, the bank having a total length of about 18m and extending for up to 4m to the south of the surviving Roman quayfront. On the surface of the bank at its eastern end were laid various planks, and the remains of a clinker-built boat, spread out so as to provide a level surface at around −0.34m OD. Dendrochronology dates one of the boat timbers to 915-55, though it is clear that its date of reuse will have been significantly later. There was no trace of a plank surface at the western end, though here the rubble and timber lacing was set around at least two rows of upright stakes, virtually all of oak, their tops tapered by

Billingsgate Lorry Park

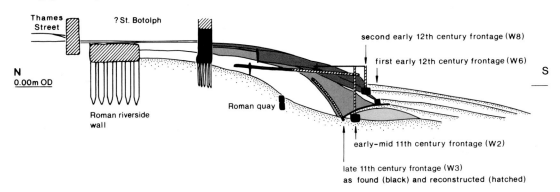

Thames Street

? St. Botolph

second early 12th century frontage (W8)

first early 12th century frontage (W6)

N
0.00m OD

S

Roman quay

Roman riverside wall

early-mid 11th century frontage (W2)

late 11th century frontage (W3)
as found (black) and reconstructed (hatched)

New Fresh Wharf

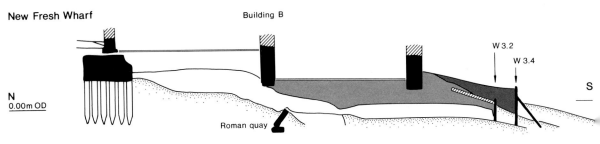

Building B

W 3.2

W 3.4

N
0.00m OD

S

Roman quay

Seal House

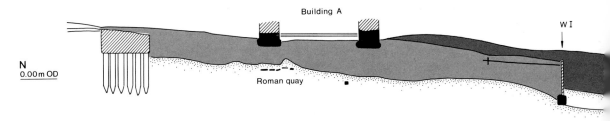

Building A

W I

N
0.00m OD

Roman quay

Swan Lane

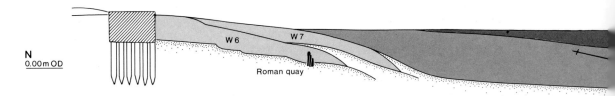

N
0.00m OD

W 6

W 7

Roman quay

0   15m

Key to dates of land reclamation

☐ early to mid 11th century

▨ late 11th century

▨ early to mid 12th century

▨ late 12th century

56. Reconstructed cross-sections through the four study sites, illustrating the different degrees of reclamation over the 11th and 12th centuries. The tidal amplitude was between +1.9m OD (HAT) and about -1.5m OD (LAT). Scale 1:200.

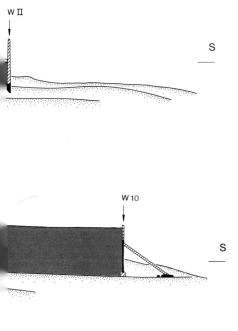

decay. North of the Roman quayfront were further, less substantial stakes which might have formed a fence or revetment along the northern edge of the bank.

Immediately west of the rubble bank was a series of driven posts in fairly regular east-west rows, running from close to the south side of the riverside wall down to a point opposite the southern end of the rubble bank, and measuring *c.*7.5m from east to west at a distance of 13m from the wall (Fig 6). The top of the highest surviving vertical timber was at 1.7m OD, but in general all the posts, whether at the base of the sloping riverbank or at the top by the wall, had survived to about the same height of between 1.2m and 1.6m OD; construction of the overlying embankments (below, p.104-5) must have had some effect on the survival of the posts, though many were left to protrude above rather than were completely sealed by them. Shorter timbers had been used at the top of the slope and longer ones at the base, the implication being that the posts were originally intended to stand to the same height, forming foundations for a horizontal timber superstructure. Whilst it was clear that attempts had been made to regulate the spacing between the east-west lines of posts, especially in those places where the posts would have stood taller, the spacing of posts within individual rows was such as to imply that they were intended to be integrated with east-west beams, rather than with beams which ran north-south. Although no trace of working survived at the tops of any timbers, even those which had later collapsed and therefore survived to greater lengths, the uprights could somehow have been fixed onto horizontal beams, the whole supporting a planked surface. The wall had survived to a lower level at this point than it had elsewhere over its observed length on the site, varying from 2m OD to over 2.3m OD across the projected width of the planking. It is impossible to determine whether a conveniently low area of the wall had been chosen or had been specially created: although some of the material in the rubble bank could conceivably have derived from the creation of such an access, some of the stone, such as the large boulders, was clearly unworked. The planked surface could well have been at a level higher than 2m OD originally, with the posts up to half a metre longer before decay, and the beams and planking bringing it up to the required height. Alternatively there may have been a short step down from the surviving stub of wall onto the planking.

Aside from retaining the timber lacing, those

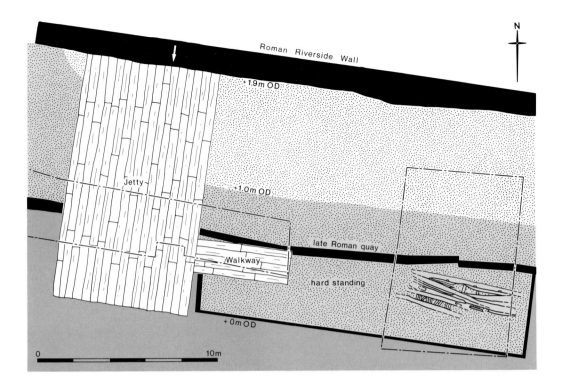

rows of posts which were set within the rubble bank may also have functioned as supports for a second planked surface running at least part of the length of the bank. These rows continued the lines of two of the rows further west, though the timbers used were smaller and the intervals between them shorter. These posts had rotted at a lower level than those to the west; although this could have been the result of activities subsequent to the disuse of the rubble bank, which would necessarily have involved the removal or truncation of upstanding earlier timbers, those timbers to the west which occupied similar positions survived consistently higher. If, as is reasonable to assume, all the posts had been subject to the same environmental conditions during their use and after, those in the rubble bank may never have stood as high; the fact that smaller timbers were used may support this possibility. The full extent of these posts in plan is not known, though it seems reasonable to suppose that their eastern limit was the edge of the plank surface at the eastern end of the rubble bank; there may only have been one more row, if any, to the south of those recorded, since they were not seen in the small area of bank just to the south recorded in the watching brief.

The post structures as a whole seem to have comprised a platform, or jetty, about 7.5m wide

57. *Interpretation of the post structures and rubble bank at New Fresh Wharf (Areas II and III), the blue illustrating the depth of water over the various elements at different points in the tidal cycle (approximately equivalent to contours at 0m, 1m and 1.9m OD). The walkway would have been covered only at the highest tide. The arrow indicates a possible access across the line of the riverside wall, but this part of the wall was not recorded. Scale 1 :200.*

and 13m long, extending southwards into the river, in conjunction with a narrow walkway at a lower level running parallel to the river. Integral to them was the bank of rubble, at its highest in the west around the posts of the walkway, and with a plank surface on its flatter eastern end, presumably a hard-standing for the berthing of boats. The surface of the bank was up to 1m above the foreshore on which it had been constructed, and this difference in level would have ensured that, for several hours before and after low tide, the boats would have been out of the water, allowing for loading or unloading. If the rotting of the tops of timbers of the jetty is in any way indicative of the river levels at the time of use, then the walkway would probably have stayed just above water during most high tides, whilst the jetty would have remained clear of water at all times. The level of the walkway was such that it would have facilitated cargo handling over the low sides of vessels whilst they stood on the hard-standing. The jetty, on the other hand, would have allowed boats to dock during the few hours before and after high tide. Its relatively large surface area would have allowed short-term storage or stockpiling of goods prior to distribution. The inlet on its western side may already have been used for the berthing of boats, and the platform may also have increased access to that area.

It has been said that vessels of this period did not require anything other than a sloping beach for berthing, being either unloaded at low tide when they had settled on the foreshore, or dragged above the level of high tide for a prolonged stay (McGrail 1981, 19, 22). However, there are examples of piers or jetties from such places as Birka (mid 10th century; Ambrosiani 1985, 66-8), and Ralswiek (8th to 10th century; Herrmann 1985, 56-7), as well as later examples from Bergen (12th century; Herteig 1985, 69-78), albeit of different constructional types, which testify that beaching was certainly not the only method of berthing. The use of horizontal timbers as a hard-standing for boats is known elsewhere: at Graveney (Fenwick 1978, 181-5), it was suggested that they prevented vessels from becoming stuck on mud beaches, whereas the plank surface on the rubble bank at New Fresh Wharf was presumably intended to protect the hulls of berthing boats from wear on the rubble. The width of the hard-standing, about 4m, and its near vertical southern edge, make it likely that vessels berthed parallel to the river. At its western end the walkway would have reduced the width of the rubble bank available for berthing, though it could still probably have accommodated one of the larger vessels of the period (McGrail 1981, 22). The jetty, walkway and hard-standing at New Fresh Wharf would, in combination, have provided a means whereby boats could load or unload during much of the tidal cycle.

As mentioned above, there are other excavated examples of jetties from western Europe, though there are only a few similar post structures which can be interpreted as jetties, such as those at Dorestad (Van Es & Verwers 1981, 72-6). The latter, although of an earlier date than the New Fresh Wharf example, comprised a whole series of parallel jetties or causeways, repeatedly extended into the river, and were constructed on regular grids of driven piles, of similar dimensions to those used at New Fresh Wharf. It was noted that the posts of these structures had been driven very deeply into the bed of the river, up to five-sixths of their length, and this was presumed to have been necessary to support the weight of traffic carried on a platform or wooden road, in contrast to the smaller timbers used in the construction of the associated houses, which had only a third of their length set in the ground; the posts from New Fresh Wharf, although only driven in for up to half their lengths, may also have been expected to take a considerable weight, and carts may have been driven directly on the surface. As at Dorestad, no direct evidence was found as to the manner in which the posts were attached to the superstructure. Reconstruction of a 12th-century jetty from Gdansk (illustrated in Smoralek 1981, 57) suggests that a grid of driven posts, set into a sloping riverbank like those at New Fresh Wharf, might be jointed into horizontal beams with mortice-and-tenon joints, which in turn supported a plank surface.

The sparse dating evidence indicates a probable late 10th- or possibly early 11th-century date for the New Fresh Wharf structures, but excavation gave no real indication of the length of time during which they were in use, nor was there any clue as to the reason for their disuse. The group of pottery recovered from silts and gravels which are thought to have accumulated during or after the use of the structures was of early to mid 11th-century date (CP3, 1020-50), though these deposits would have been exposed up to the time of the construction of the overlying embankments. The condition of the posts suggests that the site was probably abandoned following the disuse of the structures, the timbers having been allowed to decay for some time before most were completely covered by the embankment material. Comparison of the tree-ring sequence of the dated retaining stake within the rubble bank with that of a timber used in a boundary between two of the embankments which overlay the jetty and bank, allows for as little as seven years between the construction of the two (see dendrochronology report below, p.158); the pottery implies that the difference is unlikely to have been much more than 50 years.

The surface area of the jetty (c.100 sq m) was sufficient to have functioned as a temporary depot, or even as a market, for riverborne goods. In that event it would seem to have marked a departure from the apparently common practice at this period of beaching and unloading vessels directly onto the sloping shore with very little formal preparation (Ellmers 1981, 91). This practice appears to have applied a century earlier at the *ripa emtoralis* ('trading shore') and *statio navis*

58. Plan showing the mid 11th-century extent of the embankments constructed at New Fresh Wharf and Billingsgate Lorry Park (based on Figs 11 and 20), with tenement numbers. Arrows indicate possible points of access across the line of the riverside wall. On Figs 58 and 60-4 the blue tone indicates probable extent of the river at proposed mean high tide of +1m OD. Scale 1:1250.

('shipping station') referred to in the two late 9th-century charters for Queenhithe (above, p.18).

The location of the jetty is also notable. Its eastern edge coincided with the line of a medieval alleyway which separated the later Tenements **2** and **3** at New Fresh Wharf (above, pp.28-9, 40-3). First recorded in the early 12th century as *Rederesgate*, this alley represented a southern continuation of Pudding Lane, itself first known as *Rethereslane* or *Retheresgatelane*, on the north side of Thames Street. Lane and jetty are likely to have been complementary, the former providing access to the latter, and the literal meaning of 'cattle-gate' (Ekwall 1954, 154-5) suggests an early association with the landing and distribution of livestock. Secondly, the boundary between the City wards of Billingsgate and Bridge lies on the line of this jetty, and it has been conjectured that the wards and their boundaries emerged in London in the first half of the 11th century (Brooke & Keir 1975, 170). Even if the jetty no longer functioned in its original form at this period, its site evidently remained a prominent local feature (below, p.105). It has already been suggested (above, p.95) that the western and eastern limits of Bridge Ward coincided with the

ends of the embankments to either side of the bridge (on the Swan Lane and New Fresh Wharf sites respectively); here were the conspicuous features of access to the foreshore, Ebbgate and *Rederesgate*, the latter marked in addition by its jetty. It is therefore possible that the jetty at *Rederesgate* formed part of the ward boundary between Bridge and Billingsgate wards as early as the first decades of the 11th century.

The early to mid 11th-century embankments

(Figs 58-9; *cf* Figs 11-16)

Following the period of abandonment of the jetty structures at New Fresh Wharf, the whole stretch of waterfront from there to Billingsgate Lorry Park was now subjected to extensive activity. This involved the construction of embankments sloping down from the riverside wall to the river, laid over the remains of the rubble bank and jetty and elsewhere over the sloping riverbank and foreshore, though preserving the positions of the two inlets. The embankments were not of uniform construction, and this was reflected in the property divisions which continued into the medieval period. The archive report for the excavations at New Fresh Wharf (Miller 1985) identifies six properties between the church of St Magnus to the west and the church of St Botolph, which bordered the site to the east, referred to as Tenements **1** to **6** (see also the documentary survey, pp.72-4 above). For the purposes of this study, the numbering of tenements has been extended eastwards across the Billingsgate Lorry Park site, where the two properties separated by the retained inlet will be referred to as Tenements **7** and **8**; the church of St Botolph lay together with St Botolph's Wharf within the western of these properties (Tenement **7**) and would therefore have directly adjoined Tenement **6** on New Fresh Wharf. With the creation of the embankments, the two sites between them covered parts of six adjoining waterfront properties (Tenements **2-7**), with part of a seventh (Tenement **8**) on the east side of the inlet at Billingsgate Lorry Park. Tenements **7** and **8** were united to form St Botolph's Quay in the late 13th century.

At the western end of the New Fresh Wharf site, on Tenement **2**, the embankment comprised alder roots and discarded worked timber fragments in a matrix of clay, with a capping of clay on its higher parts. It covered most of the area of the earlier jetty, with many of the remaining posts protruding above its surface, and extended south from the riverside wall to an edge marked by vertical posts, where the clay and timber directly overlay the earlier foreshore. It sloped down to the inlet on the west, and also to the east, where it lay up against the closely spaced posts of the boundary between this property and Tenement **3**. This line of posts, incorporating some from the eastern edge of the earlier jetty, was formed into a rough fence or revetment by the addition of planks, worked timbers and branches (Fig 35). Against its eastern side, in Tenement **3**, was a thick layer of clay containing some cut branches, which, like that in Tenement **2**, sloped down from the riverside wall to a point just under 20m south of it, with a clay capping to the north. The clay and timber dump also sloped gradually down from east to west, and along the western edge of the property was a distinct linear hollow which may have served as a pathway down to the water's edge. The discontinuities in the bank material and the nature of the boundary may be indications that the embankment on Tenement **3** was constructed before that on Tenement **2** and that, perhaps for only a short period, the area of the abandoned jetty was avoided, presumably because the posts presented an obstacle to construction. The closely set posts of the boundary do seem to have been somewhat excessive merely to separate one clay bank from another, and indeed none of the boundaries between the embankments on the other properties were of such sophistication or strength. Several timbers from the boundary are dated by dendrochronology to after 1020, though ceramic dating

evidence from the embankment material is not sufficient to indicate any difference in the construction dates of the two embankments, and both are therefore dated to the early to mid 11th century (CP3).

The eastern limit of the clay embankment of Tenement **3** was not marked by any fence or similar timber structure, but changed along a line marked on the surface by a strip of rubble and organic material, which may have been a path leading down to the river as well as a boundary marker. The Tenement **4** embankment was based on a layer of mostly unworked timber and the consolidated upper clay layer had a compacted gravel surface at just over 2m OD; the southern limit of this upper clay bank was recorded over 11m south of the riverside wall, having sloped down steeply onto the brushwood base. In contrast to the embankments to the west, that on Tenement **5** was composed of one thick deposit of clay, with a thin brushwood base only south of the line of the Roman quay. A gravel metalling overlay the upper parts of the bank at 1.95m OD. Concentrations of north-south timbers marked the division between this embankment and that on Tenement **6**. Here it was based on a thick dump of organic material capped by clay. A step in the level of the bank, coinciding with the line of the Roman quay, was marked by an east-west row of posts. Compact deposits of gravels and mortar formed a surface on the bank at around 2m OD. The eastern boundary was not excavated, but it is assumed to have been on the line of a 19th-century property division. The dumping forming all these embankments contained pottery assignable to CP3 (1020-50).

The embankment on Tenement **7** (Billingsgate Lorry Park Waterfront 2) differed from those further west in several ways (Fig 23). Following some consolidation of the earlier riverbank at least three tieback braces (absent to the west) were set on the bank, retained by cross-pieces passing through mortices. These are assumed to have functioned with a grooved base plate which ran perpendicular to them 6.5m south of the cross-pieces, and which would have supported what was probably a low stave-built structure. The tiebacks were then sealed by dumps of limestone rubble, some fragments with mortar still adhering, interleaved with organic deposits (Fig 41); this material is unlikely to have come from demolition or collapse of the riverside wall, which was built of ragstone. This rubble served as the base for a thick deposit of clay and timber, both unworked and reused (Fig 15). The relationship between this and the low stave frontage was removed by later activity, and it is not clear if the staves would have retained the bank material, giving it a vertical front, or if they merely protected the foot of the sloping bank from erosion, as was the case later on the same site (below, p.109). The eastern end of the bank was marked by a line of posts with some horizontal elements set around and against them, serving as a lining of the western side of the pre-existing inlet. The excavation at Billingsgate Lorry Park did not extend as far north as the extensive watching brief at New Fresh Wharf, so that the relationship of the embankment to the riverside wall can only be assumed. The clay and timber reached a level of over 2m OD near the northern limit of excavation, where it began to peter out over the rubble layers below, and it is assumed that this embankment, like those at New Fresh Wharf, would have remained at about that level until it reached the wall, and then sloped down from this relatively level area to the inlet lining to the east and towards the stave frontage to the south. This embankment was shorter than those to the west, with a projected maximum length of about 16m from the wall to the point where the stave front would have met the boundary with Tenement **6**, though it was the widest, measuring around 16m east-west. The timbers within the bank were extensively sampled for dendrochronology, and the bulk of them came from trees felled in the winter or early spring of 1039/1040. The pottery includes types diagnostic of CP3 (1020-50), con-

sistent with the dendrochronological dates, confirming that this embankment was broadly contemporary with those at New Fresh Wharf.

A small area of another embankment (Billingsgate Lorry Park Waterfront 4) was recorded on the east side of the inlet, on Tenement **8**. Here, a clay dump containing random timbers was retained along its western edge by a closely-spaced line of piles. The limited extent of the embankment which lay within the excavation area meant that only the slopes of the bank were seen, and very little of the southern edge; there was no trace of a well-built timber frontage as found on the embankment to the west. One of the posts in the lining was felled some time after 1008, and although no dating evidence came from the bank material itself, this would not exclude the possibility that this bank was contemporary with that to the west; the next phase of clay and timber bank on this property included at least one timber which had been felled at the same time (1039/1040) as those in the western bank, and it is conceivable that it had been salvaged from its predecessor.

With the construction of both these embankments the pre-existing inlet was narrowed and its position formalised, becoming a 5m-wide revetted channel with roughly parallel sides. This directly continued the line of Botolph Lane to the north, and access to the foreshore is confirmed by the presence of a hard-standing within the narrowed inlet. This deliberately-created beach would have allowed the berthing of boats, with distribution

59. *Profile of one of the New Fresh Wharf embankments (Tenement 4) as found. Scale 1 : 100.*

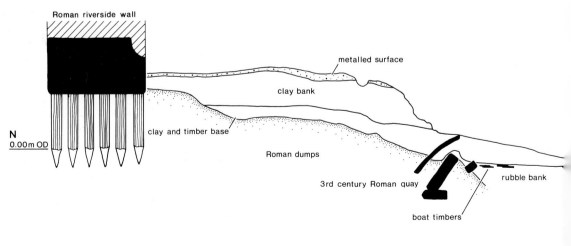

of goods to and from the centre of town via Botolph Lane.

On the Tenement **7** embankment, the rubble and organic layers which continued to the north of the clay and timber may have served as a surface. A layer of organic material was recorded over most of its exposed parts, presumably a combination of trample from the use of the bank and decay of refuse and vegetable matter deposited by the river; the lower slopes of all the embankments would have been exposed to river action, and their surfaces, particularly those composed of undulating spreads of brushwood, would have been subject to the growth of riverbank flora, providing numerous places where silt and other waterborne material could be deposited and remain. The upper parts of the banks, those areas above the reach of the tide, would have been dry land and it was these areas, generally at around 1.9m OD or above, which were surfaced.

The existence of deliberately-laid surfaces on the upper parts of the embankments and paths leading down to the river are indications that there may have been several points of access across the line of the Roman riverside wall, in addition to openings opposite the two inlets. The possible path down the western side of Tenement **3** could have led from the gap in the wall which had provided access to the earlier jetty, but there is no evidence of any alternative thoroughfare leading from this point across the tops of the other properties, though that area of the site was only covered in a watching brief. Instead, it seems that Tenements **4**, **5** and **6**, all of which had formal surfaces, may even have been accessible by means of openings through the riverside wall from a road or track which ran behind it; in effect a precursor of Thames Street. The implication is that the stretch of the riverside wall at New Fresh Wharf

did not survive intact at this date and is unlikely still to have served as a defensible barrier; although the remains of the wall were not actually sealed by any layers until the 12th century (below, p 111), there is no reason to suppose that the wall stood to any great height immediately prior to this. Indeed, a detailed, though not contemporary, account of the siege of London during the Norman invasion in 1066 stated that the city was protected by the river, and made no mention of a riverside defensive wall (*Carmen de Hastingae Proelio* by Guy, Bishop of Amiens, probably dating from the second quarter of the 12th century; quoted by Dyson in Hill, Millett & Blagg 1980, 8).

Late 11th-century alterations to the embankments

(Fig 60; *cf* Figs 17, 26-33)

Whether due to the need to replace decayed structural elements or because of the partial collapse of the inlet lining, both frontages on the Tenement **7** embankment were replaced at this period (Billingsgate Lorry Park Waterfront 3). The tiebacks were sawn through and all other elements of the earlier stave-built frontage, except the base plate, were removed. The surface of the bank was consolidated with gravel dumps and further clay and timber deposits; staves, set in trenches, fronted the bank, though whether they stood vertically or were raked back against its slope is not determinable. The staves of the southern frontage were taller than those lining the inlet, and were footed against the retained base plate. South of the staves, a low wattle-reinforced bank was constructed on the foreshore, and this may have provided beaching facilities for boats, creating a hard upon which the vessels could have settled at low tide. The pile frontage of Tenement **8** was also replaced at about the same time (Billingsgate Lorry Park Waterfront 5). The earlier line of piles had collapsed, due presumably to slippage of the retained material, and following heightening with further clay and timber, the bank was faced both along the inlet and to the south with staves and reused planks which, like those to the west, may have been vertical or set against the slope of the bank. The inlet continued to provide access to the foreshore.

These alterations to both embankments have been dated to the second half of the 11th century; some of the timber dumped on the Tenement **7** embankment was felled in 1054/1055, which accords well with the felling date range of 1049-70

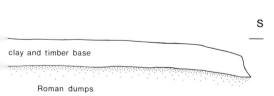

S

clay and timber base

Roman dumps

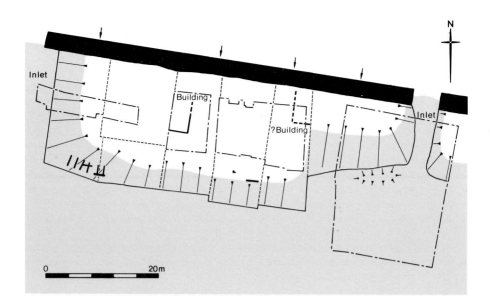

60. *Plan of the late 11th-century waterfronts at New Fresh Wharf and Billingsgate Lorry Park (based on Figs 17 and 24), with tenement numbers. Arrows indicate possible points of access across the line of the riverside wall. Scale 1 : 1250.*

for the staves, and confirms the dating of pottery recovered from the accumulation on the earlier bank, the wattle-reinforced bank and the bank material itself, all of which contained types diagnostic of CP4 (1050-80). The lining of the Tenement **8** embankment, and the timbers within it, are given felling dates of 1045-90 and 1047-70 respectively, and it also contained CP4 pottery in an accumulation on its surface. The replacement of the linings on both sides of the inlet at the same time suggests, as did the initial construction of the embankments here, that both sides may have been owned or maintained by a single individual.

This mid-late 11th-century reconstruction of the embankments flanking the inlet at Billingsgate Lorry Park was apparently not paralleled on the embankments at New Fresh Wharf, presumably because the repairs were a purely local phenomenon. On the other hand, replacement or repairs of the frontages at the latter site may have escaped detection because they lay within an area which was recorded under watching brief conditions. Some small amounts of pottery of CP4 (1050-80) were recovered from dumping over the embankments, though this dumping is assumed to be associated with later, 12th-century, revetments.

The 12th century

(Fig 61; *cf* Figs 19, 42)

On Tenement **2**, the upper parts of the slope were consolidated with clay and timber and extensive spreads of organic material extended over most of the area, partially overlying an arrangement of horizontal timbers which may have represented a walkway down to the river; the organic material presumably represented dumping and accumulation on the bank surface. It did not extend as far south as the earlier clay bank, and a timber structure with a planked surface at 0.85m OD at the base of the slope indicates that if there was a new frontage, it was of no great height. Presumably this structure was a platform to facilitate the loading or unloading of boats at low tide, with the plank pathway providing access to the upper slopes. A robbing trench along the edge of the inlet implies that this side was revetted. Despite this further consolidation of the bank, the only dry land would probably have been to the extreme north, by the remains of the Roman riverside wall, whilst the remainder would have been subject to flooding at high tides. The boundary between this property and the adjacent Tenement **3** was heightened after the raising of the level of the embankment. Tenement **3** was covered by thick deposits of organic material, in places consolidated with brushwood, and here also there was a possible plank walkway to the river adjacent to the boundary, whilst further south there was a rough internal revetment of tim-

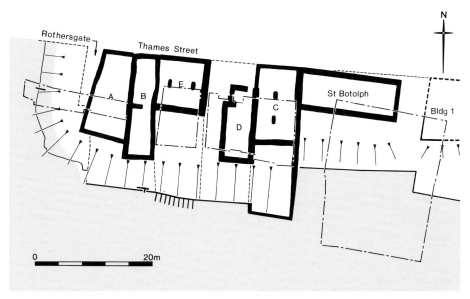

61. Plan of the late 12th- and early 13th-century buildings and waterfronts at New Fresh Wharf and Billingsgate Lorry Park (based on Figs 19 and 41), with tenement numbers; the outline of St Botolph's church is conjectured, based partly on the line of the later rebuild. Scale 1:1250.

bers aligned east-west. The southern limit was marked by what was undoubtedly the robbing cut of a low vertical revetment frontage. Dating evidence was sparse, but a piece of waste timber used as a chopping block before its incorporation in the organic material was felled some time after 1055, implying that the date of the dumping was significantly later. A timber dated to 1084+ may have derived from the dismantling of the revetment; it was found within dumping associated with the succeeding revetment on this property, and may confirm the early 12th-century date for the revetment on this and the other tenements.

The other properties exhibited similar structural development. Tenements **4** and **5** were both covered with dumps of organic material consolidated by random timbers packed with clay. On Tenement **4**, there were fragments of a planked surface and other structural features on the crest of the bank. It is possible that they represented the sparse remains of a small waterfront building, standing just clear of the water at high tide, with timber walls based on rubble spreads, though they may only have been parts of a working platform. Much of the sloping area to the south was covered by a cobbled surface. No revetment was detected to the south, though the material had slumped in that direction presumably after the removal of a vertical revetment.

Tenement **5** also contained traces of what may have been a wooden platform at 0.75m OD, with a cobbled surface to the south. The dumping on Tenement **4** contained dating material of CP5 (1080-1150), whilst Tenement **5** produced no dating evidence for this phase. Tenement **6** produced further evidence for buildings: a burnt mortar and clay floor associated with two post-holes on the upper surface of the bank implied the existence of an insubstantial structure. To the south of it were dumps of organic material against the slope of the earlier clay bank. The dumping contained pottery of CP3/CP4 (1020-80), which may have been residual.

The evidence indicates that on most of these properties there was no attempt to reclaim additional land by advancing further into the river; nor were any revetments designed to retain horizontal surfaces; instead the change in the profile of the banks allowed for the creation of slightly larger areas of dry land (see Fig 56). Although raised in level, the embankments retained a gently sloping profile, and the cobbled surfaces and wooden platforms constructed on these slopes attest to the continued exploitation of the waterfront, boats probably being pulled up onto the lower slopes when not in use. Although dating evidence was generally sparse, due largely to the fact that much of this phase was recorded under salvage conditions, it does seem probable that these changes on Tenements **2-6** were broadly contemporary with each other and with those on Tenements **7** and **8**, also of early 12th-century date.

The staves lining the Tenement **7** embankment

collapsed southwards some time after 1080, on the evidence of coin trial-pieces from within the foreshore deposits trapped beneath them. Their collapse was probably due initially to movement of the material behind them, but they may then have been pulled further over, to lie on the foreshore over the low bank in front. The main bank material, as a consequence, spilled outwards and its southern edge was retained by a line of reused base plates (Billingsgate Lorry Park Waterfront 6). On the upper slopes a well-consolidated gravel surface was created, based on a framework of reused house timbers (studied in detail in Milne in prep) and stakes, and with its own pile frontage (Fig 28). The compacted surface was virtually all above 2m OD, and must always have been above tidal level, as were the surfaces on the first embankments to the west, though these were later in date. It is possible that this construction was contemporary with St Botolph's Church. The south wall of the church was located in the excavation at Billingsgate Lorry Park, though the wall recorded then was probably part of a late 14th-century rebuild on an earlier alignment; the area of Tenement 7 to the south and east of the church was the site of St Botolph's Wharf. The earliest allusion to both church and wharf dates from c.1140 (above, p.77). The gravel bank may have consolidated the ground south of the church and protected its south wall, whilst creating a level surface adjacent to the waterfront; access to the waterfront would have been along the east end of the church. This would imply that the church was established by the late 11th or early 12th century; it must therefore have had a structural relationship to the still surviving Roman riverside wall, if only to contribute to its disappearance. The surface south of the church continued to be used until the late 12th century, with additional repairs and resurfacing; the main structural activity of the intervening period was south of it, below high tide level, and east of it, in the area of the inlet and Tenement 8.

The embankment on Tenement 8 underwent reconstruction (Billingsgate Lorry Park Waterfront 7) slightly later, and for the first time it extended further south than its western counterpart. The partially collapsed staves of the earlier inlet lining retained dumps of clay and timber forming the consolidation for further dumping and trodden accumulations on its upper parts, with a fence-line marking the edge of dry land. The dumped timbers were felled between 1056 and 1101, and pottery types included within the dumping are of CP5 (1080-1150). The advance-

ment of the property on the east of the inlet further south than its neighbour may indicate an end to the coordination seen between the two sides up until this point, and perhaps reflects separate ownership of the properties. This is seen more strongly in the construction of subsequent waterfronts; Tenement 8 was in private ownership until the late 13th century when it was incorporated within St Botolph's Wharf (Tenement 7; above, p.75).

Next, but still within the early 12th century, the embankments on both Tenements 7 and 8 received new frontages, and the inlet was reduced in width to under 2.5m. The western embankment was faced to the south with a stave-built revetment, set in base plates which directly overlay the retained edge of the earlier bank material, and which was probably at least partly front-braced (Billingsgate Lorry Park Waterfront 8). Behind this were dumped timbers set in clay, extending nearly to the edges of the earlier gravel bank. The inlet was lined on the west with a series of piles with plank cladding, whilst the eastern inlet lining (Billingsgate Lorry Park Waterfront 9), of slightly later date, consisted of driven piles with a wattle and plank cladding (Fig 51). The southern frontage of the eastern embankment did not survive later robbing, but a cruciform tieback indicates that it was back-braced, and was probably also stave-built. Like the earlier revetments both on this site and at New Fresh Wharf, these revetments did not retain horizontal surfaces, and the waterfronts presented a sloping profile from a low frontage to a more level dry area further north. The lower parts were within the tidal range, and this was clearly demonstrated by the accumulation of mixed marshy deposits behind the revetments and in the inlet. The narrowed inlet was no longer a viable place to berth boats of any great size, and it is debatable whether the 6m of sloping ground between the revetment on Tenement 7 and the gravel surface to the north would have been any more effective. Larger boats could still have berthed directly on the foreshore, with sloping access to dry land via the inlet during low tide. Such vessels could not have moored alongside the low revetments.

This conclusion needs to be set against the documentary evidence of Botolph's Wharf as a harbour important enough in 1200-1 for royal customs on goods imported from outside London to be collected there (above, p.75). The explanation is presumably that goods were transferred to land by means of smaller boats, which the 12th-century embankments at Billingsgate Lorry Park would have suited. The trouble taken to reinforce the sides of the inlet, albeit in a much narrowed form, implies that it was still a feature worth maintaining, until the mid to late 12th century when it was blocked with a low stave-built revetment (Billingsgate Lorry Park Waterfront 10); the staves used within the base plate have a felling date of 1144-83. The western inlet lining, now obsolete, was removed, but the eastern remained to function as a property division (later renewed south of the blocking as Billingsgate Lorry Park Waterfront 11), the western property apparently having annexed the area of the inlet. The unified frontage created by the blocking of the inlet was well maintained, with cruciform tiebacks being added at intervals to give additional support to the staves; the levels at which they were constructed clearly indicate that they were supporting a low revetment. Drains led into the former inlet, which was clearly marginal land within the tidal range, despite being blocked off, and it remained a marshy hollow until sealed beneath land reclamation associated with the construction of a major revetment across the site in the early 13th century. The cribbaged surface remained in use despite erosion of its southern edge, and foreshore material, mixed with dumps of organic material, accumulated on the slopes below it and behind the low frontage to such an extent that more braces had to be added to support and maintain the revetment, though the area of surfacing at the top of the bank could be extended a short distance to the south. This low revetment therefore, although not directly supporting horizontal surfaces, would have allowed natural accumulation of material behind it, protecting the slope of the riverbank and ultimately the dry land above. Several probable mooring posts were situated in front of the blocked inlet, and at one stage a line of wattle panels was laid as consolidation on the foreshore parallel to the frontage. These indicate that despite the apparent lack of direct access to the foreshore, smaller vessels were still being berthed there, perhaps taking advantage of the corner formed by the change in the alignment of the waterfront, where the eastern property extended further south.

There are hints that the part of Tenement **8** which lay within the excavation adjoined an area of more intensive structural activity, and this is confirmed by the construction, at one stage, of a building of which insubstantial traces remained: a brickearth floor, a doorway leading directly onto the slope of the bank, and the west wall built directly over the property division. On Tenement **7** high-quality external surfaces replaced the early cribbaged surface south of the church of St Botolph.

The recording conditions and the comparative sparsity of dating evidence from the excavations at New Fresh Wharf make comparison of the sequence recorded there with that from the more fully excavated sequence at Billingsgate Lorry Park difficult, and this is particularly true for the activity described below. The single dendrochronological date, for a timber from this second phase of revetment construction at the junction of Tenements **4** and **5** is late 12th century. The construction of some, or all, of the masonry buildings on the surface of the early 12th-century embankments may or may not have pre-dated the late 12th-century advancement. There was virtually no dating evidence associated with the buildings themselves; no occupation levels survived within any of the buildings, and the make-up dumps contained only 11th-century pottery. The following outline provides an introduction to the more detailed study of the medieval buildings on this site, which will be published in due course (Schofield & Dyson in prep).

Tenement **2** remained unbuilt on, though the alley of *Rederesgate* lay along its east side. Although the surface itself had been truncated, the mortar and chalk make-up dumps which prepared the ground for it were recorded over the line of an earlier timber walkway; the earliest documentary reference to the alley dates to 1108-47 (above, p.00). The slopes of the embankment, both to the river and to the inlet to the west, were further consolidated but there were no signs of any further reclamation to the south. A horizontal timber and associated piles on the edge of the inlet may have been parts of a river stair running up the slope to the alley. The Roman riverside wall was finally sealed with levelling dumps in conjunction with the creation of *Rederesgate*. This levelling also prepared the way for the construction of Buildings A and B on the adjacent Tenement **3** (Fig 61). Both were based on chalk and gravel footings, incorporating layers of timber. The aboveground walls contained ragstone and flint, and the southern wall of Building B, which must have been subject to occasional wetting at high tides, was rendered. Building B was stepped into the slope, the floors in its southern room lying over 1m lower than those of the northern room. This in turn was over 0.5m lower than the contemporary surfaces of Thames Street, located a short distance to the north. The dumping and vertical plank revetment to the south of these buildings are not dated, though it is assumed that they were contemporary with the late 12th-century revetment on the adjacent Tenements **4** and **5**; the dumping contained a timber, dated to 1084+, which may have been part of the preceding revetment, and this implies a 12th-century date for this phase of dumping.

The east wall of Building B was shared by the smaller Building E, which occupied the full width of Tenement **4**, fronting on Thames Street to the north. This had shallow foundations, most of which had been truncated by a later building, and no internal floors survived, though there were traces of what may have been two central post-pads. As with the other buildings so far discussed, Building E was constructed on the surface of the late 11th-century embankment, and there was no direct stratigraphic link between it and the late 12th-century revetment and organic reclamation dumping to the south; it could therefore have pre-dated them. The revetment was front-braced, with a corner post marking the junction between Tenements **4** and **5**; the post is dated to 1166-1211, and a slot running virtually its full height on the east side indicates that the adjacent property was advanced to the same southern limit. Following this reclamation, the ground sloped only very gradually south from Building E to the new vertical frontage.

In contrast to Buildings A, B and E, the building constructed on Tenement **5** did not occupy the full width of the property or front directly onto Thames Street, and there appears to have been provision for a small yard or forecourt sloping down from the road to the north of it, with a cobbled yard running alongside the building, presumably providing access to the waterfront. Building D consisted of two rooms, the smaller northern one being little more than a vestibule. Floor levels did survive within this building, but none produced any dating evidence. All of the plank frontage which is presumed to have retained the reclamation dumps south of the building had been robbed and, other than the slot in the corner post, only a discontinuity in the dumped material observed in section betrayed its position. The boundary with Tenement **6** was marked by a short north-south river wall with a high quality ashlar face (its base plate dated to 1130+, and possibly 1160+), which is assumed to have turned east to form the frontage; the wall presumably returned to the north along the line of the boundary with Tenement **7**, the contemporary frontage of which did not extend as far south (see Fig 61). Building C, constructed to the

north of it, shared the east wall of Building D, though it does appear to have extended further north to front onto Thames Street. Very little of the primary floor levels survived the construction of later buildings, and what little of the make-ups which did may well have been of a later date. The southern limit of the building, as well as its relationship with the river wall, was not clear. This building was not only later than Building D, but was evidently attached to the south-west corner of the church of St Botolph. Its construction is placed in the 13th century, and this provides a *terminus ante quem* for the corner of the church; though the continuation eastwards of the south wall of the church, excavated on the Billingsgate Lorry Park site, appears to date from the late 14th century.

The turn of the century

By the end of the 12th century, this waterfront area was well developed, with the boundaries of properties first laid out in the early 11th century now firmly established. The inlet at the west end remained open whilst that opposite Botolph Lane was now infilled. There had been little real advancement in the line of the waterfront from the limits set by the first embankments (see Fig 7), though there had been a gradual increase in the area of dry land created, culminating in the construction of masonry buildings on several of the tenements. The alley of *Rederesgate* was laid out adjacent to the western inlet, providing access to the foreshore via river stairs, whilst a variety of front- and back-braced vertical revetments supported reclaimed land along the waterfront to the east.

Seal House and Swan Lane

Both of these sites showed clear evidence of the rise in river levels which eroded the disused Roman waterfront structures and deposited silt and gravel foreshores. At Seal House, the first structure to post-date these deposits was of 12th-century date, overlying foreshores containing 11th-century dating material, whilst at Swan Lane there was evidence that, only a short distance to the west, there were probably two phases of waterfront embankments in the late 11th century.

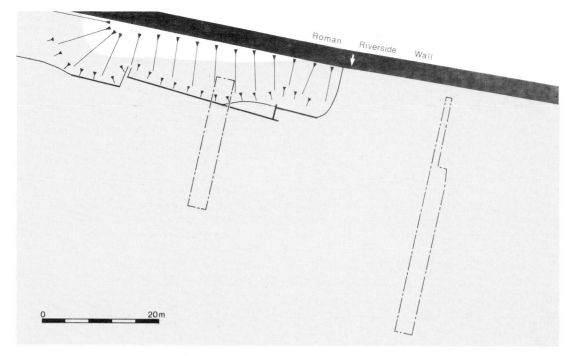

62. Plan of the first embankments, of mid 11th-century date, at Swan Lane and Seal House (based on Fig 44). Scale 1:1250.

The late 11th-century embankments

(Figs 56, 62; *cf* Figs 44-5)

At Swan Lane, directly over the eroded remains of the Roman revetments, were dumped deposits forming an embankment (Swan Lane Waterfront 6), at their thickest at the northern edge of the site, where they had a level upper surface at around 2.5m OD. This surface extended for several metres south of the Roman riverside wall, the projected course of which ran a short distance to the north of the site. From this plateau, the surface of the dumps sloped down to the south and also to the west, to a gently sloping area at between 1.3 and 1.5m OD, which in turn dropped steeply at its southern edge (see Fig 56). This southern edge was formed in various places by upstanding parts of the Roman quays, though at the eastern end, where robbing of the earlier structures had been more intensive, it appeared to swing very slightly around to the north, indicating a possible termination to the embankment in that direction. At the western end there were also indications that it may not have extended much further, and this might explain why the level upper part drop-ped away to the west. This embankment was recorded almost entirely in section, and so the dating evidence for it is sparse; the few sherds of pottery recovered from the dumps indicate a late 11th-century date (CP4, 1050-80). There were some signs of occupation on the surface of the embankment, though, apart from a trampled layer seen in one place on the upper slopes, they were restricted to the lower area. There were several stakes, which may have been mooring posts, dotted across this lower part, and some others along the crest of the steep southern edge. Assumptions as to the level of dry land at this time (based on the evidence of New Fresh Wharf, see p.120) make it clear that this lower area would have been within the tidal range and would have been ideal for the beaching and berthing of boats. Another structural feature found on this lower level was a hearth, reasonably well-built, which to judge by its position at around 0.9m OD must have been very temporary, given that it would have been submerged as the tide rose. It is possible that it was constructed for repairs or maintenance on berthed boats when tides permitted. These signs of occupation were subsequently sealed by another phase of dumping, forming another embankment.

This second embankment (Swan Lane Waterfront 7) extended the dry land several metres further south and west, and advanced around 2.5m further into the river, south of the line of the

Roman quays. The surface of the bank sloped gently south to about 1.9m OD before dropping very steeply down onto the earlier foreshores; the steep southern slope was consolidated with a capping of clay. Boats could have beached on the foreshore against the clay face of the bank; the foreshore had accumulated around at least two driven stakes, which presumably functioned as mooring posts, and the sloping surface of the foreshore seems to have been deliberately consolidated by the addition of large flint and ragstone fragments. Dating evidence from this foreshore and the bank material is also of the late 11th century (CP4). A series of internal surfaces and hearths across the northern end of the site, directly overlying the embankment surface, may have been contemporary with it, and have represented a series of buildings laid out on the expanded dry land; only one hearth however contained dating evidence, a single sherd of late Saxon pottery, and all could have been contemporary with subsequent waterfront advancements to the south.

The implied eastern limit of the first embankment, a short distance beyond the edge of the site, may have formed the edge of an inlet providing access to the foreshore through the ruined Roman wall. Swan Lane, the present-day street, represents the position of medieval Ebbgate, first mentioned in documentary sources in the mid 12th century (above, p.93), and the term '-gate' may indicate the site of an early gap through the wall (below, p.131). It is possible that the earlier embankment was related to such an access, its lower surface providing a large area for berthing of boats immediately upstream. The apparent lack of any similar construction on the other side of Ebbgate, at Seal House, confirms that even the second embankment, which straightened out the deviation in the first's southern edge, did not extend any further east. The later embankment appeared to be concerned more with reclaiming land and preventing erosion of the riverbank than with providing facilities for boats which, although they could have lain on the foreshore to the south at low tide, could not have been dragged up the slopes with any great ease, and would certainly not have settled on them as the tide retreated. A change in the function of the bank is therefore implied.

The fragmentary evidence for these embankments (Fig 62) means that no fences or other boundaries can be detected, and there was a lack of any distinctive elements within the dumping, such as the brushwood found at New Fresh Wharf

and Billingsgate Lorry Park, which might differentiate tenements. The only known property boundary confirmed by the topography of the embankments is the eastern boundary with Ebbgate, and it is possible that here, in contrast with the embankments found downstream of the bridge, separate tenements were not established until a later date, though the distribution of internal surfaces and hearths potentially contemporary with the second embankment may indicate otherwise.

The 12th-century waterfronts

(Figs 63-4; *cf* Figs 46-52)

The date at which the waterfront at Swan Lane was subsequently advanced is difficult to determine due to the recording conditions, subsequent robbing and the general scarcity of finds in contexts directly relatable to structures, and this inhibits comparison of the structures on this site with those at Seal House. There is however no reason for close similarity between the two sites, given the presence of Ebbgate between them. At New Fresh Wharf there was also an access to the river, *Rederesgate*, with embankments only on one side, to the east.

The earliest structures of possibly late 11th- or early 12th-century date at both Swan Lane and Seal House were simple plank constructions of uncertain height and function: a single *in situ* edge-set plank on the east side of the Swan Lane site (Waterfront 8), with other disturbed timbers adjacent, and a few large planks held by driven posts at Seal House. The fragmentary survival of both makes them difficult to interpret, and projection of their alignments problematical; it is possible that both may represent temporary revetments intermediate to the main phases of reclamation, especially since there were similarities in the structural components of the subsequent revetments.

At Seal House, the first substantial post-Roman revetment, Waterfront I, is dated by dendrochronology to 1133-70. It consisted of a grooved base plate, which would have supported vertical staves, later robbed, with several cruciform tie-backs which would have helped support the frontage; in addition, there were indications that there had also been front-braces. The dumped material retained by it extended all the way to the north of the excavation, and presumably to the line of the riverside wall; it contained pottery of CP5

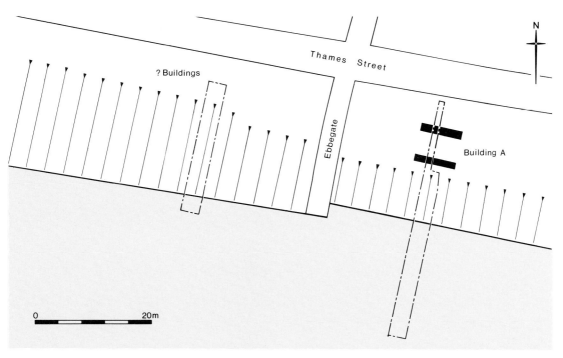

63. *Plan of the early 12th-century waterfronts at Swan Lane and Seal House (based on Figs 46 and 48). The width of Thames Street in Figs 63-4 is conjectural. Scale 1 :1250.*

64. *Plan of the late 12th-century waterfronts at Swan Lane and Seal House (based on Figs 47 and 50). Scale 1 :1250.*

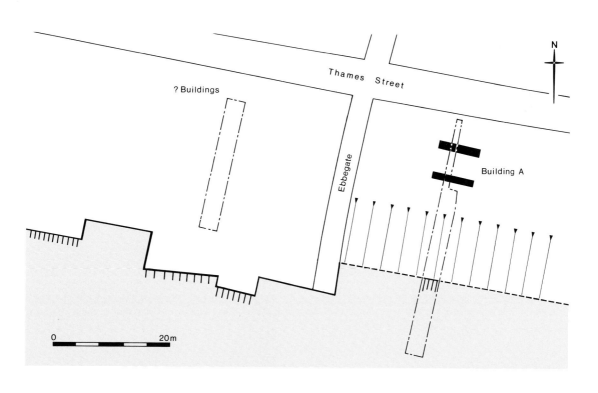

(1080-1150). Building A was constructed on this reclaimed land; two east-west walls were recorded, running for several metres parallel to the river, perhaps extending east from Ebbgate, a street first recorded in 1147-67 (above, p.93) but which could have been established much earlier. Several hearths lay south of the building, on level ground north of the slope down to the revetment frontage. At Swan Lane, the frontage had been completely robbed, but there were traces of probably two cruciform tiebacks which could have supported a revetment (Swan Lane Waterfront 9; Fig 62) of similar construction to that found at Seal House. These tiebacks were both in the eastern half of the site, whilst on the west side a line of vertical planks and a couple of posts were all that was observed. The land behind this waterfront seems to have sloped gently down to the south from a point near the top of the steep southern slope of the second embankment, probably to a low frontage such as those seen at Billingsgate Lorry Park. The sparse dating evidence for this phase at Swan Lane was also of CP5 (1080-1150), and it is likely that this and the reclamation at Seal House were contemporary, representing a phase in the development of the waterfront over a length of at least 75m, which included the extension of Ebbgate to the south of Thames Street; the total distance from Thames Street to the river was now over 20m. The revetments constructed either side of Ebbgate were not in line, and the western side continued to maintain the lead which was first established with the construction of the embankments.

The possible contemporaneity in the advance of the waterfront on the two sites is echoed in the next phase of reclamation, though by this stage the establishment of separate tenements is clearly seen in the stepped appearance of the waterfront at Swan Lane (Waterfront 10), where the presence of four or five different properties is indicated. A variety of different constructional techniques was practised, most of which involved front-bracing. A late 12th-century date is likely for these structures, and means that this waterfront, albeit divided between various property owners, was probably of similar date to the second revetment at Seal House (Waterfront II), dated by dendrochronology to 1163-92, and probably also to its front-braced successor (Waterfront III), built in c.1210. Waterfront II was of an unusual boxed construction, with compartments formed by planks set in the vertical grooves of upright posts; the area within and behind them was backfilled with organic material to reclaim further land, though there was no structural activity here south of Building A.

The turn of the century

After the apparently unified phase of reclamation seen at the start of the 12th century, which appeared to even out irregularities in the waterfront, the establishment of separate tenements (their configuration shown in sketch form, from later documentary evidence, in Fig 53) led to more staggered, though broadly contemporary, advancements of the frontage. This pattern, now established here by the late 12th century, continued throughout the medieval period. Masonry buildings were being built on the reclaimed land behind these frontages, and on either side of Ebbgate; these will be discussed more fully in the forthcoming study of these sites after 1200 (Schofield & Dyson in prep). The profusion of front-braces on the revetments would have limited their use for the docking of vessels, and no jetties or stairs were located to the south of them. In the case of the property at Seal House, the presence of large hearths on land immediately fronting the river would seem also to argue against the regular use of that area for the loading or unloading of boats.

5 : THE LATE SAXON EMBANKMENTS AND THE RIVER

The construction techniques employed on the
earliest embankments discussed above were based
on traditions which, already well-established by
this period, were used in a variety of contexts,
including defensive works as well as waterfronts.
This is particularly true of the use of layers of
uncut timber or brushwood as a means of consolidating areas of unstable ground, and examples
have been found in this country from as early as
the Bronze Age. The excavations at Runnymede
Bridge produced evidence of a sloping brushwood
layer of the 9th to 8th centuries BC, interpreted
as a beaching ramp or hard for use at low water
(Needham & Langley 1981, 48). Nearer both
geographically and chronologically to the
embankments under discussion, is the clay and
timber bank excavated recently at Northumber-
land Avenue near Covent Garden, which was
dated by dendrochronology to 670-90 (Cowie &
Whytehead 1989, 710), part of an embankment
from the mid Saxon town. The 9th- or 10th-
century embankment excavated in 1950 at the
Hungate in York (Richardson 1959) made extensive use of brushwood in what has been variously
interpreted as a military installation, or perhaps
more likely, a flood-dyke (Hall 1978, 33). At
Norwich, layers of brushwood were laid over the
unstable gravel river bank, purely to consolidate
and stabilise, and were thought unlikely to have
served as beaching platforms (Ayers 1985, 50-1).
The use of this construction technique, requiring
little carpentry skill and using readily available
waste timber, was therefore certainly not specific
to one function.

The use of dumps of pure clay in the embankments, in combination with brushwood in most
cases, implies that the structure was supposed to
be impermeable to water, and resistant to erosion.
The consolidation of the banks with wattling,

such as was used on the low bank on the foreshore
in front of the Waterfront 3 embankment at Billingsgate Lorry Park, was also recorded at
Hungate, as well as in the low flood-dyke as
excavated at Wood Quay in Dublin (Wallace
1981, 110). On the latter site, a series of banks
were constructed from the natural underlying
boulder clay, incorporating not only wattle fences
but dumped organic refuse. One of the banks was
partly faced on its riverward side with boards,
pinned against the body of the bank by stakes
driven through mortices, and these are
reminiscent of the staves used at Billingsgate
Lorry Park in the construction of Waterfront 3
(above, p.53). Although devoid of mortices, they
could conceivably have been pinned at an angle
to the embankment below, though it is just as
likely that they were set vertically, retaining some
of the bank material. They were of insufficient
height to have supported a horizontal surface at
the level of the upper embankment surface and
could only have protected the foot of the bank.
Successive waterfronts of vertical earthfast staves
have recently been excavated on the Thames
Exchange site in Upper Thames Street (site code
TEX88; report forthcoming), though the degree to
which they would have retained material behind
them is not clear.

The late Saxon embankments in the City have
been variously described as flood-dykes (Miller,
Schofield & Rhodes 1986, 73), platforms for
beaching boats, beach markets (Hobley 1981, 7),
and sloping beaches (Marsden 1981, 14). The
need to exploit the Thames waterfront as a landing place for boats would have increased as the
population of the late Saxon town grew and its
trade flourished. The shelving riverbank, with its
various indentations, would, at least initially,
have provided beaching areas for the small vessels
involved in the predominantly up-river trade,
and a number of topographical features would no
doubt have been considered in the selection of the
best areas: access from the riverbank through the

Roman riverside wall, an area of foreshore devoid of the protruding timbers of Roman structures, and a location at the western end of the walled area and closer to the direction of the trade. It may be that Queenhithe, the subject of the two late 9th-century charters, fulfilled all of these criteria, and the topographical details supplied in the documents seem to confirm this. It was on such a site as this that beach markets would have occurred. These have been described, as they are known to have existed, on the Rhine in the 9th century (Ellmers 1981, 91); the merchants beached their boats, then pitched their tents, on the edge of the sloping riverbank between the former Roman town walls and the river. No formal structures were required, and very little archaeological evidence would be expected to survive. The markets of late Saxon London could have taken the form of the 'trading shore' referred to at Queenhithe in the 9th century. The embankments under consideration here, however, are of a significantly later date.

The continued expansion of trade throughout the 10th century, and in particular the recovery of international markets (Vince 1988, 90-2), would have placed increased pressure on available land suitable for beaching the larger vessels involved in coastal trading or trading with the Continent, vessels perhaps similar in size to those found at Skuldelev in Denmark (Crumlin-Pedersen 1985, 83-93), or nearer home at Graveney (Fenwick 1978), where the vessel had a reconstructed length of 14m and a beam of 3.9m. Berthing at the western end of the city would have had less appeal for such traffic coming upstream, particularly if they had to make use of the tides to bring them to the port and the construction of the bridge would have increased the need for adequate facilities at the eastern end of the town. The harbour at Billingsgate, as well as the sites of New Fresh Wharf and Billingsgate Lorry Park just downstream of the bridge, would have served that need.

The rebuilt bridge would have presented a physical barrier to river traffic at high tides, increasing the demand for docking facilities in the area downstream of it, though it should be noted that French and German merchants, who used some of the largest ships of the period, patronised the Dowgate district (upstream of the bridge) from at least the mid 11th century. The presence of the bridge would also have provided an obvious point of interaction with the major road system; and this, along with the existence of the officially regulated harbour at Billingsgate, must have encouraged commercial activity on the New Fresh Wharf and Billingsgate Lorry Park sites. The late 10th- and early 11th-century jetty at New Fresh Wharf certainly suggests as much, as does the general character and development of the embankments of Tenements **2** to **8** from the mid 11th century. Other direct evidence of trade in the form of small finds is lacking, however, most particularly at Botolph Wharf (Tenement **7**) which on documentary evidence was clearly a notable harbour at the turn of the 12th and 13th centuries and which appears to have been in existence by the 1140s (above, p.75). Its special role and status may be reflected in the use of back-braces, not found in Tenements **2-6** to the west, and perhaps more clearly in the carefully pre-pared level surfaces and the wattle-reinforced foreshore hards of the late 11th or early 12th century, but the scale of subsequent revetments and the enclosure of the inlet to the east are not readily reconcilable with the written evidence. Perhaps, as already suggested, smaller boats now served to bring the cargoes to land, but it may be that the introduction of a single, continuous revetment across its entire frontage was intended to increase its accessibility. There is nevertheless an ambivalence in the status of Botolph Wharf at this period which could help to explain the ruinous state into which it had fallen by the end of the 13th century and the need for its rebuilding (above, p.76). Its temporary decline in the 13th century may well have resulted from the cramped conditions and changes observed on site, as well as from competition on the part of Billingsgate.

The provision of access to the river and consolidated surfaces above high-tide level would tend to imply that the lower slopes of the embankments were used for the berthing of boats, in conjunction with the upper, dry areas for loading or unloading of goods (above, p.107); the situation may have differed on the embankments on Tenements **7** and **8**, where the proximity of the hard within the adjacent inlet would have made up for any deficencies of space for berthing on the slopes or for any obstruction caused by the stave-built frontage (above, p.106). However, not all the embankments were surfaced, whilst the protruding stakes of the earlier jetty on the embankment on Tenement **2** would have made it potentially hazardous for any vessel to attempt to beach on anything but its lowest parts, and would have hindered any transport of goods from there to the upper parts (above, p.105).

It is clear, therefore, that aside from any commercial considerations, the embankments must have fulfilled other functions. Principal amongst these must have been the countering of erosion by the river. This would no doubt have required some measure of coordination and cooperation between neighbours to provide a united front against the tides and could of course have been a purely local initiative on the part of the property owners. It is possible that there was some degree of official intervention to provide adequate river defences at certain points, with individuals being made responsible for consolidating a short stretch of riverbank. It was certainly the case later in the medieval period (Dyson 1985, 23) that whereas the large public quays, such as Billingsgate, were the focus of the bulk of the trade which occurred, the frontages of the privately owned tenements were officially regarded as tidal defences, and were not capable of engaging in anything other than small-scale commercial activities. Though there is reason to believe that for much of the period with which this report is concerned trade was practised more widely than was to be the case later (below, pp.136-7), it would be reasonable to suppose that the protection of the waterfront from the tides was also an important priority. The bridge must have affected the flow of the river and increased erosion of the riverbank just downstream of it; the piers of the late 12th-century stone-built bridge were so closely spaced as to act as a weir, retaining a head of water and encouraging erosion, and its timber predecessor would have produced similar results, to a lesser degree. This may explain why the embankments on the properties nearer to the bridge extended further into the river, and why the nearest embankment to it (that on Tenement **2** at New Fresh Wharf) was constructed on the densest layer of clay and timber (above, p.29). The need to protect the riverbank here must have been important, particularly in view of the effect erosion might have had on the harbour at Billingsgate.

In contrast to the situation at New Fresh Wharf and Billingsgate Lorry Park below the bridge, the construction of the embankments above the bridge at Swan Lane showed little evidence of the influence of individual property owners, and they were presumably the work of one landowner in possession of a substantial area of the waterfront, responding to the existence (or creation) of the public access through the wall at Ebbgate. By the late 12th century, however, the stepped line of the waterfront revealed different degrees of reclamation on individual properties, strongly indicative of the existence of separate tenements. This apparently was not an entirely new development;

hearths and floors recorded behind the lines of the earlier frontages hint at the presence of late 11th- or early 12th-century buildings ranged across the site, and imply that the area behind was in the hands of several individuals. Perhaps they mark an intermediate phase of development.

Elsewhere, although the riverside wall was probably not maintained as a viable defensive structure by the 11th century, it would have served as a protection from periodic flooding in areas where there were no embankments. Evidence of the maintenance of the riverbank against inundation and erosion has been seen elsewhere on the waterfront, for instance at the extreme west end, where the protection afforded by both the *in situ* and collapsed fragments of the riverside wall was apparently augmented by the addition of a thick dump of clay containing timber and ragstone; it is conceivable that this infilling was of late Saxon date, an attempt to fill in gaps and consolidate the riverbank (layer 201 on Fig 20 in Hill, Millett & Blagg 1980, 39 and 42). The first embankments therefore fulfilled several functions connected both with protection of the riverbank and its commercial exploitation.

RIVER LEVELS IN THE 11TH AND 12TH CENTURIES

In recent years the large number of excavations which have taken place on the City's waterfront have allowed some estimates to be made of river levels at various times. This process principally involves noting the upper and lower levels of revetments, the levels at which they have decayed, and the lowest levels of what are assumed to have been contemporary dry areas. These observations can then be compared with those made of present-day waterfront structures in relation to the known river levels. This was first attempted using data from 14th-century revetments excavated at Trig Lane upstream of Queenhithe (Milne & Milne 1982, 60-2), and these results, together with estimates of the tidal levels derived from Roman revetments of the 1st century AD, were then superimposed on graphs produced for tidal levels in the inner and outer Thames estuary (Devoy 1980; Milne *et al* 1983). The exercise has recently been extended to include waterfronts from throughout the Roman period (Brigham 1990), graphically illustrating the continuous decline in the level of the river during that period. Work on strata in the south-western Baltic has shown that there the water level dropped significantly between the 1st and 8th centuries before rising again (Jankuhn 1985, 19). For the Thames, there remains a gap between the end of the Roman period and the 14th century for which the process has not as yet been attempted. The waterfront structures described in this report provide the basis for estimating such levels for the 11th and 12th centuries.

The first structure which gives any indication of contemporary water levels is the post-built jetty at New Fresh Wharf, dated to the late 10th or early 11th century. It has been suggested that the posts of the jetty must have been significantly higher when in use than the level to which they survived, and that their reduction is due either to erosion during use or to subsequent incorporation in the embankments. The posts generally survived to between 1.2 and 1.6m OD; the base of the decay zone of timber waterfront structures has been considered to be an indication of the level of the Mean High Water Neaps (MHWN), and it can be seen that the lowest levels at which these posts decayed is very similar to the levels of decay of the medieval revetments at Trig Lane (Milne & Milne 1982, 61). The lowest levels of the occupation surfaces associated with the waterfronts are presumed to give an indication of the level of the Highest Astronomical Tide (HAT); although reached only a few times in any year, this would undoubtedly have influenced the level at which anything other than the most temporary surfaces or structures could have been constructed. The early to mid 11th-century embankments were only surfaced above c.1.9m OD (or at least surfaces only survived erosion at such a level), and so it is likely that the level of the HAT was just below 1.9m OD. Once again this is comparable to the levels for Trig Lane, being only slightly lower. There were indications that some land as low as 1.7m OD might have been dry land for some of the time, including areas enclosed by fences, and the fact that they were not provided with high-quality external surfaces may indicate that they were above the Mean High Water Springtides (MHWS) but below the HAT. It would appear therefore that the 11th-century HAT, MHWN and MHWS were at levels similar to those estimated for the 14th century.

Estimating the Lowest Astronomical Tide (LAT) is more problematical; Milne noted that the difference between the values of the present-day HAT and MHWN was about a quarter of the total tidal variation, and applying this ratio to the medieval figures arrived at a figure of at least

−1.2m OD, and probably about −1.5m OD (as indicated on the published graph). This accorded well with the level above which the base plates of the Trig Lane revetments had been laid, as they are assumed to have been above water at low tide. The level at which the base plates were laid is perhaps more likely to have been a reflection of the Mean Low Water (MLW), rather than the lower, but less frequent, LAT, unless the land-owners delayed construction of the revetments specifically until the times of lowest tides; this would obviously have depended on whether the new structure was for the purpose of reclaiming more land and increasing the depth of water by the quayfront, or merely for maintaining the frontage.

The base plate of the stave frontage to the first embankment on Tenement **7** (Billingsgate Lorry Park Waterfront 2) was laid horizontally with its upper surface at around −1.4m OD, having been set into the foreshore to a depth of below −1.9m OD; this implies that the LAT in the early to mid 11th century was at least as low as −1.4m OD, and significantly lower if this level was a reflection of the MLW. The base of the clay and brushwood layer of the Tenement **2** embankment was recorded at −2m OD near its southern extremity and although this need not necessarily imply that the LAT was that low (the clay and brushwood could have been dumped into shallow water), this evidence and the level of the Tenement **7** base plate could point to a LAT of that order. The implication is that MLW and LAT in the 11th century are likely to have been lower than the estimated levels for the 14th century.

The 12th-century revetments and associated occupation surfaces provided similar results. The level at which the base plate of Waterfront I at Seal House was inserted (c.−1.5m OD) implies that the LAT was at least that low in the mid 12th century, whilst it is clear that contemporary occupation surfaces on this site, and on the others discussed here, were all above 1.9m OD. At Billingsgate Lorry Park the brickearth floor of a late 12th-century building (Building 1) was laid just above 2m OD.

Comparison of the above results with those from Trig Lane shows that there was little real difference in the river levels from the 11th to the 14th centuries, except that there were probably slightly lower low tides in the 11th century; post-Roman river levels may well have reached their peak by the early medieval period and remained fairly stable thereafter. This has obvious implications for our understanding of the mechanism of reclamation in the medieval period, when, if the level of high tide was fairly constant, the situation was in stark contrast to that in the Roman period, when the primary impetus behind the successive advancements out into the river appears to have been the pursuit of steadily dropping tides in an ultimately vain effort to maintain sufficient depth of water for the docking of cargo vessels (Brigham 1990). A more accurate reassessment of river and tide levels in the Saxon and early medieval period will follow from a more comprehensive study, now underway, of silt deposits from sites in the Vintry area and from the south bank of the Thames (James Rackham, pers comm).

6. THE EARLY LONDON WATERFRONT AND THE LOCAL STREET SYSTEM

Arising from the preceding sections of this report are two issues of particular relevance to the development of the London waterfront as a whole. The first of these concerns the inter-relationship between the various centres of activity on the foreshore and the emergent pattern of streets communicating with them from the north; a line of enquiry suggested by the juxtaposition of the late 10th- or early 11th-century jetty and Pudding Lane, and of the subsequent mid 11th-century embankment and Botolph Lane. The second issue concerns the origin of Thames Street, whose existence in some form during the later 11th century is implied, and in the early 12th century actually established, by the evidence of the New Fresh Wharf site; the date of Thames Street, relative to that of the streets which continued (or failed to continue) across its line, is of considerable importance in charting the early development of the waterfront and its impact on the topography of the southern half of the City.

The jetty at New Fresh Wharf, which may have been constructed as early as the 970s, was quite unlike anything else discovered in the bridgehead area. It lay within 50m of the late Saxon London bridge, itself perhaps of comparable date, and apparently antedated the earliest activity recorded on the Lorry Park site to the east. The jetty, or its site, was evidently sufficiently prominent to determine the line of a ward boundary when wards emerged in London, probably during the first half of the 11th century (above, p.95), and its relation to Pudding Lane to the north is perhaps even more suggestive. Jetty and lane are likely to have been interdependent to a large extent, and traces of a path or alley dating from the 11th and 12th centuries were found to follow the eastern edge of the former jetty (above, pp.40-3, 105, 111) and the division between tenements **2** and **3**. This alley can be identified with *Rederesgate*, first recorded in the first half of the 12th century (above, p.74), which continued the line of *Redereslane*, or Pudding Lane, southwards to the river.

Towards the middle of the 11th century the jetty and the rubble on its eastern side were abandoned in favour of a more ambitious installation: an embankment which included most of the frontage of both the New Fresh Wharf and Lorry Park sites and extended from the site of the former jetty in the west to a natural inlet in the east, located at the foot of Botolph Lane. Beyond the inlet the embankment reappeared, evolving in tandem with the westerly portion until the early 12th century. In all probability it continued beyond the limit of the Lorry Park excavations towards Billingsgate, some 55m further downstream. Indeed, the overall effect of the new embankment was to shift the focus of foreshore activity eastwards, away from the bridge and closer to Billingsgate; an impression strengthened by the apparent neglect of the jetty upstream, whose surviving vertical supports for some time afterwards rendered its site unusable for the handling of vessels and their cargoes (above, p.118). A conspicuous feature of the new embankment was the inlet incorporated within it, superficially similar to the one at the western end adjoining the former jetty. By the end of the 13th century the site of both the inlet and the portion of the embankment immediately to the west (Tenement **7**) was occupied by St Botolph's Wharf, a public quay comparable in status, though not in size, with Billingsgate and Queenhithe, and at that period readily distinguishable from the private tenements further to the west (Tenements **2-6**; above, p.118). The fact that this harbour was certainly in existence by *c.*1200, and apparently by the 1140s also, raises the possibility that it had formed the centrepiece of the embankment as first constructed in the mid 11th century.

Though the account of the excavations shows that there was no fundamental contrast in form and character between Tenement **7** and its neighbours to the west, several differences were noted.

Throughout the period covered by this report Tenement **7** extended less far into the river than **2** to **6**, and its frontage, unlike theirs, was revetted by vertical staves and secured by tieback braces (Figs 27, 31, 35, pp.59-60). From the late 11th century the foreshore in front of the staves was consolidated by wicker-reinforced panels presumably intended to serve as hards for vessels moored against the frontage (above, pp.53-4, 56-7, 60): these panels were absent elsewhere, except across the mouth of the inlet to the east, following its enclosure after the mid 12th century (above, pp.67-8). Again in contrast with **2** to **6**, no buildings were recorded on Tenement **7** apart from what was apparently part of the south wall of St Botolph's Church, and from the turn of the 11th and 12th centuries special attention was given to its open surfaces, which were carefully consolidated and levelled (above, p.72). Along with the wattled panels on the foreshore, the well-prepared open space seems consistent with the role of public harbour indicated later in the 12th century, while the earlier differences apparent between Tenement **7** and its neighbours to the west could, taken together, point to some such special function from the first appearance of the embankment.

One external factor favouring this interpretation is the location of Tenement **7** and the inlet to the east (both later represented by St Botolph Wharf) at the foot of Botolph Lane. This lane was already fully formed and occupied by the mid 11th century (Horsman, Milne & Milne 1988, 12-16) having most probably been established *c*.900: a new harbour at this point would therefore have had the important advantage of a ready-made access to and from the rest of the city, much as the jetty at *Rederesgate* was served by the predecessor of Pudding Lane.

This relationship of early harbours and street system is of great interest, all the more so where Thames Street might not initially have existed as an alternative means of communication between isolated points on the waterfront. The origin of Thames Street remains obscure: it existed by *c*.1130 (below, p.130), but prior to that date definitive evidence of any kind is lacking. A further important aspect of the present sites is therefore the recording at New Fresh Wharf of sand and gravel layers overlapping the truncated footings of the Roman riverside wall to the north of the early 12th-century Building B (above, pp.45-6). It is possible that these layers represent the first appearance of Thames Street at the turn of the 11th and 12th centuries, not least because this

period also broadly coincides with the first definite traces of *Rederesgate* between Tenements **2** and **3**, with the occurrence of the earliest buildings on the south side of the street on these and neighbouring tenements, and also with the likely date of origin of the church of St Botolph, which adjoined the street in the north-west corner of Tenement **7**. Each of these developments could have stemmed directly from the introduction of Thames Street as a formal thoroughfare running parallel with the waterfront, greatly increasing its accessibility and encouraging its further development. The inevitability of such a street is shown by the existence, from soon after the construction of the embankments, of paths leading down the length of most of the New Fresh Wharf tenements towards the river (above, p.107).

STREETS LEADING TO THE THAMES FROM THE
CENTRE OF THE CITY

The relationship of landing places such as the *Rederesgate* jetty and St Botolph Wharf with streets such as Pudding and Botolph Lanes leading away from them across the line of Thames Street towards the centre of the City, is paralleled at each of the other early London harbours, beginning with Queenhithe. There, the new hithe was linked to Cheapside by Bread Street to the west and by Garlick Hill/Bow Lane a little further to the east, both of them datable to the late 9th century either by archaeology or documents and evidently laid out immediately after, or as part of, the establishment of the harbour (above, pp.18-19). St Mary's Hill, a short distance to the east of Botolph Lane and Botolph Wharf, is not archaeologically dated but appears to have served Billingsgate in a similar fashion. Both Botolph Lane and St Mary's Hill, perhaps with their northern continuations, Philpot and Rood Lanes, formed with Eastcheap a compact grid of streets (Fig 43) broadly comparable with that between Queenhithe and Cheapside (Westcheap) and presumably designed to promote commerce on the hillside behind the embankments downstream of the bridge (above, pp.75-6). A third case, to be considered more fully in a future report, is represented by Dowgate Hill/Walbrook (Street). This linked the French and German harbours at Dowgate, apparently dating from about the middle of the 11th century (below, pp.129-30), with the eastern end of Poultry, itself an extension of Cheapside and most probably formed in the late

11th or early 12th century (Keene 1987, 3), presumably in response to contemporary developments on the corresponding section of the foreshore to the south.

These streets, serving the earliest recorded harbours in London, also shared a special characteristic: a marked continuity of alignment wholly unimpaired, as they made their way to Cheapside, Poultry or Fenchurch Street, by the courses of routes crossing their path from east to west. The likelihood that this linearity was the result of deliberate and comprehensive planning in districts where there had previously been relatively little activity is reinforced by their contrast with the many other streets which lay parallel with them by the 13th century. Though likewise leading down to Thames Street, and usually also to the river beyond, these lacked the same overall coherence, being either side-stepped or terminated altogether where they encountered such east-west routes as Knightrider Street, Distaff-Basing Lane, Cannon Street and Tower Street. As a group such streets appear to have evolved stretch by stretch in a piecemeal fashion, as if as part of a gradual process of completing the street plan within the spaces existing between the more regular streets that communicated with the early harbours. Only two streets of this second type have so far been excavated, Peter's Hill (Williams 1982, 28-9) and Pudding Lane, and it is notable that both have been shown to be of 12th-century date. The latter is taken to represent a formalisation of an earlier back-lane between Bridge Street (Fish Street Hill) and Botolph Lane, and extended no further north than Eastcheap; in this respect, and also in its irregular form, it compares closely with Lovat Lane (Fig 43). Both may share the same informal origin, the one corresponding to the jetty at New Fresh Wharf, and the other perhaps to developments on the western side of Billingsgate.

The street plan to the north of the waterfront therefore appears to have evolved between the extreme limits of the late 9th century and the 12th century, and reveals two contrasting types of street in which there seems to be some general correlation between form and relative antiquity. On the limited evidence available it would clearly be unwise to make too much of this comparison, certainly as between one individual street and another. Little Trinity Lane and Old Fish Street Hill, for example, extend no further north than Knightrider Street and might on that account be taken as late additions to the series, though their late 9th-century date is proved, or at any rate

strongly implied in the case of Old Fish Street Hill, by Alfred's Queenhithe grants (above, p.17). Nevertheless the contrast between the two types as a whole is of interest for its implication that the various parts of the street system evolved in an essentially fragmentary fashion, and very likely in tandem with the development of the local section of waterfront to the south. In such a process any single chronology would be inappropriate: the intervals between the emergence of Queenhithe (late 9th century), the Billingsgate area (late 10th to mid 11th century) and Dowgate (mid 11th century), as well as the physical distances between them, are likely to have imposed independent, if overlapping, time-scales upon the growth of individual sectors of the southern half of the city.

Even if it is not possible at present to trace this process of the 10th and 11th centuries in any detail, the relationship of the street system to the development of the waterfront can more clearly be indicated by a comparison of the basic medieval topography and toponymy on either side of Thames Street. In the later medieval period each of the streets to the north, with the notable exception of the 12th-century Peter's Hill, and probably of St Michael's (Miles) Lane, also continued south as far as the Thames. The apparent prototypes, Bread Street, Dowgate Hill, Botolph Lane and St Mary's Hill, widened out south of Thames Street to form spacious open areas at the heads of Queenhithe, Dowgate, Botolph Wharf and Billingsgate. Each of these harbours maintained its early primacy throughout the medieval period and beyond, enjoying – apart from Dowgate, which was reserved for French and German merchants (below, pp.129-30) — a special and apparently exclusive role as 'common quays' open to all shipping (Dyson 1985, 19-23). Elsewhere, however, the streets from the centre of the city continued south of Thames Street simply as narrow lanes leading down to the river. But despite differences of scale and role both the harbours and the ordinary lanes shared the same legal status as part of the public highway, flanked on either side by private properties, and were often listed or mentioned together as essentially similar entities (eg Lib Cust ii.444-53). Both also owed much of their later medieval form to the gradual southward progression of the foreshore between the 11th and 15th centuries. Although, at the period with which this report is concerned, the harbours and lanes would have amounted to little more than restricted open spaces on the foreshore at the foot of the streets from the north, the later lanes are of direct relevance here in that the names given to them in the 13th century and after preserve the original nomenclature of the access points in the 11th and 12th centuries. Thus, for example, in 1343 Trig Lane was referred to as the *venella vocata* ('lane called') *Fysshwharfe* , Ebbgate as the *venella vocata Ebbegate* and Haywharf Lane as the *venella vocata la Heywharf* (*ibid*; Fig 65, 6, 37, 32), names which record the original 'Fish-hithe' of 1006-12 (Sawyer 1968, no. 940), the *Ebbegate* of 1147-67 (Hodgett 1971, no. 394) and the *Heiwarft* of 1197 (Feet Fines 9 Ric 1, no. 81).

Some of these names extend the list of instances where the street to the north of Thames Street and the corresponding lane to the south shared the same nomenclature, so that to Dowgate/*vicus de Douegate* (Dowgate Hill), *Rederesgate/ Redereslane* (Pudding Lane) and Botolph Wharf/ Botolph Lane can be added *Wolsiesgate/Wolsieslane* (Suffolk Lane) and *Seint Dunstones Watergate/*St Dunstan's Lane, thus underlining the sense in which the parts north and south of Thames Street were seen as constituting a single, continuous unit. This notion of continuity can, however, be demonstrated in an even more striking and comprehensive way. In all, as many as some fifty medieval lanes have been identified to the south of Thames Street (Fig 65), almost twice the number of streets leading down to it from the north. About half the waterfront lanes, in other words, did not correspond with streets opposite, but instead terminated at Thames Street. This continuity, or lack of it, is faithfully reflected in the contrasting types of name given to the two different types of lane. Those which terminated at Thames Street were almost invariably distinguished by the vernacular 'lane' in conjunction with the names of individual persons or tenements (below, pp.128-9) as in *Oxenfordeslane, Cressynghamlane, Westoneslane*. Such names are readily differentiated from those given to lanes that did continue across the line of Thames Street, which have as an equally constant basis the topographic terms 'wharf' (occasionally 'hithe') and 'gate'. Examples, in addition to the familiar instances of Queenhithe, Dowgate, Botolph Wharf and Billingsgate and the streets leading to them, include *le Estwatergate*/Addle Street (Fig 65, 3); Brokenwharf/Fish Street Hill (Fig 65, 8); Haywharf Lane/Bush Lane (Fig 65, 32); Ebbgate/St Martin's Lane (Fig 65, 33, 37); *le Watergate*/Bear Lane (Fig 65, 48). As with many rules, there were exceptions: *Rothyngslane — Oxenefordeslane* (Fig 65, 18), though named after identifiable persons, was apparently the southern extension of Garlick Hill, just as Painted Tavern

or Three Cranes Lane (Fig 65, 23) was the continuation of College Hill; while neither *Kingesgate* (Fig 65, 5) nor *Daneburghgate* (Fig 65, 7) continued north of Thames Street. Elsewhere however the correspondence between lane types and lane names is too consistent to be accidental.

In effect, the terms 'hithe', 'wharf' and 'gate' were reserved for those points of direct contact between the city's street system to the north and the river to the south; the only places on the foreshore where the public at large enjoyed access to the Thames unimpeded by private properties. 'Hithe' and 'wharf' both meant 'landing place', and many of the places so named on the London waterfront evidently handled the basic imported commodities most sought after by the public. In order of first occurrence were Fish-hithe, c.1006-12 and 1291 (HR 20/44); Haywharf, 1197; Timberhithe, c.1206-16 (Bateson 1902, 483-4); Woodwharf (perhaps St Paul's Wharf), c.1215-30 (Hassall 1949, no. 345); Garlickhithe, 1276 (*Cal Lbk B*, 260-1); *Wynwharf*, 1316 (HR 45/71), perhaps Three Cranes Lane; and Saltwharf, 1331 (HR 59/69). Names in 'gate' appear at much the same date as those in 'hithe' and 'wharf', Billingsgate being followed by *Rederesgate*, 1108-47; Dowgate, c.1140 (Cronne & Davis 1968, no. 829); *porta Sancti Botulphi*, c.1140 and *Botuluesgat'*, c.1201; Ebbgate, 1146-67; Oystergate, after 1197 (Hassall 1949, no. 255); and *Wolseysgate*, 1259 (HR 2/41). There were also several 'watergates' or 'gates of the Thames' at the eastern and western extremities of the waterfront that did not acquire permanent distinctive prefixes: *Westwatergate* at the foot of St Andrew's Hill, 1359 (HR 87/33); *le Estwatergate* at the foot of Addle Hill, 1343 (Chew & Kellaway 1973, no. 453); and four others in the parishes of St Dunstan in the East and All Hallows Barking. It seems reasonably clear that no difference in character or function was implied by the use of 'gate' rather than 'hithe' or 'wharf'. Like Queenhithe, Dowgate and Billingsgate were both notable harbours; Botolph's Wharf is first recorded in the form of a 'gate' name, and *Rederesgate* and Oystergate were both associated, like many of the wharves and hithes, with specific commodities. Both the East Watergate and Oystergate were described as *portus*, or 'harbour', in 1291 and 1332 respectively (HR 20/98; 59/148-9).

Though several of these individual place-names are recorded by the late 12th century, many others do not occur before the late 13th or even 14th centuries. All however are likely to have emerged by the early 12th century in the same

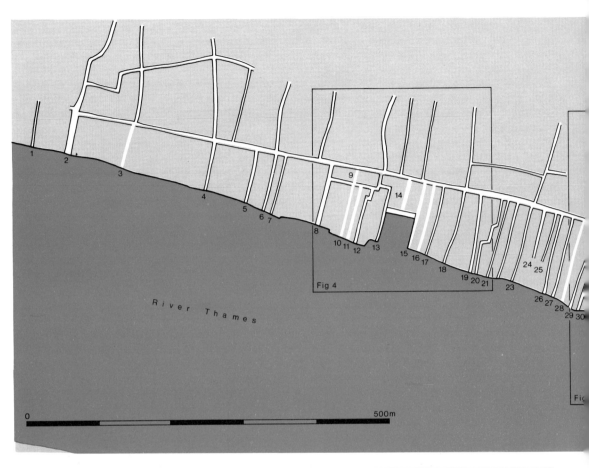

Number on map	Medieval street names (Post-medieval street names)	Continuation north of Thames Street
1	Love Lane	—
2	(West) Watergate	St Andrew's Hill
3	(East) Watergate	Addle Street
4	St Paul's Wharf	St Bennet's Hill
5	Kingsgate; Arouneslane; (Boss Lane)	—
6	Fishwharf(lane); Freshfishlane; Triglane	Lambeth Hill
7	Daneburghate; Desebournelane	—
8	Brokenwharf	Fish Street Hill
9	Timberhithestreet (High Timber Street)	—
10	Ratoneslane; Timberhithelane	—
11	Dunglane; Puddinglane	—
12	Saltwharf(lane)	Bread Street Hill
13	Pyelane; Derkelane; 'Queenhithe'	Bread Street Hill
14	'lane'	—
15	'lane'	Little Trinity Lane
16	Dibeleslane	—
17	Medelane; (Sheppard Alley)	—
18	Rothyngeslane; Oxenefordeslane	Garlick Hill/Bow Lane
19	?Fatteslane; Cressynghamlane;Sayeslane; (Anchor Lane)	—
20	Stodeyeslane; Vynteners Lane	—
21	Picardeslane; Brodelane	—
22	Sackeslane; Vannerslane; (Church Lane)	—
23	Painted Tavern Lane; (Three Cranes Lane)	College Hill
24	?Hardeleslane; Erberlane; (Brickhill Lane)	—
25	Palmereslane; Cookeslane; (Emperors Head Lane)	—

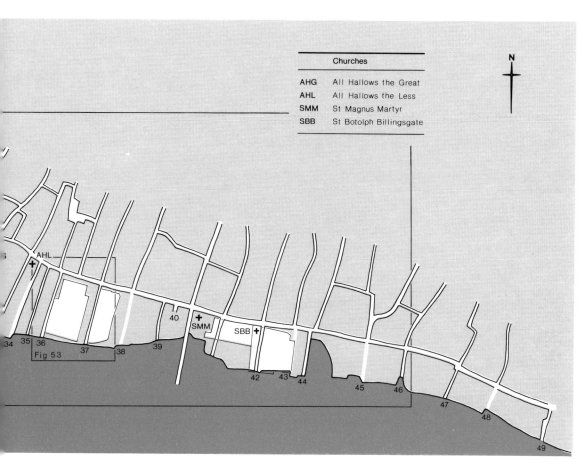

Churches	
AHG	All Hallows the Great
AHL	All Hallows the Less
SMM	St Magnus Martyr
SBB	St Botolph Billingsgate

Number on map	Medieval street names (Post-medieval street names)	Continuation north of Thames Street
26	Spiteleslane; (Tennis Court Lane)	—
27	Grenewychelane; Frerelane	—
28	Bathestereslane; Granthameslane; Brakkeleslane; (Brewers Lane)	—
29	(street of) Douegate	Dowgate Hill
30	Cosyneslane	—
31	Wancelineslane; Germeyneslane; Wendegoselane	—
32	Heywharflane; Batteslane; Chirche Lane; Allhallows Lane	Bush Lane
33	Wolsiesgate; Elselane; Wolsey Lane	Suffolk Lane
34	Sayerslane; Armenterslane; Westoneslane	—
35	'lane'	—
36	Bretaxlane	—
37	Ebbegate	St Martin's Lane
38	'Lane of Pentecost Russel'; 'Gilbert de Morden'	?St Michael's Lane
39	Stepheneslane; Chirchehawlane; (Churchyard Alley)	—
40	Oystergate	'lane' (13th century)
41	Retheresgate	Pudding Lane
42	St Botolph's Wharf	Botolph Lane
43	Treyereswharf; Wirehalelane; (Somer's Quay)	?Lovat Lane
44	Billingsgate	St Mary's Hill
45	Aubreeswatergate/St Dunstan's Watergate	St Dunstan's/Idle Lane
46	'Watergate'	Harp Lane
47	'Watergate'	Water Lane
48	'Watergate'	Bear Lane
49	'Postern next the Tower'	?Tower Bank (17th century)

general context as the earliest exemplars, Queen-hithe and Billingsgate, not merely on the grounds of analogy but because of a change in vocabulary underway shortly afterwards. In the early decades of the 13th century the existing English term 'wharf', having apparently replaced 'hithe' as a place-name element at least a century before (above, p.19) was now itself rapidly replaced by the French equivalent 'quay', which first appears in a London context in c.1190 (Kerling 1973, no. 841). As a result, 'wharf' seems to have fallen out of general use, at any rate in the language of charters, by the mid 13th century except in the case of the place-names under review, which continued to feature in such cumbersome explanatory phrases as *kayum Sancti Botolphi vocatum Bothulfeswharf* ('quay of St Botolph called Botolph's wharf') in 1334 (HR 62/52), or *kayum sive wharvum vocatum Botulphiswharf* ('quay or wharf called Botolph's wharf') in 1443 (GL MS 59, ff xxii^r-xxiii^r). The persistence of the earlier nomenclature in fixed common usage strongly implies that the places in question had already been well established before the change in vocabulary at the turn of the 12th and 13th centuries. Another example of the longevity of such usages, once applied, appears to be provided by the name 'Garlickhithe' which occurs no earlier than 1276 and which, though never attached to any specific feature on the waterfront of St James's parish, evidently preserves the memory of an early hithe at the foot of Garlick Hill (above, p.19). Incomplete as it is, the evidence for names in -hithe, -wharf and -gate suggests that all of them were current by the mid 12th century at the latest, in conformity with a general terminology which first emerged with Queenhithe and Billingsgate between the late 9th and mid 11th centuries.

That timescale closely coincides with the formation of the street system to the north (above, pp.123-4), includes the establishment of the early embankments and revetments in the bridgehead area from the turn of the 10th and 11th centuries, and enables the emergence of the streets on the one hand and of the hithes, wharves and gates on the other to be seen more clearly as closely related aspects of the overall development of the southern half of London in the late Saxon and early medieval periods. Without further evidence of the dates of individual streets to the north of Thames Street and of the character of the early foreshore elsewhere, it is impossible to detail the stages by which the whole pattern evolved. What can be suggested however is that whereas the position of the earliest streets was determined by the choice of location for the first harbours, elsewhere the reverse seems likelier to have been the case. Thus the moderately regular spacing of most of the other streets, in relation to each other and to Bread Street, Garlick and Dowgate Hills, Botolph Lane and St Mary's Hill, perhaps resulted from the need to allow for suitably sized tenement plots between them, rather than from the exact positioning of the landing places at their foot. The later and less prominent wharves and gates may therefore have emerged piecemeal as one new street after the other was added to the evolving pattern to the north. Though formed and named after the example of the major harbours, it seems unlikely that they were ever of comparable importance. Their individual names, unlike those of the major harbours, suggest that each specialised in a single commodity only, an activity of which there is little other local evidence in the written sources. By the 14th century the lanes which marked their position and preserved their names were regarded by the mayor and commonalty as little more than a means of access to the river for water-collecting, while the major harbours had consolidated their early pre-eminence to the extent of exercising a virtual monopoly on external trade (Dyson 1985, 20-3; 1989, 20-2).

65. *Previous Page: Plan of the medieval lanes south of Thames Street, together with streets to the north shown roughly as far as the line of Knightrider Street-Cannon Street-Eastcheap; derived from Leake's map of 1666, redrawn to scale using a modern base. Lanes not recorded in the medieval period have been omitted; recorded medieval lanes not shown by Leake have been added in grey. The four excavation sites are shown in outline. Sites of the four waterfront churches mentioned in this study have been added: AHG = All Hallows the Great; AHL = All Hallows the Less; SMM = St Magnus the Martyr; SBB = St Botolph Billingsgate. (Based on the 1980 Ordnance Survey 1:1250 map, and reproduced with the permission of the Controller of Her Majesty's Stationery Office: Crown Copyright.) Scale 1:5000.*

THE 'PRIVATE' WATERFRONT LANES AND THAMES STREET

In addition to the 'wharf' and 'gate' lanes which were linked with the City centre by streets on the opposite side of Thames Street, in the medieval period there were almost as many waterfront lanes again that terminated at Thames Street and did not continue further to the north. The resulting dependence of this type of lane upon Thames

Street for access to the rest of the street system suggests a separate and subsidiary origin, as does the distinctive class of names reserved for them. In place of the topographical 'wharf' or 'gate' nomenclature common to the others, such lanes almost always adopted either personal names (*eg*, *Dibeleslane* (Fig 65, 16), *Stodeyeslane* (Fig 65, 20), *Vannereslane* (Fig 65, 22), *Palmereslane* (Fig 65, 25), *Cosineslane* (Fig 65, 30), *Armenterslane* (Fig 65, 34) and *Stepheneslane* (Fig 65, 39), or the names of adjacent tenements (*Erberlane* (Fig 65,24), previously probably *Hardeleslane*; *Spiteleslane* (Fig 65, 26), from the neighbouring property of the Hospital of St Mary Bishopsgate; *Bretaxlane* (Fig 65, 36), from the tenement to the east called *la Bretasse*). A few others, recorded relatively late, were descriptive merely of themselves (*Dunglane* (Fig 65, 11) and *Derkelane* (Fig 65, 13)), and perhaps replaced earlier personal names, just as *Brodelane* (Fig 65, 21) replaced *Picardeslane* by 1335. But the general character of such names, from their earliest appearance with *Wancelineslane*, *c*.1235 (PRO E40/1791), *venella Ricardi le Gras*, 1259 (HR 2/52) and *Germeyneslane*, 1271 (HR 4/82) was overwhelmingly personal or proprietory. Moreover the persons whose names were given to the lanes are often to be found among the occupants of adjacent tenements as late as the early 14th century, when documentation is sufficient for ownership to be established. Sometimes the names of the lanes changed as one occupant replaced another, as in the cases of ?*Fatteslane* – *Cressynghamlane* — *Sayeslane* (Fig 65, 19), or *Sayerslane* — *Armenterslane* – *Westoneslane* (Fig 65, 34); and in these instances, as in others, it was the occupants of a property on one particular side of a lane who gave it its successive names. Terms such as 'the lane of Richard le Gras', the 'lane of Pentecost Russell' or 'the lane of Gilbert de Morden' imply actual ownership, and certain neighbouring property holders claimed as much in their deeds, as in the cases of *Armenterslane* in 1278 and 1364 (HR 9/70, 92/ 147) and *Stepheneslane* between 1274 and 1347 (HR 6/10, 18/33, 19/22, 45/9, 75/68).

The association between these lanes and their neighbours was evidently intimate and deep-rooted, and the contrast between them and the type with 'wharf' or 'gate' names which lay at the foot of the public streets to the north strengthens the impression that they were essentially private in character, perhaps originating with the early division of existing properties to make for a more intensive use of the waterfront within the framework of the public landing places, and acquiring the owners' names in the process. Also pointing in this direction is one further feature of this category of lanes: all of them were located in the central section of the waterfront, the westernmost represented by Boss Lane (Fig 65, 5) in the parish of St Peter the Less, and the easternmost by *Stepheneslane* (Fig 65, 39) just above the bridge in the parish of St Magnus Martyr. Most of them, however, lay between Queenhithe and All Hallows the Less, the latter a short distance upstream of Swan Lane, and even more particularly in the Vintry and Dowgate areas (Fig 65). Here the number of basic property plots between any two lanes was one in St Martin Vintry and two in All Hallows the Great, as against an average of three elsewhere on the waterfront. This greater frequency of lanes, the great majority of them not extending beyond Thames Street, was accompanied by a notably greater degree of local foreshore reclamation, amounting to some 122m, than occurred on the rest of the waterfront; three-quarters (92m) of the distance having been achieved at the site of the later Steelyard by 1301 (HR 30/39-40). The exceptional development of this part of the waterfront by a relatively early date, in terms of both the provision of lanes and depth of reclamation, is partly explained by favourable natural conditions. The gradient was comparatively gentle at this point, across the mouth of the Walbrook valley, and the resulting wider distance north-south between high and low watermarks would have lent itself more readily to the exploitation and adaptation of the foreshore.

The responsibility for this activity must lie primarily with the German and French merchants who were given special trading privileges in the area roughly half-way between Queenhithe and the bridgehead from about the middle of the 11th century (Dyson 1985, 21-2). The presence in London of the Emperor's men, and of the men of Tiel, Bremen, Antwerp, Huy, Liège and Nivelles, is mentioned by Ethelred II's fourth law code, a document which seems in part to date from the reign of Edward the Confessor (Thorpe 1840, 127-9; Richardson & Sayles 1965, 28); while the confirmation of the rights of the Rouen merchants in the port of Dowgate in 1150-1 refers to privileges which they had held there since the Confessor's day (Cronne & Davis 1968, no. 729). A German presence from the same period also is attested by quantities of Rhenish pottery of the 11th century found in the area of the Cologne guildhall close to Dowgate (Vince 1985, 39, 42, 86). The regulations of *c*.1130 for the Lorraine merchants emphasise the importance of enabling the sheriffs and the king's chamberlain to exercise the royal right of pre-emption over imported goods (Bateson 1902, 496, 499), and it was no doubt for this purpose that William Pont de l'Arche, a leading official of Henry I's chamber and exchequer, maintained a stone house next to the stalls of Dowgate before 1135 (Cronne & Davis 1968, no. 829). The same regulations also show that those traders who wished to lodge and to sell their goods beyond the wharves and Thames Street were required to make a special payment of 'shewage', and were subject to further provisions in respect of pre-emption (Bateson 1902, 497-8, 500-1). This restriction is of great interest in the present context, since its obvious purpose of confining the merchants' business as far as possible to the waterfront south of Thames Street would clearly help to account for the intensive development and occupation of the local foreshore.

An essential requirement of the concentration of lanes in the Vintry-Dowgate district and adjacent areas would have been some means of east-west communication linking them with the rest of the City's street system, to which they lacked any direct access of their own. The emerging lanes would have been dependent on just such a thoroughfare as Thames Street, and the origins of both are likely to have been closely interrelated. Direct evidence of the antiquity of Thames Street is still wanting. No sign of it appears in the detailed descriptions given by the two Queenhithe grants at the end of the 9th century: at that date any communication to east or west must have been served by the *publica strata* which defined the northern limit of the bishops' plots, and which is described in the later text as leading towards the east (Dyson 1978, 202, 212). This 'public street', identifiable as part of the Knightrider Street-Trinity Lane-Cloak Lane-Cannon Street route following the crest of the hillside behind the river, apparently offered the earliest access between the Queenhithe and bridgehead areas, just as Cannon Street must also have provided a vital link between the City's principal markets of Cheapside and Eastcheap from early in the 11th century (above, p.76). As a more direct means of communication between different parts of the waterfront, Thames Street had certainly emerged in the relatively remote area upstream of Broken Wharf by the 12th century when Peter's Hill was laid out (Williams 1982, 28-9), leading into it but not continuing beyond it to the river. The first specific mention of Thames

Street occurs in *c.*1130 as *le Ruwe qe est sur Tamise*, a unique form of the name expressive of the close proximity of street and river at that period; and the reference appears, in the regulations for the Lorraine merchants already referred to, in the context of traders who had passed London Bridge on their way to harbour, presumably in the Dowgate area (Bateson 1902, 496, 499). Though it need be no more than coincidence that the earliest allusion to Thames Street should occur in connection with this particular part of the waterfront, it nevertheless seems probable that the street did evolve as a coherent, continuous thoroughfare in this central area during the course of the second half of the 11th century. There, and at that period, it would have met two identifiable needs. First, it would have linked together with each other and with the rest of London the profusion of lanes emerging on its south side as a result of the activity of the communities of overseas merchants established there from about the middle of the century, and to which the appearance of Poultry to the north at the same period or a little later (above, pp.123-4) might be seen as a further response. Second, it would have linked the developing Vintry-Dowgate district with the existing harbours of Queenhithe to the west and of the bridgehead and Billingsgate area to the east, as well as with the smaller, specialist harbours whose commodities are recorded in many of the 'wharf' and 'gate' names.

Some such means of east-west access may already have evolved in the bridgehead area by the mid 11th century, in order to link the bridge more directly with Botolph's Wharf and Billingsgate (above, p.107). It is therefore possible that, as a result of some of the same pressures and needs which have been identified in the Dowgate area, a local antecedent of Thames Street was introduced soon after the construction of the early embankments. At New Fresh Wharf and Custom House (above, pp.96-7) and also, at the extreme western end of the intramural waterfront, at Baynard's Castle (Hill, Millett & Blagg 1980, 16-17, 71) the course of Thames Street was seen to be determined by the line of the Roman riverside wall, which at New Fresh Wharf separated the street to the north from the back of the embankments to the south. Almost certainly it is with the riverside wall also that the 'city wall' referred to in Alfred's late 9th-century Queenhithe grants is to be identified, there described as dividing the bishops' plots on one side from the trading shore and harbour facilities on the other. The streets leading down to the river from the interior of the city at this earliest period, Bread Street, Bow Lane and Botolph Lane, would therefore have encountered the riverside wall rather than Thames Street, which was only subsequently to evolve along its northern side. This seems to offer the best available explanation of the term 'gate' which was applied to several of the landing places at the foot of these streets, and it may be that its use, instead of the more usual 'hithe' or 'wharf', is an indication of the survival of the wall at these particular points as an obstacle through which gates were necessary for access to the foreshore. It is certainly notable that many of the 'gate' names occur towards the extremities of the waterfront where the wall might be expected to have survived longest: in the extreme west there was no evidence of significant modification of the post-Roman foreshore before the late 12th and early 13th centuries, following the destruction of the wall (Hill, Millett & Blagg, 71-3); and in the east none until the end of the 13th century (Tatton-Brown 1974, 128-32; 1975, 103-5).

Of the harbours and lanes reviewed here, Queenhithe, Bread Street, Garlick Hill/Bow Lane and Botolph Lane date from *c*.900, and it is possible that Garlickhithe was of similar antiquity. Other streets, like the wharves and gates at their foot, appear in general to belong to the period between the late 10th/early 11th centuries, the date of the first foreshore installations in the bridgehead area, and the mid 12th century. Their introduction was probably sporadic and piecemeal, rather than the result of any comprehensive planning, and it coincided in the latter half of the same period with the emergence of the 'private' lanes, a distinctive type of waterfront lane which extended no further north than the line of Thames Street. These, confined to the central sector of the waterfront and most numerous in the Vintry and around Dowgate, are most likely to reflect the activity of the overseas merchants who were quartered in the district from the reign of Edward the Confessor. Thames Street itself, which defined their northern limit and linked them with the rest of the City's street system, in all probability developed in conjunction with them during the second half of the 11th century. The existence of an equivalent thoroughfare of this date is indicated in the bridgehead area, serving the individual tenements at New Fresh Wharf and presumably following the north face of the riverside wall, where the metallings of the early 12th-century Thames Street were identified. On this assessment, Thames Street would seem to have emerged during the second half of the 11th century, towards the end of the period during which most of the streets leading down to the river are likely to have taken shape, and with its emergence access between the city and all parts of the waterfront would have been greatly improved. Previously, however, such access would have been wholly dependent upon the north-south streets, the origin of each of which must have been as directly and intimately linked with the development of the local foreshore as it was in the case of the earliest harbours which set the pattern.

7. CONCLUSIONS

This section, serving as conclusions to the whole report, summarises the main findings and suggestions of the preceding chapters, and briefly considers the consequences of the archaeological and historical results for the period 400-1200 at three levels: an overall impression of the use of the waterfront zone around the bridgehead, our knowledge of the wider City, and parallels with the development of other European ports in these centuries.

As this is the third volume in a series of archaeological reports on the Saxon City of London, the opportunity is also taken of reviewing the evidence so far presented in these three studies. In particular, though the pottery evidence was presented in detail in *Aspects of Saxo-Norman London II* (Vince 1991), a note of further reflection about the pottery appears here in Appendix 1 (below, p.139). It is possible that further volumes in this series will appear in the future, refining or challenging the conclusions made here.

LONDON AS A PORT, 400-886

Mid Saxon London, west of the Roman city, was a trading post to which ships came from at least the late 7th to the mid 9th centuries. Although there are hints that it might be older, such as coinage minted from the 630s, the Strand settlement can only be delineated in outline from the late 7th century, and in detail only from the 8th century (Vince 1988; Biddle 1984). Given the marshy nature of much of the land adjoining the Thames on both sides of the river, settlement seems to have been confined to available drier ground on the north bank upstream of the Roman city: from west to east, at the 8th-century royal meeting-place at Chelsea (used for royal or ecclesiastical councils at least eleven times in 785-815), at the monastic site at Westminster

(?founded in the 780s), and on the Strand. Here, in the 8th century, the port of London served as a gateway to the Continent for Mercian kings, just as Ipswich must have done for East Anglian dignitaries.

Archaeological evidence from the City itself for the 5th to 9th centuries is almost non-existent (Vince 1985, 1988; Horsman, Milne & Milne 1988). Whatever the precise state and use of the ruinous Roman buildings and their covering of dark earth, there is no evidence for substantial occupation. The nature of the earliest St Paul's (from 604) and any ancillary structures remains unknown. An argument can be made that within the walls some official and semi-official functions continued: there was a cathedral and the bishop's house, probably a royal residence, a possible place of public assembly in the Roman amphitheatre, and a small but unknown number of lesser residential enclosures (Biddle 1989, 27). The archaeological findings from the four sites considered in detail in this volume confirm the picture of a general lack of human activity in other parts of the City. On all four sites the Roman waterfront was gradually obscured by silts of the rising river; it was probably already partially robbed. The waterfront near the bridge was deserted. Thus the Roman bridge, if it still survived, probably did not form a focus of activity or communication. A recent analysis of the coins recovered from the river silts adjacent to the bridge suggests that it may have been unfrequented by traffic after the 330s (Rhodes 1991). If the route had still been open, we would expect the nearby foreshore to be littered with evidence. We therefore conclude that the bridge was broken and the north-south route across it abandoned.

Viking incursions afflicted London in the mid and later 9th century until it was occupied by Alfred in 886 and subsequently restored. From this period there is archaeological evidence of a shift in the location of settlement from the Strand to within the Roman walls, and it is clear that commercial considerations were to the fore. Documentary evidence demonstrates that at least two substantial plots of land adjoining the waterfront at Queenhithe were laid out in the last decade of the 9th century, very probably as part of a larger district bounded by Cheapside, Bread Street and Bow Lane (above, pp. 17-8). In all likelihood the occupants were engaged in the trade generated by the newly established harbour, for a beach market on the site of Queenhithe, and immediately south of a surviving section of the Roman riverside wall, was evidently the focal point of the scheme. Comparable in form and date with Bread Street and Bow Lane, but in the eastern half of the City, was Botolph Lane which led north from the river at the Billingsgate Lorry Park site towards Eastcheap (Horsman, Milne & Milne 1988, 108-16). Despite the contemporaneity of these lanes, the existence of a local counterpart to Queenhithe on the waterfront between the bridge and Billingsgate at this period seems highly unlikely in view of the excavated evidence presented here (Fig 55).

By the mid 10th century, as shown by the number of moneyers in burhs, London was the largest trading centre in southern England. Successive kings are recorded as staying in London or holding a *witan* (council) there (Hill 1981, 87-91). There is however evidence that during the 10th and early 11th centuries, London looked inland rather than abroad for its commercial well-being. London's pottery in the 10th century was supplied almost exclusively from the Oxfordshire region; very little if any imported pottery was used in London in this period (Vince 1985, 34; Jenner & Vince 1991, 40-1). This may indicate that the settlement largely restricted itself, at least initially, to local or at most to upstream trade. It is possible that embankments recently excavated at the Thames Exchange site, on the stretch of riverbank between Queenhithe and the Walbrook, later the Vintry, will throw further light on the river installations of 10th-century London and on the character and affinities of its commerce. This ambiguity is not peculiar to London; a similar scarcity of imports is a feature

of comparable towns such as Ipswich and the second Saxon settlement at Southampton, and indeed of 10th-century England generally (Wade 1988, 97; Brisbane 1988, 103-4).

This local or at best interregional trading network has parallels elsewhere in Europe (Pirenne 1925; Hodges 1982, 162-84). By the 10th century, England, like other states, had a basic network of inland market centres, their number and trading links illustrated most vividly by the distribution of their individual coinage (in 979, for instance, 53 English towns minted their own coins: Hill 1981, 131-2). Unlike the coinage of the Saxon kings in the late 7th century, this new coinage included a sharp increase in the quantity of low-value coins (Hodges 1978, 446). The development of controlled markets by the minting of coinage, within a guaranteed royal peace, is a feature of the rest of northern Europe (Ennen 1985).

After the disruptions of Viking attacks in the mid 9th century, and the campaign of English recovery in the late 9th and early 10th centuries, the development of the towns of the Danelaw shows the Vikings' 'brilliant use of commodity production as a mechanism for seducing the English' (Hodges 1988, 6). This may be the context of London's 10th-century reference to the court of *Husting* (a Northern/Viking term), where silver was weighed. But there is little archaeological evidence at present that at this period London was a large trading centre much frequented by the Northmen. Their influence was more clearly felt in the north, where epicentres of their activities included York (Hall 1978) and Irish centres such as Dublin (Wallace 1985). As in the 7th and 8th centuries, London was again on the margin of the trading network, which now had a different geographic emphasis (*cf* Vince 1990, 152).

PORT FACILITIES NEAR BILLINGSGATE, 1000-1050

The present report is largely concerned with the physical manifestations of the 11th- and 12th-century expansion of harbour works or port facilities between the haven of Billingsgate (first mentioned in Ethelred's code *c*.1000, and which lay immediately downstream of the Billingsgate Lorry Park excavations) and the rebuilt bridge (also mentioned as a point of demarcation in the code, but in a part of the text which might date from the reign of Edward the Confessor (above, p.75)). It is however suggested above (p.122) that around 1000 the embankments on the New Fresh Wharf site may have been part of the same general development as Billingsgate.

The earliest post-Roman structures discovered between Billingsgate and the bridge were the jetty and associated rubble bank from New Fresh Wharf, dated to the late 10th or early 11th century (Fig 57). It appears to have been unique; nothing of the kind has been found on the many other sites excavated south of Thames Street. The jetty's abandoned remains, the decayed vertical timbers, helped form the boundary between two of the individual plots which were subsequently constructed there, and the timbers themselves must have been a limiting factor on the use of the embankment which overlay them, due to the continued protrusion of some as late as the 12th century.

The various purposes of the embankments themselves have already been discussed (see above, Part 5). On the three sites where they were present (Swan Lane, New Fresh Wharf and Billingsgate Lorry Park), the earliest embankments were of late 10th- to mid 11th-century date. Those at Swan Lane and New Fresh Wharf had similar 'stepped' profiles, with a relatively horizontal upper surface dropping to a more gently sloping or near horizontal area which in turn sloped steeply onto the earlier foreshore, this edge being revetted in some cases. The lower areas could have been used for the berthing of boats with the upper dry land used for the unloading or loading of cargoes. At Billingsgate Lorry Park, the site of the early medieval common quay of St Botolph Wharf, the two embankments lay either side of a revetted inlet with a hard-standing, which could have provided direct landward access to the north, as well as an area for berthing boats and access for wheeled vehicles; the upper parts of these two embankments would have functioned in a similar fashion to those on the others, whilst the inlet took the place of their lower areas.

The provision of facilities for the berthing of boats would seem to be a necessary requirement for commercial exploitation, and in this respect the first embankments were well equipped. Four kinds of ship were specified as worthy of toll in Ethelred's code: the two paying most, the barque (ceol) and merchantman (hulcus), both paid eight times the rate for a small ship. More needs to be known about this variety in size before the relations between these berthing areas and contemporary shipping can be explored.

Aspects of both international and local trade were regulated by Ethelred's code (some parts of which may apply to the Dowgate/Vintry area as well as to Billingsgate). Merchants from Rouen, Flanders, Ponthieu, Normandy and the Ile de France are mentioned, implying a healthy level of cross-channel trade. This is also illustrated by the occurrence in deposits on the present sites of northern French glazed pitchers and sherds of Normandy Gritty ware (see Appendix 1). Other merchants from Huy, Liège, Nivelle and Cologne are mentioned, and their presence on these sites and elsewhere in the City may be related to the occurrence of Rhenish Red-Painted ware which is found in London from the 11th century (Vince 1985, 42-3); Andenne-type ware is found on the present sites in CP4 (1050-80). The goods being traded included timber, fish, wine, wool, cloth, gloves, fat, pigs, vinegar, and some perhaps local items: hens, eggs, and dairy products. English cheeses were themselves the subject of tolls in Flanders by 1036 (Loyn 1962, 93-6).

The development of the waterfront area south of Thames Street, between the bridge and Billingsgate, can be seen within the context of the late 10th- and early 11th-century development of the immediate neighbourhood and of the City as a whole. The formation of certain major north-south streets in the bridgehead area and the major east-west street which connected them, Eastcheap (first mentioned c.1100), during the late 9th and 10th centuries has already been proposed (Horsman, Milne & Milne 1988, 112-4 and above, p.123). In Part 6 the relationship between the street system and the waterfront as a whole is considered more broadly in the light of the street- and place-name evidence. This shows that the waterfront locations at the foot of streets leading to the river from the centre of the City were distinguished by names in -hithe, -wharf and -gate, many of them compounded with the names of particular commodities. The strong implication of this practice is that they served as localised minor markets, situated at the only places on the foreshore to which there was public access and initially co-existing with the major harbours at Queenhithe, Billingsgate and Botolph Wharf (above, p.128). The relationship of the jetty with Pudding Lane and of Tenement 7 and the inlet to Botolph Lane should be considered in this general context, and both phases of embankments and installations should also be seen in the particular context of the pattern of streets articulated by Eastcheap to the north. Here, as in the areas to the north of Queenhithe and Dowgate, the streets appear to have emerged in response to developments on the waterfront. What seems likely is that the economic vigour of the town, as illustrated by long-distance trade, spread from the waterfront area up into the City and its market-places during the 11th century; a model of development paralleled in the 12th century in Lübeck (Fehring 1985, 280). In other words, economic stimulus came by boat, not overland.

Though superficially similar to the north-south streets, New Fish Street (modern Fish Street Hill) differed from them in that it led to the bridge (and was known as Bridge Street in the medieval period); archaeological excavation on its east side in 1981 found pits of CP1 (850-1020), along the street but separated from it by a strip of unpitted strata, indicating the presence of ground-level buildings which had otherwise not survived (Horsman, Milne & Milne 1988, 113-4).

The rebuilt bridge, most probably on the same alignment as its stone successor, is first mentioned in the Code of c.1000 (though perhaps that part of the text dealing with it dates from towards the mid 11th century (above, p.125)). The building of the bridge symbolises not only London's re-established role as a distributive centre for imports or a collection-point for exports, but also its nodal position in the local and regional road network. There are currently two theories as to the date of the rebuilding of the bridge: (i) c.900 in the context both of general burh building in England, sometimes involving 'double' fortresses linked by bridges, and of the first occurrence of the name Southwark in the Burghal Hidage (Dyson 1980, 90-3); (ii) late 10th or early 11th century in the context of the general growth of trade, the appearance of the first embankments, the earliest post-Roman occupation along both Fish Street Hill and Bishopsgate (Horsman, Milne & Milne 1988, 114), and the mention of the bridge in the Code. To date, excavations in Southwark have failed to reveal significant 10th-century occupation (SLAEC 1978, 249, 189, 313; Orton 1988, 295), perhaps favouring the later date. If this is so, then perhaps the occupation along Fish Street Hill just described dates also from the late 10th or early 11th century, towards the end of the CP1 range indicated by finds in the pits.

It is quite likely that three circumstances and their effects were interwoven with each other in the late 10th and early 11th centuries: the re-establishment of the bridge on its medieval alignment, probably close to the Roman alignment; the development of the waterfront area in an advantageous position immediately downstream of the bridge, with its own inland market at Eastcheap and the harbour at Billingsgate; and the upturn in London's foreign contacts. London seems to have recovered from its contribution of one fifth of the Danegeld for the whole country in 1018. This economic resilience may have been justifiably founded on the twin decisions, which were probably parts of a single initiative, to rebuild the bridge and open Billingsgate as a controlled market.

Comparison with the results of recent work in other European ports both provides parallels and suggests further ways of looking at the London evidence. In 1000 London was part of a network of ports around the North Sea and the Baltic. A similar rise in imported pottery has been noted in 11th-century Norwich; there the City recovered from a sack in 1004 and a battle of c.1014 (Ayers 1988, 87). Ninth- and 10th-century harbour-works have been located at Hamburg (Janssen 1985, 222) and Gdansk (Zbierski 1985, 299, 306-7); the settlement at Alt Lübeck, destroyed in 1138, contained a craft quarter on one side of the river, next to the ducal stronghold, and a merchants' settlement on the other side (Fehring 1985, 269-72). In other European towns, the merchants seem to have occupied the waterfront area (eg on the Rhine at Cologne: Jankuhn 1985, 30-1; and Worms: Ellmers 1981, 91). Perhaps London was similarly divided into zones of particular character. So far the majority of large sunken-floored timber buildings have been recorded in the Queenhithe-Cheapside area, perhaps suggesting that this was the city's merchant quarter, though this impression is doubtless also partly because of the lack of evidence resulting from widespread truncation of the relevant strata. The recording of several sunken cellars on the Fish Street Hill and Pudding Lane sites, at least two of them of comparable size (Horsman, Milne & Milne 1988, 49-52), suggests that in due course further large sunken-floored buildings may be recorded in the Billingsgate and bridgehead area. There has been hardly enough excavation in either area as yet to point to any real contrast, however; what has been found could simply point to a general increase in the volume of trade in the first half of the 11th century.

The jetty and rubble embankment were over-built in the early to mid 11th century by further embankments which were constructed in identifiable individual blocks along the shore (Fig 58); these units of reclamation correspond to medieval properties as demarcated by stone foundations, and confirmed by the occasional survival of plot dimensions in the documentary record, in the 14th and later centuries.

The establishment of what are proposed here as individual properties in the second quarter of the 11th century can be closely compared with the evidence of the earliest occupation, and probably of the formation of properties, along street frontages elsewhere in the City in the 10th and 11th centuries. Nearby at Botolph Lane, and probably along Fish Street Hill, properties were established in CP1 (850-1020) (Horsman, Milne & Milne 1988, 112). On the major street of Bow Lane, laid out perhaps about 900, buildings also of CP1 have been excavated at the Well Court site, and it can be argued from the disposition of cesspits that buildings stood on the Watling Court site (Schofield, Allen & Taylor in prep). In CP2 (1000-30), buildings and perhaps property divisions can be traced at Milk Street to the north of Cheapside (ibid); and the New Fresh Wharf/ Billingsgate properties were formed at this period. They comprise the earliest evidence so far recovered for post-Roman occupation south of the Roman riverside wall, whose line was to be followed shortly after by the new Thames Street.

A feature of the sequences on the New Fresh Wharf and Billingsgate Lorry Park sites taken together is the apparent movement of the public epicentre of the harbour works (above, p.122). In the late 10th century, the jetty at the foot of *Rethereslane* and the rubble embankment (Figs 8, 57) corresponded in east-west length only to the later Tenements **1-6**, and did not stretch to the inlet excavated to the east on the Billingsgate site (Figs 12, 43). But in the succeeding periods, the rubble embankment was built over with what are proposed as private properties, whereas a large part of the appropriate strata on the Billingsgate excavation consisted of gravel spreads south of St Botolph's church. These coincide with the location of the later public wharf of St Botolph. We therefore conclude that the emphasis of public activity moved from the jetty at *Rederesgate* to the site of St Botolph's Wharf, presumably some time during the first half of the 11th century. These works were particularly impressive when the revetments of 1055 (Waterfront 3) were built on the Lorry Park site.

At Swan Lane and Seal House, the only deposits located of the post-Roman period up to the early 11th century were river silts.

THE CHANGING CHARACTER OF THE WATERFRONT NEAR THE BRIDGE AND BILLINGSGATE, 1050-1200

In the mid and late 11th century, at both Swan Lane (Figs 44-5) and New Fresh Wharf/Billingsgate Lorry Park (Fig 60), the area of dry land was increased at the expense of the lower parts of the embankments, which have been interpreted as berthing areas. Although vessels would still have docked against the southern edges of these embankments, some of which were faced with low back-braced revetments, these changes may have meant that now only smaller boats could effectively use the facilities. It is not clear whether this can be taken to indicate a reduced contribution to the level of commerce on the waterfront, or whether it reflected a shift in the manner in which cargoes were loaded or unloaded, perhaps utilising smaller vessels such as lighters.

On the evidence of the profusion of waterfront lanes, and also of developments noted at the New Fresh Wharf site, the late 11th century is likely to have seen the final demise of the Roman riverside wall and the appearance of Thames Street immediately behind (north of) its line in the central section of the waterfront (above, pp.130-1). Some of the earliest buildings to have been constructed along the northern side of the street would no doubt have been churches, and in the context of the embankments the disposition of these and of the parish boundaries offer some clues as to the general character of the wider bridgehead area (Fig 43). To the west of the Swan Lane site the churches of All Hallows the Great and the Less, like those of the other intramural parishes further upstream and the churches of St Magnus and St Botolph immediately below the bridge, were located along the line of Thames Street, close to the late Saxon foreshore (Fig 65). In almost all these cases the parishes extended only a short distance beyond the northern side of the street; their emphasis was wholly upon the waterfront, whose developing population they were clearly designed to serve, and the four churches just named actually lay to the south of the street. This pattern, however, is quite different from that of the intervening parishes of St Lawrence, St Martin and St Michael Crooked Lane, which coincided with the end of the late Saxon embankment at Swan Lane and with an area towards the bridge where, on the evidence of Seal House, the embankment was absent. These churches are located notably further to the north, closer to Cannon Street than to Thames

Street, and in the particular instances of St Lawrence and St Martin the portions of the parishes which extended southwards to the waterfront appear as incidental or token appendages. The implication of this seems to be that at least up to the 12th century the main focus of activity in these parishes was not the waterfront but Cannon (Candlewick) Street.

Ward boundaries are also of relevance here, and Cannon Street's early prominence is further shown by the fact that its eastern half formed the basis of a separate ward to which it gave its name. The ward pattern immediately to the east, where the line of Cannon Street was continued by Eastcheap, reveals a further contrast. In this area below the bridge, where the waterfront was of demonstrably early importance, the embankments reappear; and the two sides of Eastcheap were evidently regarded as part of an integral unit with Billingsgate, all being contained within a single ward named after that harbour. The varying character of the late Saxon waterfront thus appears to be reflected in the pattern of early settlement, so far as that is deducible from parish and ward boundaries.

Documentary sources of the late 11th and 12th centuries (Brooke & Keir 1975, 265-70) show that London was a bustling international port with merchants from France (especially Rouen, the source of some imported pottery of this period: Vince 1985, 47-8), Germany (Cologne and the Rhineland, source of the Badorf-type and Pafrath-type wares: Jenner & Vince 1991, 45), and Flanders (Bruges and St Omer; Andenne ware from the Meuse valley: Jenner & Vince 1991, 45). In the 12th century, the construction of several masonry buildings at New Fresh Wharf (Fig 61) seems to be an indication, however, that the waterfront on these properties was no longer used as a general landing-place to any great degree; in all but one case, the buildings occupied the full width of the tenement, denying any direct access from Thames Street, and even if goods imported at the waterfront were stored within the buildings prior to distribution, a low level of transit through the buildings is implied. The river frontages of the properties were renewed in the late 12th century, with front-braced revetments replacing the previous, probably back-braced revetments. Docking at front-braced revetments would have been severely limited by the closely-spaced braces, and there was apparently no provision of jetties or stairs to overcome this. Upstream of the bridge, this pattern was repeated at Swan Lane, where a low back-braced revetment was replaced by several front-braced examples with no additional jetties, and at Seal House, where the late 12th-century Waterfront II was based on boxes formed by planks slotting into vertical timbers.

At Billingsgate Lorry Park, by contrast, low back-braced revetments protected the base of the embankment to St Botolph's Wharf, whilst the inlet which had provided direct access from the foreshore to Botolph Lane and Thames Street was successively narrowed until it was blocked and infilled in the late 12th century (Fig 61). This seems to confirm that the public wharf of St Botolph, with its back-braced stave revetments and carefully maintained open surfaces behind, was the primary location for the docking and unloading of vessels; the closure of the inlet at the foot of Botolph Lane is likely to have been the result of an official decision, presumably making for a more effective use of the harbour. However, the role of St Botolph's Wharf as an authorised landing place for goods arriving from outside the City would not have precluded the stone buildings on the neighbouring tenements, with their capacious cellars, from all involvement in this trade. They could either have been supplied by small boat from the public quays of St Botolph or Billingsgate once custom had been paid, or, in view of their restricted access to the river, by way of Thames Street which ran past their northern frontages.

These conclusions are broadly consistent with the documentary evidence, albeit limited and of a somewhat later date, of trading practice on the London waterfront. From this it is apparent that by the mid 13th century the king, and the City authorities in his stead, were concerned to limit external trade or cargoes to the public harbours of Queenhithe, Billingsgate and Botolph Wharf (Dyson 1985, 20-1; 1989, 20). An important text in this connection is an item in the Eyre of 1244, in which the royal justices enquired into encroachments upon the Thames. To this the City replied that it knew of none

'save that the wharves were lengthened and extended towards the current of water and this was permissible by all custom because thus their lands and tenements could be protected against the sea ebbing and flowing night and day, and in the current of the Thames they placed no wharf save that they ought and might to the advantage of the king and the City and of the great ships fully loaded coming towards the City . . .' (Chew & Weinbaum 1970, 343).

In this passage a clear discrimination is made between, on the one hand, the ordinary extension of the frontage *towards* the river (permissible as a general means of protecting it from the tide) and, on the other, extensions *into* the body of the river itself (seen as the prerogative of the king and City alone in their own interests and for the benefit of fully-laden shipping). Inherent in this is a distinction between the generality of privately occupied waterfront tenements whose revetments were primarily regarded as tidal defences, and the handful of public harbours catering for external commerce. The same contrast is also reflected in the fact that, as was common elsewhere on the waterfront, most of the known 13th- and early 14th-century occupants at the New Fresh Wharf, Swan Lane and Seal House sites were fishmongers, ironmongers, dyers and tanners; people who certainly needed access to water but not because of external trade. Those who did have an interest in trade, such as mercers, merchants, and vintners, tend to be found in tenements adjoining the public harbours. The contrast between the private tenements (New Fresh Wharf/Billingsgate **2** to **6**) and Botolph Wharf (**7**) would suggest that the specialised role of the public harbours was already operative by the mid 12th century, and that they were perhaps beginning to supercede the series of commodity markets recorded in the names of several of the wharves and gates which lay at the foot of the City's streets (above, pp.125-8).

The continuing development after 1200 to the Great Fire of 1666 of these waterfront tenements, in private hands but near public installations, is the subject of another volume (Schofield & Dyson in prep). This will also deal in detail with the stone buildings on the Seal House and New Fresh Wharf sites and with St Botolph's church on the Billingsgate Lorry Park site. A discussion of 12th- and 13th-century stone buildings from recently excavated sites in London appears meanwhile in the study of the Cheapside area (Schofield, Allen & Taylor in prep).

In conclusion, therefore, the two pairs of sites above and below the bridge demonstrated different patterns of development in the period 1000-1200. Above the bridge at the Swan Lane site, there was some development in the 11th century with embankments in two phases; but east, beyond the landing-place of Ebbgate, the first identified revetment at Seal House was of the mid 12th century. Downstream of the bridge at New Fresh Wharf and Billingsgate, in contrast, a process in four parts can be observed: firstly, by 1000, an embankment and jetty probably for public use adjacent to, and perhaps an outlier of, the establishment of Billingsgate as a harbour and toll-station; secondly, by about 1050, the overbuilding of the embankment with further embankments which were divided into individual plots, the origins of medieval tenements, and the possible establishment of St Botolph's Wharf; thirdly, by about the turn of the 11th and 12th centuries, the final demolition of the Roman riverside wall, and the construction of the churches of St Magnus and St Botolph south of the new thoroughfare Thames Street; and fourthly, the erection of stone buildings on the reclaimed land during the 12th and early 13th centuries, concomitant with the crystallisation of St Botolph's Wharf as an entry-point of civic and broader significance, a place where royal customs were received in 1200-1.

APPENDIX 1 : FINDS CATALOGUE

Alan Vince, with contributions by Lucy Bown

The full catalogue continues in microfiche in the back pocket of this volume

INTRODUCTION

This appendix is in two parts: a conventionally-printed section (below), which summarises the Ceramic Phase dating framework for the study area as a whole, and a microfiche section, which contains a catalogue of pottery and small finds from each site, arranged by Group or Phase. The appendix is an abbreviated version of the appendix in *Aspects of Saxo-Norman London 2 : Finds and Environmental Evidence* (Vince 1991), with further notes to cover those phases described here, of the 12th-13th centuries, which go beyond the brief of that study. Some of the 12th/13th-century small finds have already been published, however, in the Department of Urban Archaeology's medieval finds series, *Medieval Finds from Excavations in London*, and others are in the process of publication; for knives and scabbards, see Cowgill, de Neergaard & Griffiths 1987, for shoes and pattens, Grew & de Neergaard 1988. In the present catalogue, residual Roman pottery is noted only as present, without further specification. Roman small finds are not catalogued, and details can be found in the archive held in the Museum of London; they will be published separately in due course.

DATE RANGES FOR POTTERY WARES AND THE FRAMEWORK OF CERAMIC PHASES

The ceramic dating framework rests on the identification of pottery wares, which are distinguished by four-letter (occasionally three- or five-letter) codes or acronyms (for discussion of the wares, see Vince 1985; Jenner & Vince 1991). The codes used in the present study, with their suggested date-ranges, are as follows:

*Chaff-tempered ware from the Strand area all dates from the 7th and 8th centuries, but in the area west of London is all early Saxon (450-650). It seems likely that finds of this ware from the City date to around and after 604.

Code	Pottery wares	Date range
ANDE	Andenne ware	1000-1200
BLGR	Blue-grey ware	1000-1200
BORDY	Border ware (yellow-glazed)	1550-1750
CHAF	Chaff-tempered ware	450-850*
CBW	Coarse border ware	1340-1500
CROW	Crowland Abbey type bowl	1050-1150
DEVS	Developed Stamford ware	1150-1250
EMCH	Early medieval chalky ware	1050-1150
EMCW	Early medieval coarse white ware	1000-1150
EMFL	Early medieval flinty ware	1000-1100
EMGR	Early medieval grog-tempered	1050-1150
EMIS	Early medieval iron-rich sandy	1000-1150
EMS	Early medieval sandy ware	900-1050
EMSS	Early medieval sand/shell ware	1000-1150
ESUR	Early Surrey ware	1000-1150
KING	Kingston ware	1230-1350
LANG	Langerwehe stoneware	1350-1500
LCALC	Calcareous London-type ware	1100-1200
LCOAR	Coarse London-type ware	1080-1200
LMU	Late medieval Herts glazed ware	1350-1450
LOGR	Local grey ware	1000-1150
LOND	London-type ware	1080-1350
LOND-NFR	London-type North French style	1200-1250
LOND-ROU	London-type Rouen-style	1200-1250
LSS	Late Saxon shelly ware	850-1000
MG	Mill Green ware (fine)	1270-1350
MISC	Miscellaneous wares	900-1500
NEOT	St Neots ware	900-1100
NFM	North French monochrome	1150-1200
NFRE	Miscellaneous north French wares	850-1200
NFRY	North French yellow-glazed ware	1080-1150
NMDX	North Middlesex ware	1050-1200
NORG	Normandy glazed ware	1100-1300
NORM	Normandy gritty ware	1000-1250
REDP	Red-painted ware	950-1250
ROUE	Rouen ware	1150-1300
RPOT	Roman wares (residual)	50-400
SAIN	Saintonge ware	1250-1500
SAIU	Saintonge unglazed ware	1250-1650
SATH	Sandy Thetford-type ware	1000-1150
SEMS	South-east Midlands shell-tempered	1100-1300
SHEL	Early medieval shell-tempered	1020-1150
SHER	South Herts ware	1150-1300
SIEG	Siegburg stoneware	1300-1550
SPAN	Spanish amphorae	1200-1250
SSW	Shelly sandy ware	1150-1200
STAM	Stamford ware	900-1150
THET	Ispwich Thetford-type ware	900-1100
WINC	Winchester ware	950-1100

The Ceramic Phases themselves are identified by the presence or absence of specific wares; the current (1991) date ranges used in this report are as follows:

CP	Likely date range	New wares (in quantity)
1	850-1020	LSS
2	1000-1020	EMS
3	1020-1050	EMSS
4	1050-1080	ESUR, EMCH, ANDE
5	1080-1150	LCOAR, LOND
6	1150-1180	SSW
7	1180-1240	LOND-ROU, LOND-NFR
8	1240-1270	KING
9	1270-1350	MG
10	1340-1360	CBW

SUMMARY OF THE POTTERY EVIDENCE

The late Saxon and early medieval pottery stratified in 10th- to 12th-century deposits on sites along the Thames waterfront provides the best evidence for the pottery sequence in London during that period, as well as confirmatory evidence that the sequence of development suggested by stratigraphy, dendrochronology and other means is correct. In order to ensure that there is no circularity of argument the chronological framework is summarised below. This is then followed by a discussion of the importance of this chronology for refining the dating of the ceramic sequence. Finally, the contribution, though slight, of the ceramic finds to the understanding of the function of the waterfront sites is summarised.

The site chronologies

(*cf* Fig 3)

Late 10th to early 11th centuries (CP1 to CP2)

There are no pottery assemblages from this collection of waterfront excavations which can be assigned to the first two Ceramic Phases defined for the City of London, CP1 and CP2. Activity on the waterfront is represented by the Period 2.2 jetty and bank at New Fresh Wharf which incorporated fragments of a boat dated by dendrochronology to the middle of the 10th century.

Given this dating, a late 10th-century date is almost certain for the New Fresh Wharf structure. However, there is no late Saxon pottery associated with or earlier than the waterfront, nor is there any recognisable difference between the pottery stratified in the silt sealed beneath the subsequent waterfront (Period 2.3) and that found within that waterfront (Period 2.4).

Early 11th century (CP3)

Assemblages dating to the early 11th century were found at New Fresh Wharf (Period 2.4) and Billingsgate Lorry Park (Waterfronts 2 and 3). Tree-ring dating of these waterfronts suggests strongly that the latter two were contemporary and dated *c*.1039-40, and leaves open the possibility that the New Fresh Wharf waterfront might be contemporary or slightly earlier, *c*.1020. It should be noted, however, that the New Fresh Wharf and Billingsgate sites were adjacent and that on plan it seems likely that they formed a single structure. The New Fresh Wharf excavation established that the Period 2.4 waterfront was built in sections corresponding to the later tenement divisions but there is no evidence from the pottery that these sections differed substantially in date.

Mid 11th century (CP4)

Occupation overlying waterfront 2 at Billingsgate and silting in front of the Period 2.4 waterfront (Period 3.1) both produced pottery assemblages of CP4. At Billingsgate this occupation could be dated to *c*.1039/40 to *c*.1055. The absence of LSS ware from this small assemblage is thought to be significant, especially as there are no definite occurrences in London of LSS in groups containing wares first found in CP4 such as ESUR and EMCH.

Parts of the New Fresh Wharf waterfront may have been rebuilt in the mid 11th century (Period 3.2) but the patchy nature of the archaeological evidence and the small quantity of pottery associated with it means that this site cannot be used to establish the ceramic chronology. At Billingsgate, on the other hand, Waterfronts 4 and 5 are precisely dated to *c*.1055, although the presence of some later timbers and some probably intrusive pottery in deposits associated with the construction of Waterfront 4 should be noted. The small bank which stood on the foreshore in front of Waterfront 3 contains the largest and cleanest assemblage but is only assigned to *c.*1055 on the grounds that it is most likely to be a primary feature to protect the base of the waterfront. Theoretically, it might be slightly later, contemporary with the use of the waterfront. Despite these minor reservations, it is quite clear that by *c.*1055 pottery of CP4 was in use.

Late 11th to mid 12th centuries (CP5)

Activity along the waterfront in the late 11th and mid 12th centuries is represented at Swan Lane, Seal House (Waterfront I, dated *c.*1133-70 by dendrochronology, and preceding foreshore), New Fresh Wharf (Period 3.2) and Billingsgate (Foreshore preceding Waterfront 6 – *c.*1080; Waterfronts 6 and 7 – *c.*1080-90; Waterfronts 8 and 9 – *c.*1108). Billingsgate provides the only dated sequence covering the late 11th to early 12th centuries. Seal House Waterfront I provides two assemblages dated by dendrochronology to the middle of the 12th century and this helps to fill what may be up to a fifty-year gap in the Billingsgate sequence. All of the pottery associated with these structures belongs to CP5 or CP5/6. Attempts to refine the chronology within this period have been made but it is clear that the same range of wares was present from beginning to end, whilst the relative proportions of these wares may well vary through site-specific circumstances. Shelly-Sandy ware (ssw), which is one of the type-fossils of CP6, occurs remarkably early at Billingsgate, in Waterfronts 6 and 7, whilst being absent from deposits contemporary with the use of Waterfront 3. It seems therefore that the London area pottery industry began quite early although making little impression on existing industries.

Late 12th century (CP6)

Later 12th-century activity was represented at Swan Lane, Seal House (Waterfront II, dated by dendrochronology between 1163 and 1192), New Fresh Wharf and Billingsgate (modification of Waterfront 9; Waterfront 10, *c.*1144-88; Waterfront 11, *c.*1172 or later, and subsequent alterations). Of these sites, as before, only Seal House and Billingsgate have both clear dating evidence and associated ceramic assemblages.

Early 13th century (CP7)

Early 13th-century activity along the waterfront was represented at Swan Lane, Seal House (Waterfront III, dated *c.*1203-15 by dendrochronology; the construction and occupation of Building B, dated *c.*1203 or later) and Billingsgate (rebuilding of Waterfront 11, before *c.*1187; abandonment of Waterfronts 10 and 11 and of Building I in *c.*1215).

Dating the London ceramic sequence

These waterfront sites significantly improve our knowledge of the dating of the ceramic sequence in London from the early 11th century (CP3) to the early 13th century (CP7). There are two types of evidence: firstly, there are pairs of deposits which date the transition from one Ceramic Phase to another and, secondly, there are deposits which date the duration of a Ceramic Phase. Since the phasing of the ceramic sequence in London depends on recognising the introduction of new types of pottery and the replacement of older ones, there will be a limit to the accuracy of any dating scheme, beyond which it can be refined no further. For the period in question there are only four potential fixed points: the transitions between CP3 and CP4; CP4 and CP5; CP5 and CP6; and CP6 and CP7. That these points were events separating periods when the same range of forms and wares were in use is itself potentially a simplification, especially for CP5/6. However, these waterfront excavations give the following dates:

Transition	Date
CP3/4	between *c.*1039/40 and *c.*1055
CP4/5	between *c.*1055 and *c.*1080
CP5/6	between *c.*1080 and *c.*1108 (for the introduction of ssw) or between *c.*1133 and *c.*1187 (for the collapse of the handmade coarseware industries)
CP6/7	between *c.*1172 and *c.*1187

It is clear that the transition between CP5 and CP6 is capable of being dated with much greater precision in the future, whereas the remaining dates are probably as accurate as one can expect to achieve. A word of caution is required however. Since these dates are based in most cases on a single dated deposit or a single sequence there is a need to duplicate the evidence before they become accepted as fact. Nevertheless, they provide a very useful working model.

Pottery and the function of the London waterfront

The pottery from these waterfront sites can be divided into two groups: firstly, potsherds from dumped deposits which might have been in use elsewhere in the City and, secondly, potsherds from silting, foreshores and occupation deposits which ought to have derived from activity on or close to the waterfront. It is quite likely that much of the pottery in the redeposited assemblages also came from waterfront sites but this cannot be proved.

Another difference between the two types of assemblage is that the dumps contain material deposited in a single operation, whereas the other deposits may have accumulated over a period of time. However, given that the dumps themselves probably contain material which itself accumulated over a period of time (for example in rubbish middens), this difference may not be significant.

Crucible fragments occur in small quantities throughout the sequences on all sites but form less than one percent of all but two assemblages: they form two percent of pottery in the silts pre-dating Seal House Waterfront II and 12 percent of pot-

tery associated with the final use of Building 1 at Billingsgate. Both deposits indicate that non-ferrous metalworking took place close by but the Billingsgate assemblage seems to indicate that metalworking took place in or around Building 1 itself.

Sherds of imported pottery should also have an interesting distribution since they might indicate discarding of reject cargo or vessels broken during unloading of craft. However, there is no concentration of imported sherds from any of these sites to compare with that found at Dowgate in 1959. Nevertheless, it does seem that the rare sherds of French origin (NFRE, NORM, NORG, ROUE) are more common at both New Fresh Wharf and Billingsgate in foreshore/silting deposits than they are in dumps from the same sites. Conversely, Rhenish and Low Countries wares (REDP, BLGR, ANDE), which form the majority of the Dowgate imports, are as common in dumps as they are in foreshore/silting/occupation deposits at Billingsgate. Local concentrations where they occur seem to be a product of the small size of some assemblages, since the presence of a single large sherd can make a significant difference to the overall composition of the group.

APPENDIX 2: TREE-RING ANALYSIS OF OAK TIMBERS

Jennifer Hillam

Jennifer Hillam

INTRODUCTION

Tree-ring analysis of Saxon and early medieval timbers from the City of London has been carried out in the Sheffield Dendrochronology Laboratory for over ten years. Although the majority of samples have come from Billingsgate Lorry Park, samples from Custom House, New Fresh Wharf (Area III), Seal House and Swan Lane have also been examined. Archive reports containing full details of the work have been produced for all the sites except Custom House, and these are stored at the Museum of London and the Ancient Monuments Laboratory. The following report is a summary of the archive reports but also includes a re-evaluation and synthesis of the results, particularly for the three sites excavated in the 1970s: Custom House, Seal House and New Fresh Wharf.

A general description of dendrochronology is given in Baillie (1982), whilst details of methods used at Sheffield can be found in Hillam & Morgan (1986) and Hillam (1985a). The analyses are described site by site in the present report, but a step-by-step account of how each timber was dated is too lengthy to include here. Generally, ring sequences were dated against reference chronologies such as City Med (Hillam unpublished), Southwark (Tyers pers comm) or Ref 6 (Fletcher 1977), or they were dated against their site master.

Details of the samples are given site by site in Figs 75-8, together with sketches of the cross-sections, showing the method of timber conversion. Estimates of felling dates in the absence of bark or bark edge are based on the sapwood estimate of 10-55 rings (see Hillam *et al* 1987 for further details). The ring width data from all the measured samples is stored in the Sheffield Dendrochronology Laboratory where it can be consulted. To avoid confusion with dates and measurements, in the following report context numbers are cited in italics.

The interpretation of the waterfront sequence has changed several times since the initial tree-ring analyses, often due to the tree-ring results themselves, and discrepancies in phasing and nomenclature will be noted between the original archive reports and the present text; but the tree-ring dates themselves are unaltered.

BILLINGSGATE LORRY PARK

(Figs 66-71, 75)

Work on the 421 samples from Periods IV-VII began in 1985 and was completed in 1988. The first samples examined were those taken from the major structures, the timbers of which were stored at the Museum of London where they awaited conservation (Hillam & Groves 1985). All the other samples were taken during the excavation. Full details of the analysis of samples from Periods IV and V are given in Hillam 1987a and 1988a respectively, whilst those for Periods VI and VII are in Hillam 1988b.

Period IV (Waterfronts 2-5)

Oak timbers (*Quercus* spp) were uncovered from phases 1, 2, 4 and 7; 128 were sampled for tree-ring dating.

The IV.1 timbers from the west bank of the inlet were subdivided into two groups, both from Waterfront 2:

(a) timbers related to apparently primary tie-backs;

(b) timbers from the east side of the revetment.

The IV.2 timbers from the east bank were subdivided into three groups:

(a) an initial pile in the clay bank, *7576*, contemporary with Waterfront 4;

(b) timber lacing in the clay bank, Waterfront 5;

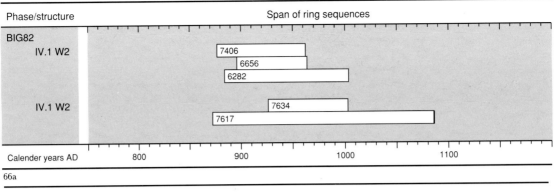

66a

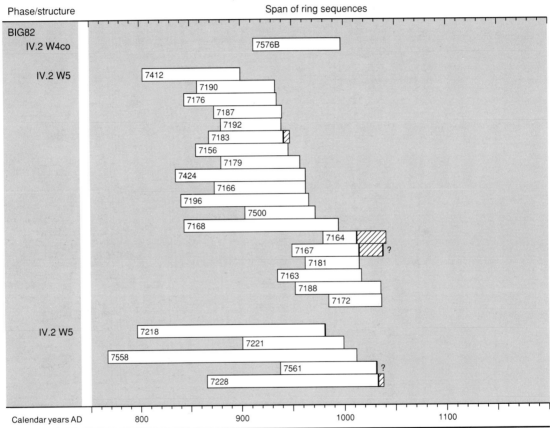

66b

(c) plank cladding on the west side of the revetment, Waterfront 5.

The IV.4 timbers were from:

(a) north-south elements in the main body of the timber and clay bank, Waterfront 2;

(b) east-west and random timbers in the main bank, Waterfront 2;

(c) stave frontage of the large stave Saxon revetment, Waterfront 3.

66. Bar diagram showing the relative positions of the dated ring sequences from Billingsgate Lorry Park Period IV: (a) IV.1; (b) IV.2; (c) IV.4 and IV.7. The following conventions are used in Figs 66-73: numbers = context numbers; hatching = sapwood; thick line before the hatching = heartwood-sapwood transition; thick line at the end of the bar = bark edge (and so actual year of felling).

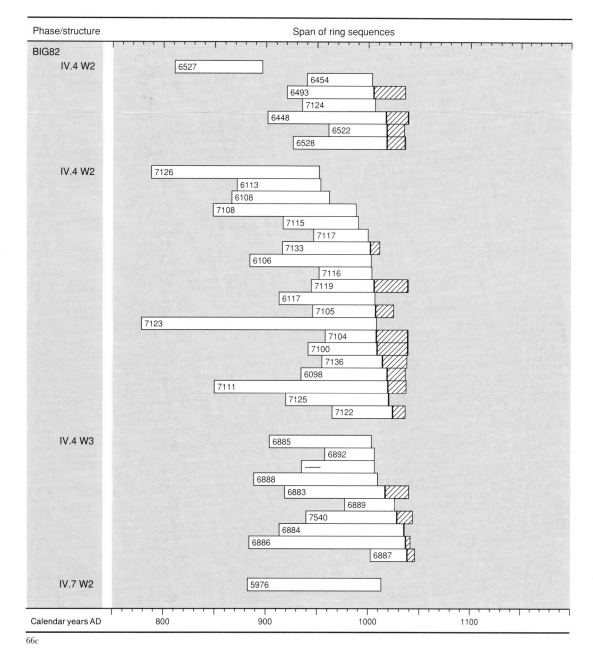

Phase/structure	Span of ring sequences

BIG82

IV.4 W2

IV.4 W2

IV.4 W3

IV.7 W2

Calendar years AD   800   900   1000   1100

66c

The latter were added to the front of the west bank, effectively sealing most of the IV.1 and IV.2 levels. Three of the timbers (*7536*, *7540*, *7542*) were sampled on site; the remainder were sampled at the Museum of London where they had been taken for conservation.

The IV.7 timber *5976* was a stake on the surface of Waterfront 2.

Period IV.1

Three of the timbers related to primary tiebacks were dated, but none of them had sapwood (Fig 66a). They were felled after 973, 975 and 1015 respectively. At the east side of the revetment, there were two dated timbers. *7634* was felled after 1014, and *6717* has an estimated felling date range of approximately 1097-1142.

Period IV.2

The only timber to be dated from the initial piles in the clay bank was *7576*. Its last measured heartwood ring dates to 998, so that it was felled some time after 1008.

Most of the dated timbers come from the timber lacing, and there are at least two phases of felling. In the early group (Fig 66b: *7412* to *7500*), the timber with sapwood has a felling date of 954-999, but if the group is regarded as a single felling phase (see Baillie 1982, 56) the date becomes 983-990. *7168* was felled after 1005, and may be of similar date to the initial piles. The other six timbers are later in date. *7167* was felled in 1039/40, as were the Waterfront 2 timbers (IV.4) on the other side of the inlet. *7164* also has sapwood, but its outer measured ring is 1042, giving a felling date in the period 1042-1070. *7163* and *7181* were felled after *c*.1027 and after 1026 respectively. There is therefore no way of knowing if they were felled in 1039/1040 or at the later date of 1042-1070. The last measured heartwood ring of the remaining timbers, *7172* and *7188*, is 1037. These timbers cannot have been felled in 1039/1040, since the *terminus post quem* for felling is 1047. They may belong to the same phase of felling as *7164*, which would give a felling date of 1047-1070 for this phase.

Two felling phases are also indicated from the five dated timbers from the plank cladding. The heartwood-sapwood transition of *7218* is *c*.982, which gives a felling date of approximately 992-1037. *7228* and *7561* were felled in the period 1045-1090, and are therefore of similar date to *7172*, *7188*, and possibly *7164* from the timber lacing. *7221* and *7558* were felled after *c*.1010 and 1027 respectively, and could belong to either felling phase.

Period IV.4

Six of the seven dated timbers from the north-south timbers in the clay bank appear to be contemporary (Fig 66c), and one was definitely felled in the winter or early spring (referred to as 'winter felled' hereafter) of 1039/1040. The seventh timber (*6527*) ends in 897, and has no sapwood. It was therefore felled some time after 907, and could have been reused.

Re-used material was probably also used for the east-west and random timbers in the main bank, since *7126*, *6113* and *6108* were felled after

963, 964 and 973 respectively. The remaining 17 dated timbers are probably contemporary. Four of them had bark edge, although the outer rings of *7105* could not be measured. *7100* and *7119* were felled in the winter of 1039/1040; *7104* was felled in 1039 or 1040 but the season of felling could not be determined.

Nine of the samples from the conserved stave frontage (Waterfront 3) were dated in 1985 (Hillam & Groves 1985). A combined felling date of 1049-1071 was indicated, although it was suggested that there could be two phases of felling if there was archaeological evidence to support it: one in 1040-1071, the other 1049-1091. Three new samples from stakes or piles were examined in 1986. *7536* and *7542* remain undated, but *7540* has a heartwood-sapwood transition of 1030 (Fig 66c). This falls roughly in the middle of the range of heartwood-sapwood dates produced for the conserved samples, and therefore supports the theory that there was just one felling phase rather than two. The date of felling is therefore 1049-1070.

Period IV.7

The only timber to be examined from this phase was *5976* (Fig 66c), a stake on the embankment surface of Waterfront 2. Although the sample was dated, it contained no sapwood, and the *terminus post quem* for felling (1024) does not help to date the later development of the bank.

Period V (Waterfronts 6-7)

Two hundred and seven timbers were sampled from Period V, which represents a further development of the inlet and includes Waterfronts 3, 6 and 7. The bulk of the samples came from the V.3 bank (Waterfront 3), where about ten percent of the unworked and most of the worked timbers were sectioned. In addition, two samples came from V.1 (Waterfront 6), five from V.2 (Waterfront 3), seven from V.4 (Waterfront 3), 19 from V.6 (Waterfront 6), and 27 from V.8 (Waterfront 7). The samples were analysed in 1987, first those from V.1, V.4, V.6 and V.8, and then the 147 samples from V.3.

Two timbers were sampled from the V.1 revetment (Waterfront 6), one of which was an upright squared post (*6788*). The function of the other (*7530*) is unknown. The V.3 timbers were aligned north/south, parallel to the inlet, changing to east/west at the south end following the main direction of the frontage. The timbers tended to become larger towards the bottom of the layers. With the exception of *7074*, which was recorded as a boat or house timber, the V.3 timbers were not recorded separately. Some were worked and others unworked, but these details were not available until towards the end of the study.

The V.4 timbers were all worked. Timber *5659* was found above three planks (*5714, 5765, 5812*); *6026* and *6027* were found a little to the east of these, whilst *5626* was one of five robbed-out stakes scattered to the north.

The V.6 timbers were worked horizontal timbers or upright stakes/piles from a revetted bank above the earlier Period V embankment. A group of the piles were set in clusters around north/south horizontal timbers and extending beyond them to the south. The clay and timber consolidation of the V.8 east bank was mostly represented by north/south horizontal timbers, 27 of which were sampled. The east bank structure was similar to that on the west side except that it contained reused timbers from the Period IV frontage.

Period V.1

The two V.1 timbers had relatively few rings. *7530*, with 36 rings, was rejected, but *6788* was dated, its 47 rings spanning the period 1024-1070 (Fig 67). Even though the sequence is relatively short, the dating is reliable since the visual matching was good, and the *t*-values produced by the computer program CROS (Baillie & Pilcher 1973) were relatively high: *eg* 6.7 with City Med, 5.2 with Southwark and 6.0 with BIG4.2, the Billingsgate master derived from the IV.2 samples. The timbers of the V.1 revetment therefore are unlikely to have been felled before 1080.

Period V.2

Two of the five samples were dated from this group. *7259* ends in 934 and was therefore felled some time after 944. The outer ring of *7233*, which was thought to be bark edge, dates to 1039, giving a felling date of 1039/40 and possibly indicating that the timber was reused from Waterfront 2.

Period V.3

After preparation of the cross-sectional surfaces, 32 of the samples were rejected. During measurement of the remainder it became apparent that, not only were the rings generally narrow, but also that some of the ring patterns were almost identical. The patterns of *6623, 6674* and *6731B*, for example, were recognisable by a very wide ring, which was later dated to 837. Other ring patterns were also found to be similar, and on the basis of the high *t*-values between them (greater than 8.0, and often greater than 10.0; see Hillam 1987b, Table 2), as well as the similarity of the samples themselves, it is suggested that as many as 14 timbers were cut from the same tree. Another possibility is that the 14 samples come from one or two trees which were growing close together, but the three named above are definitely from the same tree, and some of the other comparisons give higher *t*-values.

Comparison of the 115 measured samples with dated reference chronologies resulted in the dating of 84 ring sequences (Fig 68). The degree of correlation with the reference chronologies was very variable. Some of the samples gave the highest agreements, as expressed by *t*-values (Baillie & Pilcher 1973), with non-Billingsgate chronologies, but the majority were dated by comparison with master curves made up from Billingsgate data as well as by comparison with City Med and Southwark. As the study continued, various V.3 masters were constructed which contained an increasing number of ring sequences (BIG5.3 mark 1-6, and finally BIG5.3). However, some V.3 sequences matched better with the Period IV master (BIG4) than with any of the V.3 masters.

There is little evidence from the tree-ring results that any of the timbers were reused. The only obvious exception is *6312*, which has a felling date of 1039/40, and was probably reused from Waterfront 2. Eleven of the remaining samples probably had bark edge. Ten of these were felled either in the winter of 1054/55 (*eg 6340*) or in the late spring/summer (hereafter 'summer felled') of 1055 (*5904*). This could in fact represent a difference in felling of only a few weeks. It seems likely therefore that the bank was constructed in 1055, since the timbers would probably have been used green (Baillie 1982, 138, 167).

Two timbers were definitely felled after this date. *6635* was felled in the winter of 1061/2, and *6316* has an end date of 1057. The latter was probably felled some time after this, since the date of

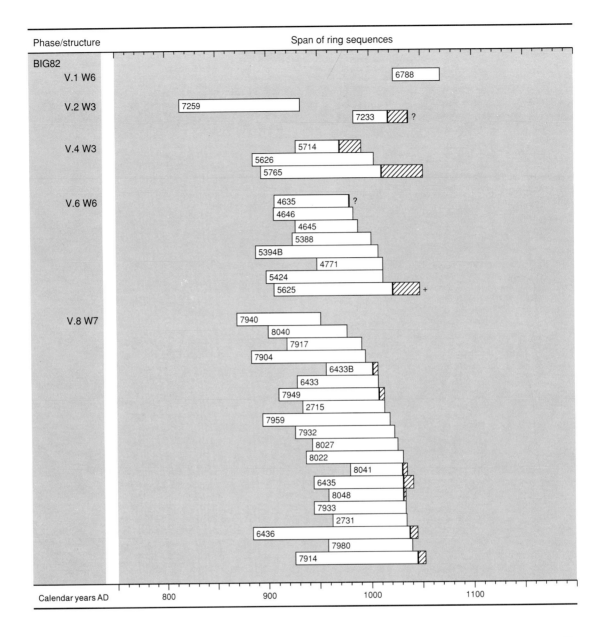

Phase/structure | Span of ring sequences

BIG82

V.1 W6 — 6788

V.2 W3 — 7259, 7233 ?

V.4 W3 — 5714, 5626, 5765

V.6 W6 — 4635 ?, 4646, 4645, 5388, 5394B, 4771, 5424, 5625 +

V.8 W7 — 7940, 8040, 7917, 7904, 6433B, 6433, 7949, 2715, 7959, 7932, 8027, 8022, 8041, 6435, 8048, 7933, 2731, 6436, 7980, 7914

Calendar years AD   800   900   1000   1100

its heartwood-sapwood transition ranges from 1040 to 1054, giving a likely felling date range of 1063-1094.

Of the 83 measured samples without sapwood, the end dates show a gradual fall-off from 1034 to 818. These probably represent timbers with sapwood removed or, in the case of the earlier date spans, timbers taken from the inner part of the trunk. For example, of the timbers which may have come from the same tree, *5914B* dates to 649-866 and *6679B* to 893-1005, thus representing two portions of a trunk. *6701*, *6709* and *6625*B have similar end dates to *6679B* (1015, 1014 and 1008

67. *Billingsgate Lorry Park: Period V, excluding V.3. For conventions see Fig 66.*

68. *Billingsgate Lorry Park: Period V.3. For conventions see Fig 66.*

respectively), suggesting that these all come from the outer part of a tree from which the sapwood has been removed.

Thirty-one samples remain undated. Although tentative dates were obtained for some, they could not be confirmed by reference either to other chronologies or to other V.3 ring sequences.

Phase/structure   Span of ring sequences

BIG82
V.3 W3

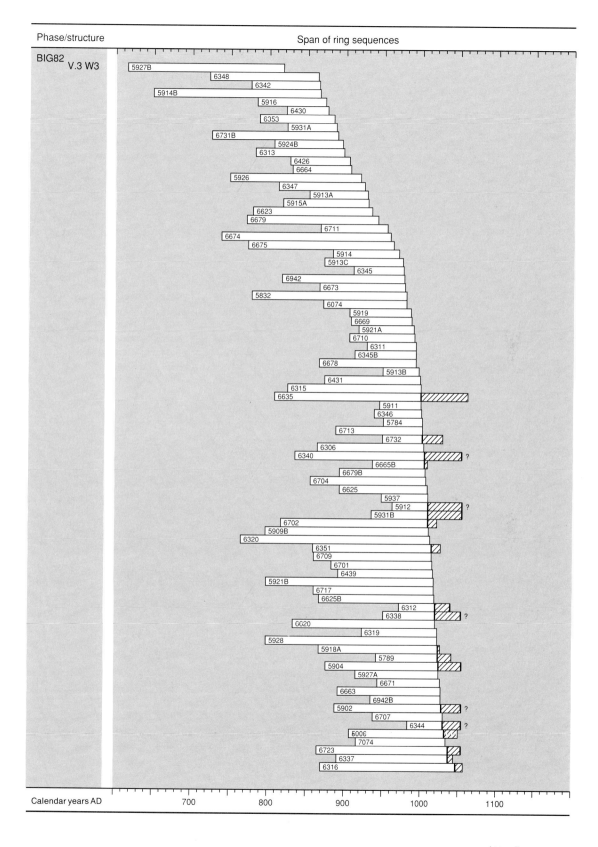

Calendar years AD   700   800   900   1000   1100

Period V.4

Of the three dated timbers from this phase, *5714* and *5765* had bark edge, although the outer one or two rings were damaged and could have been missing on sections of the sample's edge. The last measured rings of *5714* and *5765* were 993 and 1053 respectively. Their felling dates are therefore 994-6 and 1054-6, and it seems likely that *5765* is contemporary with the V.3 timbers which were felled in 1055, whilst *5714* was reused.

Period V.6

Sixteen out of the 19 samples were measured, giving sequences of 51-143 years. *5625* had complete sapwood, and the outer edge of *4635* may have been the heartwood-sapwood transition, but the remainder had heartwood rings only. Nine sequences were dated (Fig 67), most of them matching with Southwark, City Med and BIG4. The *t*-values for the matches were very variable, ranging from 3.5 to 8.5. *5394*B did not match well with Southwark or City Med but gave *t*-values of 4.4 and 6.4 with BIG4 and BIG5.3 respectively.

The end dates for the dated samples without sapwood range from 947 to 1013. *4635* has a possible heartwood-sapwood transition date of 982, and *5625* ends at 1049. However, about 10-15 sapwood rings on *5625* were too narrow to measure accurately; it was therefore felled in *c*.1059-64, making it slightly later than the V.3 and V.4 timbers but earlier than V.1. *4635* was felled after 991 and probably before 1036, indicating that late 10th-century timbers might also have been used in V.6.

Period V.8

Fourteen timbers were dated from the Waterfront 7 clay and timber dump, eight (possibly nine) of them with sapwood (Fig 67). The dates of the heartwood-sapwood transitions range from 1002 to 1046. The probable felling date range for *6433B* is 1011-1056, whilst that for *7914* is 1056-1101, indicating that there are probably at least two felling phases amongst the V.8 timbers. The first felling phase presumably represents reused timbers since timbers from Period IV were found in this phase.

Periods VI and VII (Waterfronts 8-11)

In Period VI the surface of the west bank was consolidated with timbers (VI.1; construction of Waterfront 8). Twenty-four timbers were sampled: most of them came from the timber dump but *5855B* was a stray timber, and *5416* was a grooved base plate from the stave revetment in front of the west bank. Three timbers were sampled from the VI.2 west inlet lining (construction of Waterfront 8), thought to be contemporary with VI.1, whilst fourteen samples were taken from the VI.4 east bank lining (construction of Waterfront 9), which is stratigraphically later than Waterfront 8. The VI.2 timbers were piles, but those from VI.4 were either piles (*eg 2713*) or cladding (*eg 2666A*). The VI.4 timbers were also differentiated into those from an interim line of piles (*eg 2713*) and those from a new east inlet lining (*eg 6866*).

The first phase of Period VII is represented by the small stave Saxon revetment (Waterfront 10) which was built at the mouth of the inlet. Some samples from this revetment had already been analysed (Hillam & Groves 1985), but another two were examined for this study. *5082* was a pile from the west bank, whilst *5448* was thought to be a reused stave from the revetment. One of the conserved timbers, the back-brace *6585*, was not original, and is now allocated to Period VII.6.

Period VII.4 is represented by the construction of a drain in the inlet, from which one stray reused sample (*6690*) was taken. Four samples were taken from the new construction of Waterfront 11 (VII.4), which is an extension to the east bank revetment. This post-dates the VII.1 revetment, although both structures were in use simultaneously. *6042* was a plank fragment and *6378* was a pile from the north/south revetment, but the function of *6559* and *6594* is unknown. One timber (*6245*) was sampled from VII.6, which represents the addition of tiebacks to Waterfront 8/10, and three (*6327, 6552, 6659*) from VII.7.

In VII.8, the VII.1 structure was modified, whilst the VII.5 structure was reconstructed in VII.9. Period VII.13 seals and post-dates the VII.9 activity. Four samples were taken from the VII.8 modifications, although one of them (*6325*) was a stray timber. Three planks (*4524, 6380, 6482*) were sampled from VII.9, and two timbers (*5985, 6064*) from VII.13. *5985* was a replacement for a VII.8 tieback, whilst *6064* was a pile from either a drain or a fence.

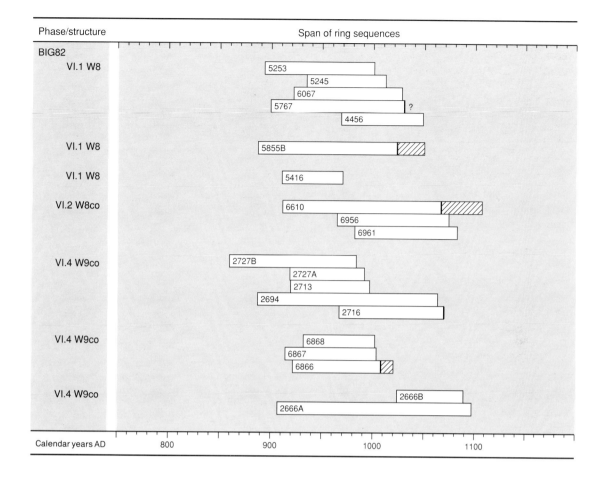

Phase/structure	Span of ring sequences

BIG82

VI.1 W8 — 5253, 5245, 6067, 5767, ?, 4456

VI.1 W8 — 5855B

VI.1 W8 — 5416

VI.2 W8co — 6610, 6956, 6961

VI.4 W9co — 2727B, 2727A, 2713, 2694, 2716

VI.4 W9co — 6868, 6867, 6866

VI.4 W9co — 2666B, 2666A

Calendar years AD: 800, 900, 1000, 1100

69. *Billingsgate Lorry Park: Period VI. For conventions see Fig 66.*

Period VI.1

Eight sequences were dated (Fig 69). *5262* from the timber dump was dated by comparison with the BIG5.3 chronology, which is made up of sequences from Period V.3. The match between BIG5.3 and *5262* gives a *t*-value of 10.2 when the latter sequence covers the period 611-725. This surprisingly early date is explained by examining the match between *5262* and the V.3 sequence *5927*B. The ring patterns are almost identical ($t = 10.1$), and may indicate that the two timbers came from the same tree or group of trees. Certainly *5262* must be residual from Waterfront 3 (V.3).

Five other timbers from the dump were dated. They have end dates between 1002 and 1050 but,

with the exception of *5767* which may have two sapwood rings, none of the timbers had sapwood. If the outer two rings of *5767* are sapwood, the timber has a probable felling date range of 1039-1084. The *terminus post quem* of the most recent dated timber in the dump, *4456*, is 1060, but the actual felling date could be much later.

The only dated timber which definitely had sapwood was the stray timber *5855B*. Its outer ring dates to 1056 and its heartwood-sapwood transition to 1024, which gives a probable felling range of 1056-1078. The grooved base plate *5416* has a *terminus post quem* for felling of 971, and is probably reused.

Period VI.2

The three VI.2 timbers had 102-197 rings, and all the sequences were dated. Since the outer ring of *6610*, which dates to 1108, appeared to be bark edge, the date of felling is either 1108 or one or two years later.

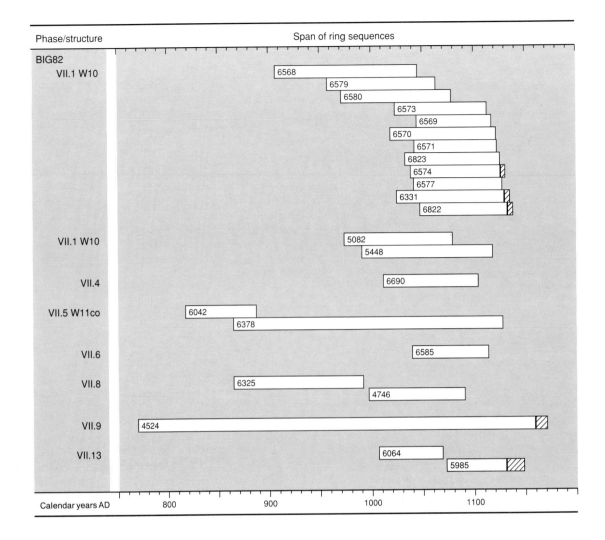

Phase/structure	Span of ring sequences

BIG82

VII.1 W10 — 6568, 6579, 6580, 6573, 6569, 6570, 6571, 6823, 6574, 6577, 6331, 6822

VII.1 W10 — 5082, 5448

VII.4 — 6690

VII.5 W11co — 6042, 6378

VII.6 — 6585

VII.8 — 6325, 4746

VII.9 — 4524

VII.13 — 6064, 5985

Calendar years AD — 800, 900, 1000, 1100

70. Billingsgate Lorry Park: Period VII. For conventions see Fig 66.

Period VI.4

Ten sequences were dated: five from the interim line of piles, and five from the eastern line of piles, which was parallel to the Period VI.2 western line. Both groups seem to be made up of timbers with two phases of felling. The earlier group (*2727A/B, 2713, 6868, 6867, 6866*) was probably felled within the period 1021-1063, and is therefore residual from Period V. The later group (*2694, 2716, 2666A/B*) comprises primary timbers with end dates of 1065, 1070, 1090 and 1098 respectively. This gives a *terminus post quem* for felling of 1108. However, the heartwood- sapwood transition of *2716* dates to 1071, which indicates that the timber was probably felled in the period 1080-1125. The combined felling date for Period VI.4 is therefore 1108-1125, which is consistent with the date of 1108 or shortly afterwards for VI.2.

Period VII.1

Tree-ring analysis of the conserved samples from the small stave revetment indicated a felling date range of 1144-1183 (Hillam & Groves 1985). The two new samples (*5082, 5448*) were both dated but, as neither had sapwood, their dating does not help to refine this range (Fig 70). The reused stave *5448* had a *terminus post quem* for felling of 1129.

Period VII.4

The single sample from this phase, *6690*, was from a reused grooved timber. It had 94 rings, which were dated to 1012-1105, giving a *terminus post quem* for felling of 1115.

Period VII.5

6042 dates to 818-888, and was clearly reused, whilst *6378* ends in 1129 and was therefore felled after 1139. Since the VII.5 extension post-dates the VII.1 revetment, *6378* is likely to have been felled after 1144.

Periods VII.6 and VII.7

The VII.6 timber which was used as a replacement back-brace in the VII.1 revetment (*6585*) has a *terminus post quem* for felling of 1125. The tree-ring results therefore do not distinguish between the primary and secondary timbers of VII.1 (Waterfront 10). None of the three VII.7 samples were dated.

Period VII.8

The ring sequences of *4746* and *6325* date to 997-1091 and 865-992 respectively, indicating that the timbers were probably reused.

Period VII.9

The dated sample from this phase (*4524*) had 403 rings, of which the last 11 were sapwood. Whilst samples with over four hundred rings have been found amongst the bog oaks of Northern Ireland (Baillie 1982), it is unusual to find such samples amongst archaeological timbers, and it is the first time a sample with more than four hundred rings has been examined at Sheffield. *4524* was dated to 770-1172, and its likely felling date range is 1172-1216.

Period VII.13

Both samples from this phase were dated: *5985* to 1073-1149 (heartwood-sapwood transition – 1133), and *6064* to 1007-1070. The latter may have been reused since its *terminus post quem* for fel-

ling is 1080. The likely felling range for the tieback *5985* is 1149-1187, but since phase VII.13 post-dates VII.9, the date must be later than 1172.

The Billingsgate timbers

Since not all the excavated timbers were sampled for dendrochronology and the excavated assemblage itself is only a small part of what must have been used at 10th- to 12th-century Billingsgate, this section is limited to a few general remarks. Many of the timbers from the major revetments, for example, were not sampled but kept instead for conservation and display, and only ten percent of the 'unworked' timbers from the Period V.3 bank were sampled. However the V.3 group is the largest assemblage from Billingsgate that was sampled for dendrochronology, and it is worthwhile examining this group in more detail.

The timbers from the V.3 clay and timber bank of Waterfront 3 were very variable in size, shape, number of rings, and ring pattern. Contrary to information recorded at the time of excavation, most of the timbers appear to have been worked to some degree, and were often sections cut from larger tree trunks. If the section was taken from towards the outside of the trunk, then the sapwood was often left on (*eg 5904, 5912*). Other timbers were wedge-shaped segments covering the complete radius of a smaller trunk (*eg 6312*), indicating that trees of various diameters were used. *5909A* and *6726* came from trees with diameters of less than 180mm, whilst *5914B* and *6709* were cut from a tree, probably the same tree (see below), with a diameter of more than 500mm.

Age of tree is difficult to determine with any accuracy. *6635* had well over 254 rings because many inner rings were too narrow to measure. Even then the centre of the trunk was not present so that the tree must have been over three hundred years old when felled. By contrast, the tree producing *6719* was under a hundred years old. Between these extremes there are many samples, representing trees of many different ages. This variety is reflected by the number of rings per sample (Fig 71), although the bulk of the samples had between 60 and 100 rings. The number of rings does not seem to affect whether a sample is dated or not.

The average ring widths of the measured samples tend to be narrow (Fig 75). Three samples (*6635, 6704, 6726*) have average widths under 0.5mm. This is extremely narrow, and in the past it has not been possible to measure such rings with

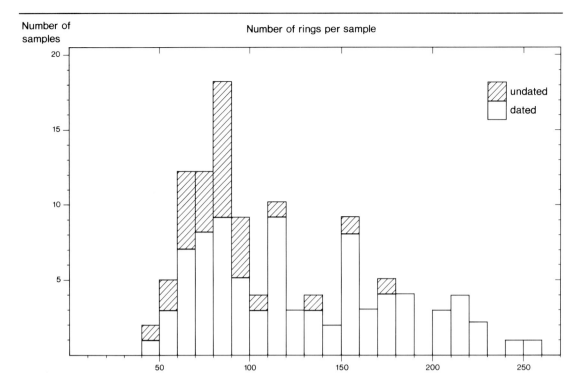

71. *Billingsgate Lorry Park Period V.3: distribution of ring sequence length in relation to the number of dated and undated samples. The 32 rejected samples have not been included because it was usually impossible to determine the number of rings.*

any accuracy. Several other V.3 samples were rejected for just this reason (see above). Two of the samples were successfully dated, but the third (*6726*) remains undated. Of the remaining samples, 87 have average widths in the range 0.5-1.49mm, and 24 are greater than 1.5mm. This is much lower than, for example, timbers from the Waterfront site at Dundas Wharf, Bristol (Nicholson & Hillam 1987).

It is difficult to draw any conclusions about the timbers from the remaining phases of Period V because there are relatively few compared with V.3. All have been worked in some way, although the degree of working is variable (Fig 75). As in V.3, the shape and size of the cross-section, and the age of the tree from which they were taken, are very variable. Sapwood was removed more often from the V.6 timbers than from those in V.4: five out of eight V.4 timbers had sapwood, compared with two or three out of 19 in V.6.

The timbers from Periods IV, VI and VII were also very variable. Some of the Period VI samples were knotty and of poor quality, but there was good-quality timber available, particularly in Period VII. The Period VI timbers tend to have fewer rings than those from Period VII. Most of the parent trees were probably felled between one hundred and two hundred years of age, but a few

(*eg 5049, 5413, 5855A*) were younger than this, and others (*2666A, 2964, 6610*) were older. The average ring widths are variable but the samples tend to be wider-ringed than those from Period V. This suggests that faster-grown but younger trees were being selected in Period VI.

The Period VII timbers also came from parent trees of various ages. *6245* and *6482* were probably felled when less than a hundred years old, but at least four timbers (*4524, 6378, 6380, 6544*) came from trees older than two hundred years. *4524* must have been well over four hundred years old because the sample had incomplete sapwood and no pith. The quality of its timber is comparable with that used for panelling or furniture.

The growth rates of the Period VII trees tended to be slower than those from Period VI, but faster than those from Period V. The fact that none of the Period VII samples were rejected because of knots or very narrow rings also points to the timber being of good quality. All the samples tended to have straight grain with a regular growth rate. Thus, although the size of the sample is small, it seems that the Period VII timber is generally superior to other Billingsgate timber so far examined, and particularly to the Period VI timbers.

The chronology of the Billingsgate waterfront, Periods IV-VII

Most of the activity in Period IV occured in the mid 11th century, but at least some of the timbers were felled in the late 10th century (Fig 74). The only timber with sapwood from this earlier period is *7183*, which was reused in the timber lacing on the east bank of the inlet (Waterfront 5; IV.2). It was felled between 954 and 999, but if the other reused timbers in the lacing are grouped together, the possible felling range becomes 983-990. Reused timbers, probably of the same date, were also found in Waterfront 2, and possibly Waterfront 3, on the west bank.

Most of the remaining timbers from Waterfront 2 were felled in the winter or early spring of 1039/1040, and presumably were used very soon afterwards. In 1049-1071, a stave front (Waterfront 3; IV.4) was added, and on the east of the revetment a timber pile (*7617*) was added in c.1097-1142. This last timber probably relates to a later period of activity. Development along the opposite (east) bank of the inlet probably took place at the same time. *7167* from the timber lacing of Waterfront 5 seems to have been felled in 1039/1040, whilst other timbers were felled in 1047-1070.

In Period V, the fact that the timber for the V.1 revetment was felled considerably later than the timber for V.2, V.3 and V.4 has led to a reinterpretation of the site's stratigraphy. The V.1 timbers are now asigned to Waterfront 6, whilst V.2-V.4 are from Waterfront 3. Many of the V.3 timbers were felled in 1055, which indicates that the stave frontage of IV.4, which was in front of the V.3 bank, was also added in 1055. At roughly the same time, timbers were added to the structure east of the inlet (IV.2). More timbers were added at a later date on both sides of the inlet: in 1059-64 on the west side (Waterfront 6: V.6), and some time in the second half of the 11th century on the east (Waterfront 8; V.8). Finally, a new revetment was constructed on the west bank some time after 1080. This could be contemporary with the activity on the V.8 bank.

The felling date for the V.1 revetment can be refined to 1080-1108/10, since Period VI activity started in 1108 or just after, when timbers were felled for the lining of the western bank (VI.2). Period VI.1 is thought to be contemporary with VI.2, which suggests that the surface of the bank was also consolidated in 1108 or one or two years later. On the east side of the inlet, timbers for the lining of the bank (VI.4) were felled in 1108-1125, so that both sides of the inlet could have been lined at the same time. The eastern lining also included piles from earlier phases.

The staves for the new VII.1 revetment were felled in 1144-1183. The VII.5 extension to this eastern revetment was constructed some time after this (*ie* later than 1144), but the revetment and extension continued in use together. In VII.8, more modifications were made to the VII.1 revetment, but the tree-ring evidence is vague as to their date. Again it must have been later than 1144.

Plank *4524*, which was used in the Period VII.9 reconstruction of the VII.5 extension, was probably felled between 1172 and 1216. However, the VII.13 tieback *5985* has an estimated felling date range of 1149-1187. Since VII.13 seals VII.9, Period VII.13 must date to after 1172, but the timber for VII.9 must probably have been felled before 1187. This gives the same likely felling date range for VII.9 and VII.13 but, within this period of 1172-1187, VII.13 must be later than VII.9.

As in the earlier periods, several reused timbers were identified from Periods VI and VII. Some were identified by their unexpectedly early dates, such as *5262* from VI.1, which is dated to 611-725, or *6042* from VII.5, dating to 818-88. Others, such as some of the piles from VI.4, were not exceptionally early but were still too early with respect to the stratigraphy; some of these were identified during excavation, such as stave *5448* from VII.1.

The next activity precisely dated by dendrochronology is the construction of the revetment from VIII.2. The timbers of this were felled in 1215/6, although a random stake from a possible revetment in VIII.1 was felled between 1168 and 1205. The details of these results are beyond the scope of this report and will be described elsewhere.

CUSTOM HOUSE

Tree-ring samples from the medieval waterfront at Custom House were examined in the early

1970s by John Fletcher (1974). The timbers, mostly posts, were from trenches IV, XII and XIV. All but one of the timbers were fast-grown and unsuitable for dendrochronology. A vertical post from trench XII, however, contained 159 rings, and was later dated to 977-1135 (Morgan & Schofield 1978). The post did not have sapwood, and was therefore felled some time after 1145.

In 1978 an additional four samples from trenches IV and VI were examined at Sheffield (Hillam unpublished). They all had less than 75 rings and were not dated. All these samples plus those measured by Fletcher have been compared with the numerous reference chronologies which have become available since the original studies. No further dating has been obtained.

SEAL HOUSE

(Figs 72, 76)

Tree-ring samples from the three medieval revetments at Seal House were examined at Sheffield in 1977. Most of the samples were analysed by Ruth Morgan (1977), although a few were examined by the author (Morgan 1978; Morgan & Schofield 1978). Dating was achieved by comparing the ring sequences with a dated chronology from Germany (Hollstein 1965). As there are now many chronologies from the London area which are more suitable for dating sequences from London than the German curve, all the Seal House data has been re-examined for this paper. As a result, additional samples have

been dated, whilst others which were previously thought to be accurately datable have now been omitted. Felling dates have also been recalculated in accordance with the new sapwood estimate of 10-55 rings (Hillam *et al* 1987). The results from Waterfronts I and II are described below. A detailed description of the timbers can be found in Morgan (1978).

Waterfront I

Eleven samples were examined from this revetment. The sill beam *596* had 77 rings; three planks (*609, 626, 640*) had 157, 141+ and 77 rings respectively, and the stake *582* had 131 rings. Six braces were also sampled, although the function of *615* as a brace was queried and *637* was thought possibly to be secondary in origin. The braces had 41 to 225 rings.

Six ring sequences were dated (Fig 72). The plank *640B* and the sill beam *596* end in 1039 and 1042 respectively and, since they did not have sapwood, were felled after 1049 and 1052. The brace *611* was felled after 1096, whilst *637*, the brace with possible secondary origins, was felled after 1132. The only dated timber with sapwood was the stake *582*, which has a heartwood-sapwood transition dating to 1116. This gives a probable felling date range of 1133-1170. It is not possible to deduce from the tree-ring evidence whether *637* was primary or secondary.

Timber *615*, which was thought to be a brace

72. Seal House. For conventions see Fig 66.

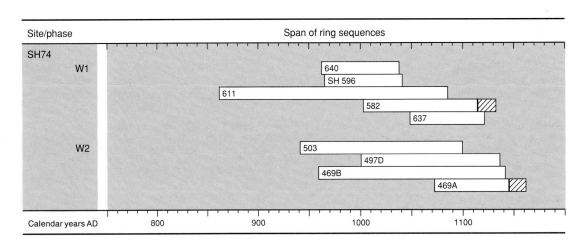

from the revetment, has a ring sequence spanning the period 1108-1181. Since it does not have sapwood, it is unlikely to have been felled before 1191. Its ring sequence matches extremely well with the timbers *387*D (*t* = 7.4) and *387*E (*t* = 7.7) from Waterfront III. This, plus the later than expected date, suggests that the timber belongs to Waterfront III rather than Waterfront I.

Waterfront II

Eight timbers were sampled from this structure. *469* was a post with 91 rings; *469B*, *497*C, *497*D and *503* were planks with 114-160 rings, and *528* with 95 rings was probably a reused post. Two braces were also sampled but these had less than 30 rings and were rejected.

Four ring sequences were dated (Fig 72). The post *469* had 16 sapwood rings with its sapwood transition dating to 1148. This gives a probable felling date range of 1163-1192. The outer rings of the planks *469B*, *497*D and *503* are 1143, 1137 and 1101 respectively. These first two dates are similar to the sapwood transition of *469*, suggesting that the timbers are contemporary and were all felled in the period 1163-1192.

The felling date ranges, and hence the construction date ranges, are broader than those originally given by Morgan (Morgan & Schofield 1978). The date of *c*.1140 for Waterfront I now becomes 1133-1170, whilst the *c*.1170 date for Waterfront II becomes 1163- 1192. This is because of a more scientific approach to the estimation of the number of oak sapwood rings (Hillam *et al* 1987).

NEW FRESH WHARF

(Figs 73, 77-8)

Excavations in 1975 (Area III, sitecode SM75) and 1978 (Areas I, IV and V watching brief, sitecode FRE78) produced tree-ring samples from the Saxon and later medieval structures (Hillam & Morgan 1981). Work on these was carried out by the author except for the reused boat timbers, which were measured and dated by Ian Tyers, and the Area III (also informally called the St Magnus trench) samples which were measured by Ruth Morgan. Some dating was achieved in the late 1970s but, as with the Seal House samples, all the tree-ring data has been reworked for this report. There is no discussion of the timbers themselves, since the sample number from each phase is too small.

Period 2.2

Of the primary timbers, only two were sampled for dendrochronology since the remainder were small and had insufficient rings for reliable dating. Both (SM273, FRE4001A) were from the construction of the first rubble bank, and neither have been dated. FRE4001A had 55 rings, of which 20 were sapwood. The ring sequence could not be dated against other London reference chronologies although it did appear to match some of the timbers from the second Saxon embankment. As a result, a tentative date of 1007 has been given for the outer ring (Hillam 1985b). However, the recent reworking of the data does not confirm this result, and the timber must remain undated.

Eight reused boat timbers from the foreshore in front of the jetty were also examined from this phase. These provided a chronology of 654-915 with a suggested construction date for the boat of 915-955 (Tyers 1990). They were presumably incorporated into the structure some time after this.

Period 2.4

In this phase the site was divided into strips which became the medieval tenements (referred to as Tenements **1-8**). Nine timbers were sampled for dendrochronology and five were dated (Fig 73). SM7, SM183 and FRE3008 were from the fence/boundary between the clay embankments of Tenement **2** and Tenement **3**. SM7 had a felling date range of 959-1004, SM183 was felled after 942, and FRE3008 after 1014, which suggests that there were at least two phases of felling. The tentative dates given for two other timbers from this fence/boundary (Hillam 1985b) were not confirmed, and therefore FRE3004 and FRE3006 remain undated.

FRE575A, from the construction of the clay bank on Tenement **5**, was felled some time after 942. The remaining dated timber, FRE3005, which was from the construction of the clay bank on Tenement **3**, was felled after 978.

Site/phase	Span of ring sequences

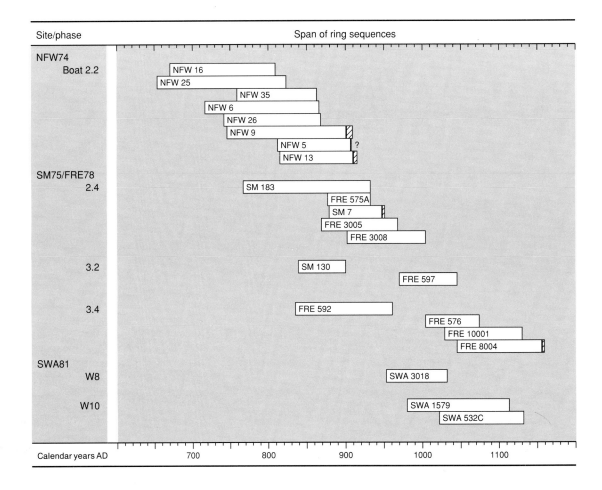

73. *New Fresh Wharf and Swan Lane. For conventions see Fig 66; FRE = New Fresh Wharf 1978; SM = St Magnus (New Fresh Wharf Area III); SWA = Swan Lane.*

74. *The chronology of the Saxon and early medieval waterfront in the City of London as represented by the felling dates for the main features. The sapwood estimate used is 10-55 rings (95 percent confidence limits).*

Period 3.2

Of the three timbers sampled from this phase, two were dated. They had very different end dates. SM130, which was from a dump behind the revetment on Tenement **3**, was felled after 910, and FRE597, part of the internal revetment in the dump on Tenement **3**, was felled after 1055.

Period 3.4

The four timbers from this phase are all dated. The corner post of the revetment on Tenement **4** (FRE8004) was felled in the period 1166-1211. The base plate of a wall on Tenement **6** (FRE10001) may be similar in date. This had an outer measured ring dating to 1130, but at least twenty to thirty outer rings were unmeasurable. FRE576 was a possible brace fragment from the 3.2 revetment, which was found in a dump. This

was felled after 1084. FRE592 was felled after 971, and was part of a platform behind the presumed line of the revetment frontage of Tenement **3**.

The chronology of the waterfront at New Fresh Wharf

The relatively small number of samples and the lack of sapwood make it difficult to provide a precise dating framework using dendrochronology.

In Period 2.4 a felling date range of 959-1004

Site/phase/structure	Waterfront construction dates

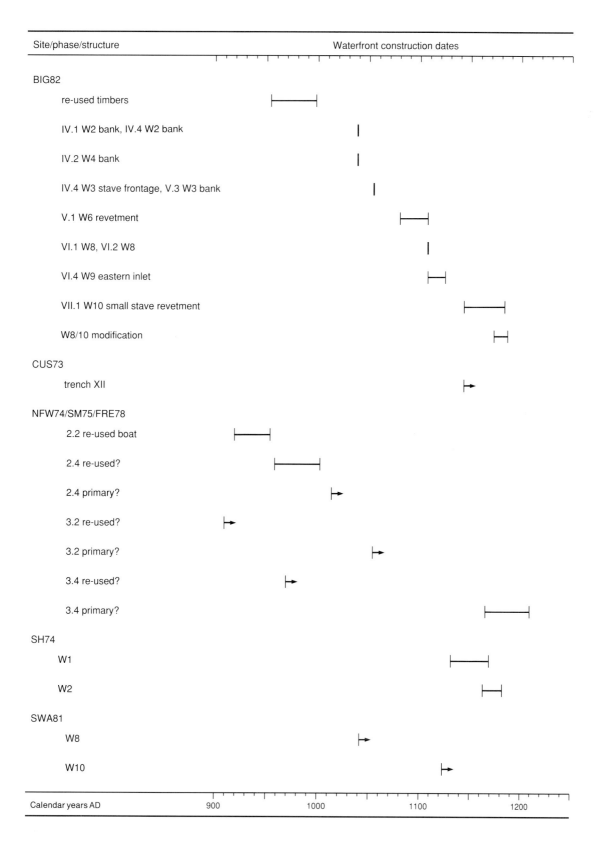

BIG82

    re-used timbers

    IV.1 W2 bank, IV.4 W2 bank

    IV.2 W4 bank

    IV.4 W3 stave frontage, V.3 W3 bank

    V.1 W6 revetment

    VI.1 W8, VI.2 W8

    VI.4 W9 eastern inlet

    VII.1 W10 small stave revetment

    W8/10 modification

CUS73

    trench XII

NFW74/SM75/FRE78

    2.2 re-used boat

    2.4 re-used?

    2.4 primary?

    3.2 re-used?

    3.2 primary?

    3.4 re-used?

    3.4 primary?

SH74

    W1

    W2

SWA81

    W8

    W10

Calendar years AD   900   1000   1100   1200

has been obtained for the fence/boundary timbers between Tenement **2** and Tenement **3**, but at least one timber was felled after this date. In both 3.2 and 3.4 there appear to be two phases of timber. Each have a timber with a *terminus post quem* in the 10th century. As at Billingsgate, it may be that the 11th-century builders were reusing 10th-century timbers. The other 3.2 timber was felled after 1045, although the date for the 3.2 revetment may possibly be refined using FRE576, which was reused in a 3.4 dump. This would give a date after 1084 for the 3.2 revetment. The 3.4 revetment on Tenement **4** is dated by FRE8004, which gives a date of felling in the period 1166-1211.

SWAN LANE

(Fig 73)

Over a hundred tree-ring samples were examined from Swan Lane, of which about eighty were medieval in date (Groves & Hillam 1986). Dendrochronologically this project was not very productive, largely because very few of the samples had sapwood. Only three of the dated timbers are relevant to this project. *3018* was part of the plank revetment Waterfront 8, and was felled after 1042 (Fig 73). *1579* was a post from the front-braced revetment Waterfront 10 on Tenement **3**, and had a *terminus post quem* of 1123. *532C* was possibly also from Waterfront 10. It was a timber in the dumping behind Waterfront 10, and felled after 1142.

CONCLUSION

Felling dates for timbers from the main features at the sites discussed above show that there was building activity in the second half of the 10th century at Billingsgate and New Fresh Wharf (Fig 74). At Billingsgate, the structures themselves were not found but timbers such as *7183*, which was felled in 954-999, were reused in 11th-century structures. Saxon structural timbers were excavated *in situ* at New Fresh Wharf in 1975 and 1978. Timber FRE575A was felled after 942, whilst SM7 was felled in the period 958-1004.

The history of the development of the waterfront structures in the 11th century relies mainly on results from Billlingsgate because, although some of the timbers from New Fresh Wharf may

date to this period, the felling dates are *termini post quem* and therefore not precise. At Billingsgate, timbers were felled in the winter of 1039/40 for use in the Period IV.1 and IV.2 banks on the west and east side of the inlet (Waterfronts 2 and 4). In 1055, timbers were felled for the IV.4 stave frontage and V.3 bank of Waterfront 3. Dates for the later part of the 11th century are not so precise, but a timber for the V.1 revetment (Waterfront 6), which replaced the IV.4 frontage, was felled between 1080 and 1108. In 1108, or just after, the VI.1 bank was consolidated and the VI.2 lining added to the western inlet (Waterfront 8). The eastern inlet lining used timbers felled in 1108-1125 (Waterfront 9). The final phases at Billingsgate which are relevant to this study are the construction and modification of the VII.1 stave revetment (Waterfront 10), the timbers of which were felled in 1144-1183, and modifications to the Waterfront 8/10 line of revetment, which date to 1172-1187. There may also have been waterfront construction at other sites in the latter part of the 12th century (Fig 74). The Custom House timber has a felling date after 1124; Seal House Waterfronts 1 and 2 have felling date ranges of 1133-1170 and 1163-1192 respectively; and a Period 3.4 timber at New Fresh Wharf was felled during 1166-1211.

ACKNOWLEDGEMENTS

The Sheffield Dendrochronology Laboratory is funded by English Heritage. The writer is also grateful to Ruth Morgan for her initial work on some of the New Fresh Wharf and Seal House timbers. Cathy Groves dated the timbers from Swan Lane and from the two stave revetments at Billingsgate; Ian Tyers dated the reused boat timbers from New Fresh Wharf and provided unpublished data from many other sites in London; both provided helpful comments during the production of this report. Thanks are due also to Ken Steedman for providing information about the rephasing.

75. Billingsgate Lorry Park: details of tree-ring analysis. Sketches are not to scale; sapwood is indicated by closer lines. [ ] = context number; ⟨ ⟩ = accession number; ARW = average ring width; BE = bark edge; HS = heartwood-sapwood transition; date in parentheses = date of heartwood-sapwood transition; all dimensions in mm.

Phase IV.1, Waterfront 2

[ ]	< >	Rings	Sap'd	ARW	Dimensions	Comments	Sketched cross-section	Date range
6282	4927	121	—	1.08	145 x 50	—		885-1005
6656	4404	69	—	1.37	85 x 65	—		897-965
7406	4259	87	—	2.70	360 x 120	—		877-963
7617	4889	200	yes	0.96	215 x 90	more outer rings		873-1072(1087)
7634	4896	78	—	1.63	250 x 225	—		927-1004

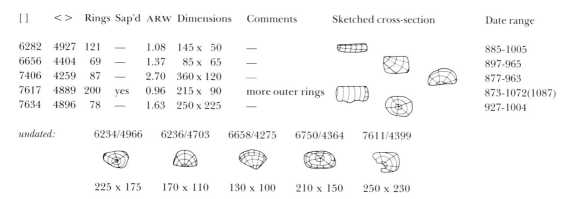

undated:

6234/4966	6236/4703	6658/4275	6750/4364	7611/4399
225 x 175	170 x 110	130 x 100	210 x 150	250 x 230

Phase IV.2, Waterfront 4 construction

[ ]	< >	Rings	Sap'd	ARW	Dimensions	Comments	Sketched cross-section	Date range
7576в	4876	76	—	1.49	205 x 195	—		923-998

undated:

7576/4906

180 x 165

Phase IV.2, Waterfront 5

[ ]	< >	Rings	Sap'd	ARW	Dimensions	Comments	Sketched cross-section	Date range
7156	4421	92	—	1.07	110 x 85	—		856-947
7163	4436	54	yes	1.43	135 x 35	more outer rings		936-989(1018)
7164	4382	63	28	1.65	105 x 55	—		980-1042(1015)
7166	4397	91	—	0.77	125 x 95	more inner rings		874-964
7167	4432	90	23	2.14	215 x 165	?felled 1039		950-1039(1017)
7168	4902	152	—	1.10	385 x 285	—		844-995
7172	4255	53	—	1.75	100 x 40	—		985-1037
7176	4408	92	—	1.25	130 x 90	—		845-936
7179	4453	79	—	1.24	110 x 65	—		881-959
7181	4401	54	—	1.28	75 x 50	—		963-1016
7183	4424	81	6	0.77	150 x 105	—		869-949(944)
7187	4444	68	—	1.37	195 x 75	—		874-941
7188	4405	85	—	0.81	125 x 125	—		953-1037
7190	4282	78	—	0.75	125 x 65	—		858-935
7192	4437	61	—	1.29	120 x 75	—		881-941
7196	4258	127	—	1.12	165 x 115	more inner rings		841-967
7218	4973	136	yes	—	215 x 205	more inner & outer rings		797-932(982)
7221	4936	80	—	0.71	100 x 85	more inner & outer rings		901-980
7228	4890	174	5	1.31	500 x 135	—		866-1039(1035)
7412	4289	98	—	1.22	260 x 150	—		804-901
7424	4398	129	—	0.79	100 x 85	—		836-964

7500	4975	70	—	2.62	270 x 225	—		904-973
7558	4882	172	—	—	310 x 35	more inner & outer rings		771-942
7561	4885	95	—	1.73	185 x 50	—		938-1032(1033)

undated:

7157/4252	7158/4457	7159/4418	7160/4926	7160/4963	7169/4466	7170/4413
240 x 170	145 x 50	250 x 140	150 x 115	130 x 125	160 x 115	205 x 205

7171/4498	7174/3812	7175/4407	7177/4281	7178/4462	7180/4483	7182/4276	7189/4464
135 x 110	170 x 60	155 x 85	140 x 120	80 x 80	70 x 60	85 x 80	145 x 90

7191/4403	7195/4426	7222/4886	7223/4887	7225/4897	7226/4985	7419/4463	7422/4367
95 x 85	115 x 70	160 x 150	240 x 215	220 x 200	185 x 170	130 x 85	115 x 95

7426/4465	7469/4984	7565/4978	7573/4879
100 x 65	175 x 130	145 x 80	140 x 115

Phase IV.4, Waterfront 2

[]	<>	Rings	Sap'd	ARW	Dimensions	Comments	Sketched cross-section	Date range
6098	4053	103	17	1.42	155 x 80	—		935-1037(1021)
6106	4704	120	—	1.05	130 x 85	—		885-1004
6108	4365	97	—	1.13	130 x 105	—		867-963
6113	4348	83	—	1.72	175 x 70	more inner rings		872-954
6117	4644	95	—	1.25	210 x 150	—		913-1007
6448	4402	138	21	0.89	135 x 75	felled winter		902-1039(1019)
6454	4295	65	—	1.03	75 x 75	—		940-1004
6493	4603	116	31	—	245 x 45	sapwood, 28-33		921-1036(1006)
6522	4647	75	16	2.37	185 x 40	—		961-1035(1020)
6527	4613	87	—	1.18	180 x 110	more inner rings		811-897
6528	3376	110	17	0.66	175 x 80	felled winter		927-1036(1020)
7100	4438	98	29	2.00	230 x 105	felled winter		942-1039(1011)
7104	4433	82	30	0.65	180 x 120	felled winter; more inner rings		958-1039(1010)
7105	4439	80	17	1.46	230 x 180	*c.*12 rings to BE		946-1025(1009)
7108	4362	141	—	0.83	310 x 125	—		849-989
7111	4925	188	—	1.13	260 x 140	more inner rings		850-1037(1020)
7115	4280	75	—	1.73	170 x 75	—		917-991
7116	4274	53	—	2.79	170 x 80	—		952-1004
7117	4446	55	—	1.69	105 x 50	—		947-1001
7119	4443	95	32	1.65	180 x 110	felled winter		945-1039(1008)
7122	4287	73	12	0.63	155 x 105	more inner rings		965-1037(1026)
7123	4273	231	—	0.70	170 x 60	—		779-1009

[]	<>	Rings	Sap'd	ARW	Dimensions	Comments	Sketched cross-section	Date range
7124	4445	81	—	1.77	165 x 70	—		928-1008
7125	4396	102	1	0.74	150 x 75	—		920-1021(1021)
7126	4394	165	—	1.41	245 x 75	—		789-953
7133	4400	97	9	1.60	165 x 45	—		916-1012(1004)
7136	4479	84	23	1.26	110 x 60	sapwood, 20-26		955-1038(1016)

undated:

6054/4032	6102/4233	6109/4300	6114/4761	6235/4294	6452/4416	6492/4298
155 x 140	150 x 95	120 x 100	185 x 100	75 x 55	230 x 150	135 x 70

7101/4917	7108B/4417	7109/4428	7113/4427	7114/4451	7115B/4431	7121/4369	7129/4409
300 x 95	185 x 110	155 x 125	150 x 95	155 x 150	180 x 170	165 x 75	140 x 115

7130/4414	7134/4429	7154/4931
180 x 180	130 x 90	110 x 70

Phase IV.4, Waterfront 3

NB This revetment has been fully conserved. Dendrochronology was by wedges or cores, and so no cross-sectional measurements or drawings are available.

[]	<>	Rings	Sap'd	ARW	Dimensions	Comments	Sketched cross-section	Date range
—	3550	73	—	1.84	unmeasured	—		936-1008
6883	3560	122	22	1.62	unmeasured	stave; sapwood, 20-24		919-1040(1019)
6884	3559	123	—	1.07	unmeasured	stave		914-1036(1037)
6885	3558	101	—	1.86	unmeasured	stave		904-1004
6886	3555	158	4	1.47	unmeasured	stave		885-1042(1039)
6887	3554	66	7	2.68	unmeasured	stave		981-1046(1040)
6888	3553	122	—	1.26	unmeasured	stave; more inner & 2 outer rings		887-1010
6889	3552	50	—	1.97	unmeasured	stave		978-1027
6892	3546	68	—	1.37	unmeasured	stave		940-1007
7540	4950	105	15	1.47	335 x 115	—		940-1044(1030)

undated:

7536/4953	7542/4942
305 x 90	390 x 155

Phase IV.7, Waterfront 2

[]	<>	Rings	Sap'd	ARW	Dimensions	Comments	Sketched cross-section	Date range
5976	4628	132	—	0.80	100 x 90	—		883-1014

Phase V.1, Waterfront 6

[ ]	< >	Rings	Sap'd	ARW	Dimensions	Comments	Sketched cross-section	Date range
6788	4905	47	—	2.64	155 x 150			1024-1070

undated: 7530/4919

170 x 130

Phase V.2, Waterfront 3

[ ]	< >	Rings	Sap'd	ARW	Dimensions	Comments	Sketched cross-section	Date range
7233	4423	55	19	2.71	160 x 80	—		985-1039(1021)
7259	4952	120	—	1.91	300 x 100	more inner rings		815-934

undated: 7235/4458   7239/4239   7240/4256

115 x 60   100 x 65   120 x 50

Phase V.3, Waterfront 3

[ ]	< >	Rings	Sap'd	ARW	Dimensions	Comments	Sketched cross-section	Date range
5784	4508	52	—	2.00	175 x 65	—		950-1001
5789	4656	100	18	1.48	170 x 105	—		942-1041(1024)
5832	4670	202	—	1.05	215 x 60	in 2 pieces		778-979
5902	4807	167	26	1.19	190 x 190	?felled 1054/5		888-1054(1029)
5904	4811	179	30	0.89	155 x 65	felled summer 1055; in 2 pieces		876-1054(1025)
5906	4584	144	18	1.25	185 x 70	—		907-1050(1033)
5909B	4384	214	—	0.80	215 x 190	—		797-1010
5911	4700	55	—	1.25	140 x 125	—		945-999
5912	4036	93	45	0.64	85 x 65	?felled winter 1054/5		962-1054(1010)
5913A	4335	77	—	2.03	255 x 150	more inner rings		852-928
5913B	4765	48	—	1.88	85 x 80	—		949-996
5913C	4595	103	—	0.78	100 x 70	—		872-974
5914	4649	87	—	1.03	115 x 95	—		883-969
5914B	4657	218	—	0.75	180 x 55	—		649-866
5915A	4655	112	—	0.89	115 x 50	—		818-929
5916	4739	90	—	1.56	170 x 55	—		784-873
5918A	4684	160	3	0.77	140 x 100	—		867-1026(1024)
5919	4292	81	—	1.32	105 x 55	—		905-985
5921A	4297	73	—	1.35	110 x 100	—		917-989
5921B	4759	220	—	0.74	200 x 80	knot at outside		798-1017
5924B	4640	90	—	1.94	200 x 80	—		801-895
5926	4695	171	—	0.90	190 x 100	—		749-919
5927A	4738	110	—	0.87	105 x 60	—		915-1024
5927B	4656	204	—	1.02	215 x 75	—		615-818

5928	4230	225	—	0.63	145 x 55	—	798-1022
5931A	4350	65	—	1.10	125 x 30	—	823-887
5931B	4220	120	427	0.78	125 x 115	felled ?summer 1055	936-1054(1011)
5937	4037	62	—	2.84	220 x 125	—	948-1009
6074	4680	109	—	0.69	170 x 95	—	871-979
6306	4764	140	—	1.21	190 x 55	—	864-1003
6311	4803	65	—	1.95	130 x 100	—	928-992
6312	4683	69	21	1.29	250 x 115	+ inner rings; sapwood, 16-25	971-1039(1020)
6313	4599	116	—	1.49	185 x 175	—	782-897
6315	4888	175	—	1.39	310 x 90	near HS	825-999
6316	4810	188	11	0.76	165 x 95	sapwood, 4-18	870-1057(1047)
6319	4699	100	—	1.23	215 x 50	—	923-1022
6320	—	248	—	0.99	260 x 60	—	765-1012
6337	4585	154	7	1.01	225 x 85	knot at inside; more inner rings	891-1044(1038)
6338	4665	69	yes	1.40	120 x 115	+ about 34 to BE; felled c.1053	951-1019
6340	3366	219	49	0.52	125 x 90	felled winter (but narrow rings)	835-1053(1005)
6342	4614	90	—	1.12	110 x 45	—	776-865
6344	4232	72	24	1.77	135 x 85	?felled winter 1054/5	983-1054(1031)
6345	4808	66	—	1.10	140 x 130	pith	910-975
6345B	4685	81	—	1.04	160 x 155	pith	912-992
6346	—	63	—	2.01	135 x 110	—	939-1000
6347	4565	113	—	0.99	130 x 90	—	812-924
6348	3365	142	—	0.92	130 x 90	—	722-863
6351	4757	168	12	0.73	130 x 90	20-30 to BE	859-1026(1015)
6353	4758	98	—	0.96	130 x 75	more inner rings	787-884
6426	4601	78	—	1.69	145 x 55	—	827-904
6430	4629	55	—	1.91	115 x 55	—	822-876
6431	4732	126	—	0.98	150 x 80	—	873-998
6439	4636	125	—	1.28	175 x 45	—	892-1016
6620	4801	187	—	0.89	200 x 105	—	833-1019
6623	4760	156	—	0.84	145 x 75	same tree as 6674	779-934
6625	4050	116	—	1.57	205 x 70	—	893-1008
6625B	4754	152	—	1.07	190 x 60	—	867-1018
6635	4296	254	62	0.41	130 x 45	more inner rings	808-1061(1000)
6663	4643	136	—	1.07	230 x 155	pith; nr HS	892-1027(1028)
6664	4802	77	—	1.17	110 x 50	—	830-906
6665B	4755	73	4	1.07	85 x 45	—	936-1008(1005)
6669	4679	80	—	1.45	160 x 155	pith	907-986
6671	—	83	—	1.44	195 x 55	—	944-1026
6673	4043	112	—	0.72	150 x 95	more inner rings	866-977
6674	4688	221	—	0.83	215 x 80	same tree as 6623	738-958
6675	4659	190	—	0.71	165 x 60	unmeasured rings at inside	773-962
6678	4560	127	—	1.38	200 x 130	—	866-992
6679	4676	172	—	1.04	205 x 85	—	771-942
6679B	4639	113	—	1.06	140 x 65	—	893-1005
6701	4536	133	—	0.72	110 x 70	—	883-1015
6702	4766	205	12	0.61	140 x 65	—	817-1021(1010)

6704	4561	152	—	0.49	245 x 65	—		855-1006
6707	4652	83	—	1.45	155 x 60	c.10 unmeasured heart rings		938-1020
6709	4033	155	—	1.25	220 x 50	—		860-1014
6710	4702	86	—	1.04	105 x 40	—		905-990
6711	4645	88	—	1.51	150 x 65	—		867-954
6713	4696	114	—	1.12	150 x 90	unmeasured rings at inside		888-1001
6717	4096	158	—	0.80	150 x 55	—		860-1017
6723	4698	190	17	0.68	180 x 135	near pith; BE		865-1054(1038)
6731B	4604	165	—	0.84	160 x 60	same tree as 6623/6674		725-889
6732	4090	80	27	1.00	125 x 95	about 22 rings to BE		949-1028(1002)
6942	4731	160	—	0.68	135 x 90	—		817-976
6942B	4730	93	—	1.00	110 x 75	—		935-1027
7074	4452	119	—	1.03	280 x 130	—		916-1034

undated:

5799/4891	5861/4689	5871/4393	5873/4516	5901/4797	5908/4804	5909A/4690
250 x 125	140 x 95	230 x 185	125 x 85	100 x 100	145 x 75	135 x 130

5915B/4232	5917/4302	5918B/4664	5920/4672	5922/4600	5924A/4336	5925/4671	5932/4547
190 x 100	175 x 90	130 x 105	190 x 75	110 x 70	130 x 70	155 x 85	100 x 100

5934/4231	6045/4691	6305/4806	6307/4630	6307B	6309/4692	6310/4583	6334/6486
215 x 85	200 x 180	170 x 110	110 x 75	110 x 90	260 x 250	175 x 75	280 x 145

6335/4651	6341/4041	6344B/4913	6349/4351	6350/4677	6352/4299	6419/4564	6420/4637
165 x 105	205 x 65	140 x 130	85 x 45	140 x 70	165 x 115	170 x 130	140 x 75

6421/4653	6424/4693	6427/3367	6428/4591	6434/4648	6615/4669	6619/4042	6619B/4752
135 x 90	150 x 125	110 x 35	155 x 70	170 x 55	180 x 80	225 x 140	130 x 70

6624/4049	6627/4039	6629/4694	6631/4095	6632/4733	6634/4092	6665/4038	6666/4610
220 x 115	155 x 70	120 x 40	165 x 70	145 x 80	135 x 95	285 x 145	185 x 150

6667/4762	6668/4661	6671B/4242	6671C/4093	6677/4559	6700/4650	6706/4675	6708/4658
125 x 115	180 x 90	200 x 55	180 x 55	140 x 90	160 x 75	205 x 50	120 x 40

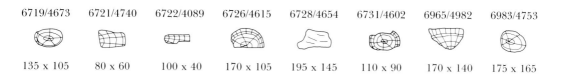

6719/4673	6721/4740	6722/4089	6726/4615	6728/4654	6731/4602	6965/4982	6983/4753
135 x 105	80 x 60	100 x 40	170 x 105	195 x 145	110 x 90	170 x 140	175 x 165

Phase V.4, Waterfront 3

[ ]	< >	Rings	Sap'd	ARW	Dimensions	Comments	Sketched cross-section	Date range
5626	4576	119	—	1.37	175 x 105	—		887-1005
5714	4487	65	21	1.88	135 x 50	nr BE; 2 radii		929-993(973)
5765	4492	159	40		120 x 35	nr BE;measured in 2 sections		895-1053(1014)

undated::

5659/4366	5812/4490	6026/4661	6027/4736
110 x 60	115 x 85	165 x 120	165 x 95

Phase V.6, Waterfront 6

[ ]	< >	Rings	Sap'd	ARW	Dimensions	Comments	Sketched cross-section	Date range
4635	3378	74	—	1.36	140 x 80	possible HS at 982		908-981
4645	4291	62	—	1.16	85 x 65	—		928-989
4646	4668	79	—	1.44	110 x 110	—		907-985
4771	4697	65	—	2.19	180 x 95	—		949-1013
5388	5388	78	—	1.03	90 x 45	—		925-1002
5394B	4593	120	—	0.81	115 x 100	—		889-1008
5424	4567	114	—	0.87	135 x 85	—		900-1013
5625	3314	143	26	1.04	200 x 135	10-15 rings to BE; +inner rings		907-1049(1024)

undated:

3269/4557	4643/4556	5304/4641	5334/4606	5387/4496	5389/4809	5392/4293
115 x 50	80 x 75	135 x 75	100 x 70	240 x 70	245 x 60	90 x 85

5394/4592	5423/4674	5750/4520	5981/4760
90 x 45	150 x 85	330 x 150	140 x 75

Phase V.8, Waterfront 7

[ ]	< >	Rings	Sap'd	ARW	Dimensions	Comments	Sketched cross-section	Date range
2715	4626	81	—	2.18	210 x 115	—		934-1014
2731	4378	73	—	0.86	110 x 65	—		963-1035
6433	4881	80	yes	1.32	135 x 70	25-30 rings to HS		929-1008

[]	<>	Rings	Sap'd	ARW	Dimensions	Comments	Sketched cross-section	Date range
6433B	4097	51	6	1.15	115 x 75	—		957-1007(1002)
6435	4594	98	9	1.28	145 x 65	—		945-1042(1034)
6436	4734	162	8	1.27	225 x 95	knotty		885-1046(1039)
7904	4971	112	—	2.12	280 x 85	knotty		884-995
7914	4958	128	18	0.92	190 x 70	+ at least 3 rings; & more at inside		926-1053(1046)
7917	4957	74	—	1.03	200 x 80	more inner rings		919-992
7932	4938	98	—	1.28	140 x 75	—		927-1024
7933	4932	90	—	1.24	120 x 40	HS visible		945-1034(1035)
7940	4940	83	—	1.86	195 x 170	—		870-952
7949	4920	104	5	0.83	100 x 85	—		911-1014(1010)
7959	4916	125	—	0.77	110 x 80	—		895-1010
7980	4928	83	—	1.74	160 x 40	—		958-1040
8022	4894	96	—	1.33	150 x 70	near HS		937-1032
8027	4937	84	—	1.30	120 x 60	—		943-1026
8040	4979	78	—	2.01	165 x 80	—		901-978
8041	4924	57	4	1.40	150 x 100	more inner rings		980-1036(1032)
8048	4988	76	1	1.58	140 x 75	—		959-1034(1034)

undated:

6432/4681	7969/4893	7970/4930	7979/4502	7984/4943	7987/4944	8031/4971
200 x 140	175 x 95	100 x 100	165 x 90	165 x 145	115 x 65	90 x 85

Phase VI.1, Waterfront 8

[]	<>	Rings	Sap'd	ARW	Dimensions	Comments	Sketched cross-section	Date range
4456	4539	82	—	1.89	150 x 105	—		969-1050
5245	4678	79	—	1.71	185 x 90	—		935-1013
5253	4546	109	—	1.20	150 x 65	—		894-1002
5262	4504	115	—	1.12	150 x 60	—		611-725
5416	4741	61	—	1.41	105 x 90	—		911-971
5767	4491	132	—	0.97	150 x 85	—		900-1031(1030)
5855B	4667	164	28	0.83	150 x 135	+ at least 5 rings		888-1051(1024)
6067	4607	107	—	0.95	115 x 65	—		922-1028

undated:

5047/4542	5049/4969	5244/4541	5260/4390	5406/4562	5410/4370	5413/4537
115 x 75	145 x 125	180 x 135	135 x 75	140 x 120	160 x 65	155 x 95

5475/4884	5478/4507	5485/4390	5653/4494	5662/4493	5715/4505	5717/4355	5855A/4503
125 x 105	245 x 185	140 x 120	140 x 125	130 x 75	140 x 75	260 x 195	100 x 90

6072/4301

100 x 65

Phase VI.2, Waterfront 8 construction

[]	<>	Rings	Sap'd	ARW	Dimensions	Comments	Sketched cross-section	Date range
6610	4441	197	38	0.76	165 x 155	sapwood, 35-41; ?felled 1108		912-1108(1071)
6956	4956	111	—	1.30	165 x 140	—		965-1075
6961	4877	102	—	1.59	180 x 155	—		982-1083

Phase VI.4, Waterfront 9 construction

[]	<>	Rings	Sap'd	ARW	Dimensions	Comments	Sketched cross-section	Date range
2666A	4586	192	—	0.90	325 x 35	unmeasured inner rings		907-1098
2666B	4544	67	—	2.53	290 x 140	—		1024-1090
2694	4623	178	—	1.01	210 x 185	—		888-1065
2713	4625	79	—	1.17	175 x 155	pith		920-998
2716	4385	104	yes	1.30	140 x 120	HS at 105		967-1070(1071)
2727A	3382	74	—	2.22	175 x 30	—		919-992
2727B	4229	125	—	1.83	260 x 110	—		860-984
6866	4912	100	12	2.08	215 x 120	—		922-1021(1010)
6867	4412	91	—	1.34	205 x 125	—		915-1005
6868	4941	71	—	0.71	140 x 120	many inner rings; unmeasurable		933-1003

undated:

2738/4306	6869A/4459	6869B/4921	6988/4956
235 x 190	210 x 125	100 x 95	110 x 100

Phase VII.1, Waterfront 10

NB This revetment has been fully conserved. Dendrochronology was by wedges or cores, and so no cross-sectional measurements or drawings are available.

[]	<>	Rings	Sap'd	ARW	Dimensions	Comments	Sketched cross-section	Date range
5082	4638	107	—	1.13	120 x 110	—		974-1080
5448	4923	129	—	1.37	225 x 60	—		991-1119
6331	3518	77	yes	1.59	unmeasured	stave; + c.35 incl. 5 sapwood		1026-1137(1133)
6568	3512	140	—	1.17	unmeasured	stave		907-1046
6569	3513	70	—	1.70	unmeasured	stave; more inner & c.4 outer rings		1045-1118
6570	3514	104	—	1.29	unmeasured	stave		1020-1123
6571	3515	64	—	2.04	unmeasured	stave; + c.18 outer rings		1043-1124
6573	3517	91	—	1.55	unmeasured	stave		1024-1114
6574	3519	94	4	1.46	unmeasured	stave		1039-1132(1129)
6577	3535	88	—	1.52	unmeasured	stave		1042-1129
6579	3525	107	—	1.43	unmeasured	stave		958-1064

[]	<>	Rings	Sap'd	ARW	Dimensions	Comments	Sketched cross-section	Date range
6580	3526	106	—	1.41	unmeasured	+ *c*.3 outer rings		972-1080
6822	—	61	yes	1.72	unmeasured	stave; + ?31 rings incl. 5 sapwood		1048-1139
6823	3536	57	—	1.05	unmeasured	stave; + inner & *c*.37 outer rings		1034-1127

Phase VII.4

[]	<>	Rings	Sap'd	ARW	Dimensions	Comments	Sketched cross-section	Date range
6690	4091	94	—	1.53	145 x 65	—		1012-1105

Phase VII.5, Waterfront 11

[]	<>	Rings	Sap'd	ARW	Dimensions	Comments	Sketched cross-section	Date range
6042	4892	71	—	1.53	125 x 30	—		818-888
6378	4411	265	—	0.99	270 x 25	—		865-1129

undated: 6559/4907   6594/4946

135 x 70   120 x 50

Phase VII.6, Waterfront 10

undated: 6245/4922

230 x 100

Phase VII.6

[]	<>	Rings	Sap'd	ARW	Dimensions	Comments	Sketched cross-section	Date range
6585	3532	76	—	1.23	unmeasured	crosspiece		1040-1115

Phase VII.7, Waterfront 11

undated: 6327/4415   6552/4909   6659/4939

245 x 145   240 x 110   185 x 35

Phase VII.8

[]	<>	Rings	Sap'd	ARW	Dimensions	Comments	Sketched cross-section	Date range
4746	4523	95	—	1.36	150 x 70	—		997-1091
6325	4880	128	—	1.11	245 x 120	pith		865-992

undated: 4193/3309   6544/4895

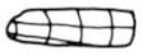

255 x 115   120 x 50

Phase VII.9

[ ]	< >	Rings	Sap'd	ARW	Dimensions	Comments	Sketched cross-section	Date range
4524	4528	403	11	0.76	335 x 25	—	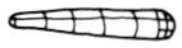	770-1171(1162)

undated: 6380/4883

300 x 25

Phase VII.13

[ ]	< >	Rings	Sap'd	ARW	Dimensions	Comments	Sketched cross-section	Date range
5985	4563	77	17	1.86	145 x 140	—		1073-1149(1133)
6064	4363	64	—	2.05	195 x 190	pith	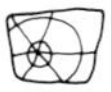	1007-1070

[]	Rings	Sap'd	ARW	Dimensions	Comments	Sketched cross-section	Date range
Waterfront 1							
582	131	18	1	120 x 90	tieback stake?		1003-1133
596	77	—	2.49	250 x 200	sill beam		966-1042
605	41	6	—	190 x 100	brace		—
609	157	—	1.19	190 x 70	plank		—
611	225	—	1.05	210 x 130	brace		862-1086
615	74	—	1.51	130 x 40	brace?		1108-1181
626	141	—	0.96	150 x 50	plank; plus outer rings		—
637	74	—	1.55	120 x 30	secondary?		1049-1122
640	77	—	2.37	180 x 60	plank		963-1039
685	58	—	2.52	150 x 60	brace		—
686	125	2	1.07	180 x 60	brace; plus outer rings		—
Waterfront 2							
469A	91	16	1.73	180 x 150	post		1073-1163
469B	184	—	0.85	150 x 30	upright plank		960-1143
497C	114	—	—	360 x 30	plank; plus outer rings		—
497D	137	—	1.55	210 x 40	plank		1001-1137
503	160	—	1.49	230 x 30	plank		942-1101
515	23	2	—	270 x 130	brace		—
527	25	3	—	170 x 130	brace?		—

76. Seal House: details of tree-ring analysis. Sketches are not to scale; sapwood is indicated by closer lines. [ ] = context number; ARW = average ring width; all dimensions in mm.

77. New Fresh Wharf: tree-ring analysis of the boat timbers (information from Ian Tyers). ARW = average ring width; HS = heartwood-sapwood transition; all dimensions in mm.

NFW74

Period 2.2, boat timbers, context no. 514

Sample	Rings	Sap'd	ARW	Dimensions	Comments	Sketched cross-section	Date range
5	6	—	1.6	160 x 145	?HS		812-907
6	150	—	1.4	215 x 25	—		717-866
9	164	8	1.2	200 x 15	—		746-909
13	101	5	1.2	130 x 20	—		815-915
16	139	—	1.5	275 x 20	—		671-809
25	170	—	1.5	255 x 20	—		654-823
26	127	—	1.2	170 x 20	—		742-868
35	105	—	2.2	250 x 20	—		759-863

[ ]	Rings	Sap'd	ARW	Dimensions	Comments	Sketched cross-section	Date range
SM75/FRE78							

Period 2.2

| FRE4001 | 55 | 20 | 1.25 | 180 x 170 | — | | — |
| SM273 | 75 | — | 3.21 | 280 x 250 | — | | — |

Period 2.4

FRE3003	76	—	1.94	230 x 160	—		—
FRE3004	57	1	1.70	190 x 190	—		—
FRE3005	100	—	2.12	320 x 220	—		869-968
FRE3006	120	—	1.89	250 x 180	—		—
FRE3008	103	—	1.51	280 x 260	—		902-1004
FRE575A	58	—	2.60	240 x 160	—		875-932
FRE575B	79	—	1.62	230 x 230	—		—
SM183	166	—	1.51	270 x 60	—		767-932
SM7	73	2	1.65	120 x 120	—		879-951(950)

Period 3.2

SM130	62	—	3.39	210 x 200	—		839-900
FRE3001	89	—	1.48	320 x 80	—		—
FRE597	76	—	1.81	340 x 130	—		970-1045

Period 3.4

FRE576	1	—	2.26	270 x 140	—		1004-1074
FRE592	127	—	1.35	270 x 90	—		835-961
FRE8004	115	3	1.83	370 x 330	—		1045-1159(1157)
FRE10001	102	—	3.30	750-280	more outer rings		1029-1130

78. New Fresh Wharf: details of tree-ring analysis. Sketches are not to scale; sapwood is indicated by closer lines. [ ] = context number; ARW = average ring width; date in parentheses = date of heartwood-sapwood transition; all dimensions in mm.

BIBLIOGRAPHY AND ABBREVIATIONS

Ambrosiani, B, 1985 Jetties in Birka and Stockholm and the changing water levels in the Malaren area, in Herteig 1985, 66-8

ASC: Anglo-Saxon Chronicle

Ayers, B S, 1985 The growth of a Saxon port, in Herteig 1985b, 46-54

——, 1988 Excavations at St Martin-at-Palace Plain, Norwich, 1981, East Anglian Archaeol, **37**

Baillie, M G L, 1982 Tree-ring dating and archaeology

——, & Pilcher, J R, 1973 A simple crossdating program for tree-ring research, Tree Ring Bulletin, **33**, 7-14

Bateson, M, 1902 A London municipal collection, English Hist Rev, **17**, 480-511

Biddle, M, 1976a Towns, in Wilson 1976, 99-150

——, (ed) 1976b Winchester in the early Middle Ages

——, 1984 London on the Strand, Popular Archaeol (July 1984), 23-7

Birch, W de G, 1885 Cartularium Saxonicum, **1**

Brigham, T, 1985 Watching Brief at Billingsgate Market, Archive Report, Museum of London

——, 1990 The Late Roman waterfront in London, Britannia, **21**, 99-183

Brisbane, M, 1988 Hamwic (Saxon Southampton): an 8th century port and production centre, in Hodges & Hobley 1988, 101-8

Brooke, C, & Keir, G, 1975 London 800-1216: the shaping of a City

Cal Charter Rolls: Calendar of Charter Rolls, **1** (1226-57), 1903; **4** (1327-41), 1912

Cal Lbk B, etc: R R Sharpe (ed) Calendar of the Letter-Books of the City of London [B, E-G] 1900; 1903-5

Cal Misc Inq: Calendar of Miscellaneous Inquisitions, **1** (1219-1307), 1916

Chaplais, P, 1961 The original charters of Herbert and Gervase abbots of Westminster (1121-1157), in P M Barnes & C F Slade (eds), A medieval miscellany for Doris May Stenton, Pipe Roll Soc New Ser, **36**, 89-110

Chew, H, & Kellaway, W, (eds) 1973 The London Assize of Nuisance 1301-1431, London Record Soc, **10**

——, & Weinbaum, M, (eds) 1970 The London Eyre of 1244, London Record Soc, **6**

Clarke, H B, & Simms, A, (eds) 1985 The comparative history of urban origins in non-Roman Europe, British Archaeol Rep, **S255**

CLRO: City of London Records Office

Colgrave, B, & Mynors, R A B, (eds) 1969 Bede's Ecclesiastical History of the English People

Cowgill, J, de Neergaard, M, & Griffiths, N, 1987 Knives and scabbards (Medieval finds from excavations in London:1)

Cowie, R, & Whytehead, R, 1989 Londonwic: the archaeological evidence for Middle Saxon London, Antiquity, **63**, 706-18

Cronne, H A, & Davis, R H C, 1968 Regesta Regum Anglo-Normannorum, **3**

Crumlin-Pederson, O, 1985 Cargo ships of northern Europe AD 800-1300, in Herteig 1985b, 83-93

Devoy, R, 1980 Post glacial environmental change and man in the Thames estuary: a synopsis, in F Thompson (ed), Archaeology and coastal change

Dolley, R H M, 1976 The coins, in Wilson 1976, 349-72

Dyson, T, 1978 Two Saxon land-grants for Queenhithe, in J Bird, H Chapman & J Clark (eds), Collectanea Londiniensia: studies in London archaeology and history presented to Ralph Merrifield, London & Middlesex Archaeol Soc Special Paper, **2**

——, 1980 London and Southwark in the seventh century and later: a neglected reference, Trans London Middlesex Archaeol Soc, **31**, 83-95

——, 1985 Early harbour regulations in London, in Herteig 1985b, 19-24

——, 1989 Documents and archaeology: the medieval London waterfront, Museum of London (Annual Archaeology Lecture 1988)

——, & Schofield, J, 1984 Saxon London, in J Haslam (ed), Anglo-Saxon towns in southern England, 285-313

Ekwall, E, 1954 Street-names of the City of London

——, 1960 The concise Oxford dictionary of English placenames (4th edn)

Ellmers, D, 1981 Post-Roman waterfront installations on the Rhine, in Milne and Hobley 1981, 80-95

Ennen, E, 1985 The early history of the European town: a retrospective view, in Clarke & Simms 1985, 3-14

Feet Fines 9 Ric I: Feet of fines of the ninth year of King Richard I . . . 1197 to 1198, Pipe Roll Soc, **23**, 1929

Fehring, G, 1985 The archaeology of early Lübeck: the relation between the Slavic and German settlement sites, in Clarke & Simms 1985, 267-88

Fenwick, V, 1978 *The Graveney Boat*, British Archaeol Rep, **53**

Fletcher, J M, 1974 The dendrochronology, in Tatton-Brown 1974, 211-15

——, 1977 Tree-ring chronologies for the 6th to the 16th centuries for oaks of Southern and Eastern England, *J Archaeol Science*, **4**, 335-52

Gibbs, M, 1939 *Early charters of the cathedral church of St Paul, London*, Camden Soc 3rd ser, **58**

GL: Guildhall Library

Grew, F, & de Neergaard, M, 1988 *Shoes and pattens* (Medieval finds from excavations in London: 2)

Groves, C, & Hillam, J, 1987 *Tree-ring analysis of timbers from Swan Lane, City of London, 1981*, Ancient Monuments Laboratory Report, **30/87**

Hall, R A, 1978 The topography of Anglo-Scandinavian York, in R Hall (ed), *Viking Age York and the north*, CBA Res Rep, **27**, 31-6

——, 1988 York 700-1050, in Hodges & Hobley 1988, 125-32

Harris, R, 1989 *Excavations at Swan Lane*, Archive Report, Museum of London

Hassall, W O, 1949 *The cartulary of St Mary Clerkenwell*, Camden Soc 3rd ser, **71**

Herrmann, J, 1985 Ralswiek – maritime trading station and harbour development from the 8th to the 10th century along the southern Baltic Sea, in Herteig 1985b, 55-8

Herteig, A E, 1985a Details from the Bergen medieval waterfront, in Herteig 1985b, 69-78

——, (ed.), 1985b *Conference on waterfront archaeology in North European towns no.2 (Bergen 1983)*

Hill, C, Millett, M & Blagg, T, 1980 *The Roman riverside wall and monumental arch in London*, London Middlesex Archaeol Soc Special Paper, **3**

Hill, D, 1981 *An atlas of Anglo-Saxon England*

Hillam, J, 1985a Theoretical and applied dendrochronology – how to make a date with a tree, in P Phillips (ed), *The archaeologist and the laboratory*, CBA Res Rep, **58**, 17-23

——, 1985b *Tree-ring dating of Saxon timbers from the City of London*, Ancient Monuments Laboratory report, **4733**

——, 1987a *Tree-ring analysis of timbers from Billingsgate Lorry Park, City of London, 1982: the Period IV timbers*, Ancient Monuments Laboratory report, **47/87**

——, 1987b Problems of dating and interpreting results from archaeological timbers, in Ward 1987, 141-55

——, 1988a *Billingsgate Lorry Park, City of London, 1982: tree-ring analysis of the Period V timbers*, Ancient Monuments Laboratory report, **94/88**

——, 1988b *Billingsgate Lorry Park, City of London, 1982: tree-ring analysis of the Period VI and VII timbers*, Ancient Monuments Laboratory report, **95/88**

——, & Groves, C, 1985 *Tree-ring dating of waterfront structures from Billingsgate Lorry Park, City of London*, Ancient Monuments Laboratory report, **4747**

——, & Morgan, R, 1981 *Tree-ring analysis of timbers from New Fresh Wharf*, Ancient Monuments Laboratory report, **3562**

——, & ——, 1986 Tree-ring analysis of the Roman timbers, in Miller *et al* 1986, 75-85

——, — & Tyers, I, 1987 Sapwood estimates and the dating of short ring sequences, in Ward 1987, 165-85

Hobley, B, 1981 The London waterfront – the exception or the rule?, in Milne & Hobley 1981, 1-9

Hodges, R, 1978 State formation and the role of trade in Middle Saxon England, in S Green *et al* (eds), *Social organisation and settlement*, British Archaeol Reports, **47**, 439-53

——, 1982 *Dark Age economics: the origins of towns and trade AD 600-1000*

——, 1988 The rebirth of towns in the early Middle Ages, in Hodges & Hobley 1988, 1-7

——, & Hobley, B, (eds) 1988 *The rebirth of towns in the West AD 700-1050*, CBA Res Rep, **68**

Hodgett, G A J, (ed) 1971 *The cartulary of Holy Trinity Aldgate*, London Record Soc, **7**

Hollstein, E, 1965 Jährringchronologische Datierung von Eichenhölzern ohne Waldkante, *Bonner Jahrbuch*, **165**, 12-27

——, 1980 *Mitteleuropäische Eichenchronologie*, Zabern, Mainz am Rhein

Horsman, V, Milne, C, & Milne, G, 1988 *Aspects of Saxo-Norman London, 1, Buildings and Street Development*, London Middlesex Archaeol Soc Special Paper, **11**

HR: Husting Roll(s), CLRO

Jankuhn, H, 1985 The interdisciplinary approach to the study of the early history of medieval towns, in Clarke & Simms 1985, 15-44

Janssen, W, 1985 The origins of the non-Roman town in Germany, in Clarke & Simms 1985, 183-216

Jenner, A, & Vince, A G, 1991 Pottery, in Vince 1991, 19-119

Johnson, C, & Cronne, H A, 1956 *Regesta Regum Anglo-Normannorum: 2*

Keene, D J, 1987 *The Walbrook Study: a summary report*, Social and Economic Study of Medieval London (typescript in library of Institute of Historical Research, University of London)

Keene, D, & Harding, V, 1985 *A survey of documentary sources for property holding in London before the Great Fire*, London Record Soc, **22**

Kerling, N J M, (ed) 1973 *The cartulary of St Bartholomew's Hospital*

Keynes, S, & Lapidge, M, (eds) 1983 *Alfred the Great: Asser's Life of King Alfred and other contemporary sources*

Lib Cust: H Riley (ed), *Liber Custumarum: Munimenta Gildhallae Londoniensis*, 2, 1860

Loyd, L C, & Stenton, D M, (eds) 1950 *Sir Christopher Hatton's Book of Seals*

Loyn, H R, 1962 *Anglo-Saxon England and the Norman Conquest*

Marsden, P, 1981 Early shipping and the waterfronts of London, in Milne & Hobley 1981, 10-16

McGrail, S, 1981 Medieval boats, ships, and landing places, in Milne & Hobley 1981, 17-23

Miller, L, 1985 *Excavations at New Fresh Wharf: ii, Saxon*, Archive Report, Museum of London

____, Schofield, J, & Rhodes, M, 1986 *The Roman quay at St Magnus House, London*, London Middlesex Archaeol Special Paper, **8**

Milne, G, 1985 *The port of Roman London*

____, in preparation *Medieval waterfront structures*, London Middlesex Archaeol Soc Special Paper, **15**

____, & Hobley, B, (eds) 1981 *Waterfront archaeology in Britain & Northern Europe*, CBA Res Rep, **41**

____, & Milne, C, 1982 *Medieval waterfront development at Trig Lane, London*, London Middlesex Archaeol Soc Special Paper, **5**

____, Batterbee, R, Straker, V, & Yule, B, 1983 The London Thames in the mid-first century, *Trans London Middlesex Archaeol Soc*, **34**, 19-30

Morgan, R A, 1977 Tree-ring dating of the London waterfronts, *London Archaeol*, **3**, 40-5

____, 1978 *Tree-ring dating of the medieval waterfronts at the Seal House site*, Archive Report, Museum of London

____, & Schofield, J, 1978 Tree-rings and the archaeology of the Thames waterfront in London, in J M Fletcher (ed), *Dendrochronology in Europe*, British Archaeol Rep, **S51**, 223-38

Needham, S P, & Langley, D, 1981 Runnymede Bridge, in Milne & Hobley 1981, 48-50

Orton, C, 1988 Post-Roman pottery, in *Excavations in Southwark 1973-76; Lambeth 1973-79*, London Middlesex Archaeol Soc & Surrey Archaeol Soc Joint Publication, **3**, 1988, 295-7

Pipe Roll 2 John: D M Stenton (ed), *The Great Roll of the Pipe for the second year of the reign of King John, Michaelmas 1200*, Pipe Roll Soc new ser, **12**, 1934

Pirenne, H, 1925 *Medieval cities*

PRO: Public Records Office

Rhodes, M, 1991, The Roman Coinage from London Bridge and the development of the City and Southwark, *Britannia*, **22**, 179-90

Richardson, H G, & Sayles, G O, 1966 *Law and legislation from Aethelbert to Magna Carta*

Richardson, K M, 1959 Excavations in Hungate, York, *Archaeol J*, **116**, 51-114

Roskams, S, 1990 *Excavations at Billingsgate Lorry Park*, Archive Report, Museum of London

Sawyer, P H, 1968 *Anglo-Saxon charters: an annotated list and bibliography*

Schofield, J, 1978 *Excavations at Seal House, 106-8 Upper Thames Street, 1974-6*, Archive Report, Museum of London

____, Allen, P, & Taylor, C, in preparation *Medieval buildings in the area of Cheapside*

____, & Dyson, T, in preparation *Medieval waterfront tenements*

SLAEC 1978: Southwark & Lambeth Archaeological Excavation Committee, *Southwark Excavations 1972-74*, London Middlesex Archaeol Soc & Surrey Archaeol Soc Joint Publication, **1**, 1978

Smoralek, P, 1981 Ships and ports in Pomorze, in Milne & Hobley 1981, 51-60

Tatton-Brown, T, 1974 Excavations at the Custom House site, City of London, 1973, *Trans London Middlesex Archaeol Soc*, **25**, 117-219

____, 1975 Excavations at the Custom House: part II, *Trans London Middlesex Archaeol Soc*, **26**, 103-70

Taxatio: Taxatio ecclesiastica ... P. Nicholai IV c 1291, Record Commission, 1802

Thorpe, B, 1840 *Ancient laws and institutes of England*, Record Commission

Tyers, I G, 1990 *New Fresh Wharf – the boat timbers*, Archive Dendrochronology Report, Museum of London

Van Es, W A, & Verwers, W J H, 1981 Dorestad: a Carolingian waterfront on the Rhine, in Milne & Hobley 1981, 72-6

Vince, A G, 1984 New light on Saxon pottery from the London area, *London Archaeol*, **4**, 431-9

____, 1985 Saxon and medieval pottery in London: a review, *Medieval Archaeol*, **29**, 25-93

____, 1988 The economic basis of Anglo-Saxon London, in Hodges & Hobley 1988, 84-92

____, 1990 *Saxon London: an archaeological investigation*

____, (ed) 1991 *Aspects of Saxo-Norman London, ii, Finds and environmental evidence*, London Middlesex Archaeol Soc Special Paper, **12**

Wade, K, 1988 Ipswich, in Hodges & Hobley 1988, 93-100

Wallace, P F, 1981 Dublin's waterfront at Wood Quay: 900-1317, in Milne & Hobley 1981, 109-118

____, 1985 The archaeology of Viking Dublin, in Clarke & Simms 1985, 103-46

Ward, R G W, (ed.) 1987 *Applications of tree-ring studies: current research in dendrochronology and related areas*, British Archaeol Rep, **S333**

Whitelock, D, (ed) 1979 *English historical documents, c 500-1042* (2nd edn)

Williams, T, 1982 St Peters Hill, *Popular Archaeol*, **4.1**, 24-30

Wilson, D M, (ed) 1976 *The archaeology of Anglo-Saxon England*

Zbierski, A, 1985 The development of the Gdansk area from the ninth to the thirteenth century, in Clarke & Simms 1985, 289-334

SUMMARIES IN FRENCH AND GERMAN

RÉSUMÉ

Dans ce volume l'on a fait la description de con-
textes datant de la période allant de *c*.400 à
c.1200; ils proviennent de fouilles situées le long
de la rivière effectuées entre 1974 et 1982 dans
la Cité de Londres. Deux d'entre elles (New Fresh
Wharf et Billingsgate Lorry Park) se trouvaient
juste en aval du pont saxon tardif et médiéval et
les deux autres (Swan Lane et Seal House) étaient
situées immédiatement en amont. Un survol des
sources documentaires et les résultats des fouilles
donnent ensemble une idée du développement du
quartier autour de la tête de pont sur la rive
gauche et du port de Billingsgate (dont il est fait
mention pour la première fois en *c*.1000) et
jusqu'à un certain point de toute la partie de la
ville faisant face à la rivière pour la période sax-
onne tardive et pour le haut Moyen-Age.

Pendant la période de 400 à 900, les indices
obtenus sur ces quatre sites confortent les
hpothèses faites récemment qui suggèrent que la
cité romaine était en grande partie abandonnée.
La partie de la ville romaine située le long des
berges était petit à petit envahie par les limons
de la rivière en crue, et le pont romain, si il existait
encore à cette époque, ne formait plus le centre
vital des activités publiques. Il y a des indices
archéologiques à d'autres endroits qui montrent
que l'agglomération est passée du Strand à l'in-
térieur des murs romains aux environs de la fin
du 9ème siècle ou au début du 10ème. Cette
observation est confirmée par des documents qui
indiquent que deux immeubles au moins ont été
construits près de la rivière à Queenhithe pendant
les dernières décennies du 9ème siècle.
Cependant, à cet endroit comme ailleurs, les indices montrent que pendant le 10ème et le début
du 11ème siècle Londres était tournée vers l'in-
térieur plutôt que vers l'étranger pour ses activités
commerciales. Ce réseau commercial local, ou au
mieux interrégional, a des parallèles dans d'autres
pays d'Europe.

Les structures post-romaines les plus anciennes
que l'on a retrouvées entre Billingsgate et le Pont
de Londres sont la jetée et les remblais de moellons
qui lui sont associés à New Fresh Wharf datant
de la fin du 10ème ou du début du 11ème siècle.
A la suite de quoi, sur trois des quatre sites, des
quais d'argile et de bois ont été construits en sections séparées qui peuvent être associées à des pro-
priétés individuelles du bas Moyen-Age. Ceci
donne à penser que chaque section de quai avait
un propriétaire différent depuis le début. Les
quais auraient pu servir au mouillage des bateaux
de petite taille qui étaient alors courant et ils form-
aient sans doute une partie du port de Londres
en expansion au 11ème siècle.

L'étude du développement des berges de la
rivière entre le pont et Billingsgate au sud de
Thames Street a été fait dans le contexte de l'expansion du quartier environnant à la fin du
10ème et au 11è siècle et de la topographie de
toute la ville. Il semblerait qu'il y avait eu
d'abord, en même temps que les ports importants
de Queenhithe, Billingsgate et Botolph Wharf,
une série de petits marchés placés comme ces ports
au bout des rues orientées nord-sud touchant à
la rivière: le seul endroit de la rive où le publique
pouvait accéder. La construction du pont au
début du 11ème siècle (bien qu'aucune date pré-
cise n'ait encore été obtenue), symbolise le rôle
retrouvé de Londres comme centre de distribution de produits importés, sans doute aussi comme
point de rassemblement pour les produits à
exporter et également comme centre d'un réseau
routier local et régional.

Le développement de deux sites en amont du
port après 1050 ne s'est pas fait sur une échelle
importante; mais, en aval du pont, on distingue
deux phases: d'abord, vers 1100, la démolition
définitive du mur romain le long de la berge et
la construction des églises de St Magnus et St
Botolph au sud de la nouvelle voie, Thames
Street, qui est elle-même placée le long du côté
nord de l'ancien mur. Deuxièmement, la construction de bâtiments en pierre sur les terrains
récupérés pendant les 12ème et 13ème siècles. Ce

processus fait que l'embarcadaire de St Botolph va devenir un port important et un point d'entrée où les douanes royales sont perçues en 1200-1.

Cette étude comprend aussi des tableaux détaillés qui montrent les dates obtenues (y compris par la dendrochronologie) et fait le résumé des artefacts.

ZUSAMMENFASSUNG

Dieser Band beschreibt Baustrukturen von ca.400 bis ca.1200 und faßt vier Augrabungen in der City von London an der Themse zwischen 1974 und 1982 zusammen. Zwei Grabungen (New Fresh Wharf und Billingsgate) liegen direkt unterhalb der spät-sächsischen und mittelalterlichen Brücke, die beiden anderen (Swan Lane und Seal House) oberhalb. Zusammen mit historischen Dokumenten geben die archäologischen Funde ein Bild der Entwicklung der Gegend um den nördlichen Brückenkopf und den Hafen von Billingsgate, der ca.1000 erstmals erwähnt wird. Zu einem gewissen Grad gilt dies auch für die Entwicklung des gesamten Flußufers von der spät- sächsischen bis zur frühen mittelalterlichen Zeit.

Die Ausgrabungen bestätigen jüngste Vermutungen, daß die römische Stadt während der Zeit von 400 bis 900 weitgehend verlassen war. Die Uferfront versandete langsam unter steigendem Wasser und die römische Brücke, falls sie noch stand, war kein belebter Mittlepunk mehr. Irgendwann zwischen dem späten 9. und dem frühen 10. Jahrhundert wurde die sächsische Siedlung vom Strand im Westen hinter die römischen Mauern verlegt. Dieses belegen archäologische Funde von andernorts und Dokumente: wenigstens zwei Grundstück-Komplexe wurden am Fluß in Queenhithe in den letzten 10 Jahren des 9. Jahrhunderts abgesteckt. Sowohl von hier als auch von anderswo ist belegt, daß während des 10. und frühen 11. Jahrhunderts die Londoner Handelsbeziehengen eher landeinwärts gerichtet waren. Ein derartiges lokales oder bestenfalls regionales Handelsnetz hat auch Parallelen anderswo in Europa.

Die frühste nach-römische Bautätigkeit, der Landungssteg und ein dazugehöriges Schotterufer von New Fresh Wharf, lagen zwischen Billingsgate und London Bridge und stammen aus dem späten 10. bis frühen 11. Jahrhundert. An drei Grabungsstellen folgten in der ersten Hälfte des 11. Jahrhunderts Böschungsanlagen aus Holz und Ton. In New Fresh Wharf waren sie unzweideutig in Abschnitte eingeteilt, die später im Mittelalter Grundstückgrenzen markierten. Es liegt nahe anzunehmen, daß dies Land von Anfang an verschiedenen Besitzern gehörte. Die Uferanlagen waren nur zur Landung kleinerer Boote zu gebrauchen und sie waren wahrscheinlich ein Teil des sich im 11. Jahrhundert ausdehnenden Hafens. Beziehungen zwischen dem steigenden Wasserspiegel und den verschiedenen Uferbefestigungen werden auch erwogen.

Die Entwicklung der Flußufergegend im 10. und 11. Jahrhundert zwischen London Bridge und Billingsgate südlich Thames Street muß auch im Zusammenhang mit der Topographie der näheren Umgebung und der gesamten Stadt gesehen werden. Anfänglich gab es eine Reihe kleiner Märkte, die in der Nähe der großen Häfen in Queenhithe, Billingsgate und Botolph Wharf, nahe am Wasser am Ende von Nord/Südstraßen lagen, der einzigen Stelle mit öffentlichem Zugang zur Themse. Der Bau von London Bridge im frühen 11. Jahrhundert (das genaue Datum ist noch nicht belegt) symbolisiert nicht nur Londons erneute Rolle als Verteilerzentrum für Importe und als Sammelpunkt für Exporte, sondern es war auch ein Knotenpunkt im lokalen und regionalen Straßennetz.

Die Entwicklung der zwei Grabungsstellen flußaufwärts von London Bridge war nach 1050 vergleichsweise unbedeutend, unterhalb jedoch gab es zwei Bauphasen: um 1100 wurde die römische Stadtmauer entlang des Flußes endgültig abgetragen und südlich der neuen Verbindugsstraße Thames Street wurden die Kirchen St Magnus und St Botolph gebaut. Die Straße lag auf der Nordseite der früheren Stadtmauer. Außerdem wurden während des 12. und frühen 13. Jahrhunderts auf dem neu gewonnenen Ufergelände Steingebäude errichtet. Alles zusammen machte St Botolph Wharf zu einem bedeutenden Hafen und Zugangspunkt zur Stadt, und zwischen 1200 und 1201 wurde es eine königliche Zollstation.

Des weiteren enthält die Studie detaillierte Zeit-Tabellen (inclusive dendrochronologischer Daten) und eine Zusammenfassung der Funde.

INDEX

by Francis Grew and John Schofield

This index covers all three volumes of *Aspects of Saxo-Norman London*, and is comprehensive in its treatment of the following subjects: (a) personal names, place names and street names; (b) excavation sites (invariably distinguished from street names by street numbers and/or Museum of London site codes: BIG82, NFW74 etc); (c) artefacts (indexed by material and type) and botanical/'environmental' samples; (d) major themes of a more general nature. It is based on the indexers' judgement as to what is likely to be useful for the archaeological reader; street names, for example, have been omitted when they are merely a guide to location, the entry contributing nothing to knowledge of the street itself. A more interpretative listing has been preferred to a strictly alphabetical one when this provides clarity. The entries under major topics such as 'buildings' are ordered by (a) general, (b) chronological, (c) site specific; London finds generally precede non-London finds, and under major excavation sites, artefacts follow structural findings. The index is intended to be used in close conjunction with the published catalogues: the microfiche catalogue to vol ii, the catalogues of small finds (ii.249-78) and coins (ii.305-24), and the tables of botanical remains (ii.356-79). For this reason, only those plant remains, coins and small finds discussed in the main text have been indexed, and the pottery entries for each major excavation site have been subdivided by ware and form only if the reference is an important one; for further cross-referencing the user should consult the appropriate catalogue or table.

Volume numbers are in small Roman numerals and figure numbers in italics; pottery is listed as far as possible under its Common Name, with its four-letter mnemonic code; names have generally been entered under their modern forms, the Latin or Old English originals being used only for reference to inscriptions or etymological discussion, or to distinguish medieval from modern streets. Unless clearly stated otherwise, all entries are to finds of 'Saxo-Norman' date.

(Peninsular House; PEN79), i.33; at
Milk Street (1-6; MLK76), i.55
Daucus carota see carrot
David I, king of Scotland, ii.303
Delgany, coin hoard, ii.285
denarii see sceattas
dendrochronology, iii.143-73, *iii.66-75*
dating of,
Billingsgate Lorry Park (BIG82),
ii.21, ii.23, ii.83, iii.143-55; Custom
House (CUS73), iii.155-6; Milk Street
(1-6; MLK76), ii.406-7, *ii.7.2-3*; New
Fresh Wharf (NFW74), ii.21, iii.157-
60; Seal House (SH74), iii.156-7;
Swan Lane (SWA81), iii.160
as a dating tool, ii.10; London and
non-London reference chronologies
correlated, *ii.7.1*; used to date pottery
type series and Ceramic Phases, *i.3*,
ii.23-4, *ii.2.3*, iii.140-2
deniers *see* coins, deniers
Deorwald, moneyer, ii.290, ii.310
Department of Environment, iii.11,
iii.48
Department of Urban Archaeology
(DUA), ii.7-8, iii.9
Derby, coin mint, ii.299, ii.311
Derkelane, iii.129
Desebourne Lane (= *Daneburghgate*), *iii.65*
Diarelm, moneyer, ii.322
Dibeleslane, iii.129, *iii.65*
dice, bone, ii.205, ii.265, *ii.3.87*
diet, evidence from botanical remains,
ii.348
Diormod, moneyer, ii.309
disc, with cloisonné enamel, ii.120
disc brooches *see* brooches
Distaff Lane, iii.124
Dolley, M, study of late Saxon coin
hoards by, ii.292-5, ii.304
Domburg,
Domburg-type/Low Countries
Greyware (DOMB), ii.114; equal-
armed brooch, ii.143
Domences, moneyer, ii.323
Domesday Book, ii.47
Aelfburh-type names, ii.184; on
buildings in Southwark and the City,
i.109; on die-cutters in London, ii.332
door,
from building at Pudding Lane
(PDN81), i.47, i.85-7, i.89-91, i.105,
i.84, i.86, ii.141; to St Botolph's church
Hadstock (Essex), *i.85*
doorframes, i.88
Milk Street (1-6; MLK76), i.53; Well
Court (WEL79), i.61
door furniture, i.89-91, ii.140-1, ii.252-
3, *ii.3.20*
doorways, i.85-7
dimensions, i.105-7; to sunken-floored

buildings, i.101; *see also* buildings
Dorchester-on-Thames,
bishopric, ii.412-3; mint, ii.292, ii.324
Dorestadt, ii.419, *ii.8.16*
combs, ii.195; jetties, iii.103; knives
with reversible blades, ii.128; lead
objects with official coin types, ii.328-
9; lead weights, ii.335
Dorking, coin hoard, ii.286, ii.320
Dover, ii.414
mint, ii.297, ii.299, ii.313
Dowgate, iii.75, iii.77, iii.118, iii.123-5,
iii.129-31, iii.134
stone house near, iii.130; ward of,
iii.93; excavations at *see* Public
Cleansing Depot (Dowgate; PCD59)
Dowgate Hill, iii.123, iii.125, iii.128,
iii.65
gold brooch, ii.124
drains, iii.69-70, *iii.41*
Roman, at Swan Lane, iii.80;
medieval, iii.85-6, *iii.47*
drapers, occupants of excavated
tenement, iii.95
dress, style of female, ii.143-4
dress fasteners *see* perforated pig
metapodia
dress pins, ii.203, ii.207
Drury Lane, early Saxon pot, ii.20,
ii.417
DUA *see* Department of Urban
Archaeology
Dublin, i.7
as a Viking centre, iii.133;
buildings, i.66
benches in, i.97; doorways, i.87;
floors, i.85; hearths and ovens, i.97-
8; partitions, i.97; post-and-plank
construction, i.79; post-and-wattle
construction, i.78; stave and plank
construction, i.103-7, *i.104-5*;
threshold, i.88; wattle, i.83
character of medieval artefact
assemblages, ii.121; complete section
of wattle walling, i.105; cultural links
of with London, ii.123; stave-built
structures, i.76, i.83; Wood Quay,
excavations, iii.117;
finds: bone implement with
zoomorphic head, ii.203; combs,
ii.198; cordage, ii.247; Crowland
Abbey-type bowls (CROW), ii.45,
ii.111; green porphyry, ii.155; ivory
carvings with glass inlay, ii.173;
leatherworking waste, ii.211; motifs
on bone motif-pieces, ii.180; Roman
glass, ii.172; soapstone artefacts
reused as moulds, ii.166; stave-built
vessels, ii.242; wood vessels, ii.240
Dudinc, moneyer, ii.342
Dulfsi?, moneyer, ii.324

Dunglane (= Pudding Lane near
Queenhithe), iii.129, *iii.65*
Duning, moneyer, ii.299, ii.314, ii.318
Dunn, moneyer, ii.309
Dunning, G C,
on Saxon pottery from London, ii.20-
1; on White Thetford-type Ware
(THWH), ii.94
Durham,
botanical remains, ii.352; buildings,
i.67, i.83; ovens, i.98
dyebaths, pottery, ii.123
dyeing, ii.168-9, ii.431
in Saxon London, ii.123-4; evidence
from York, ii.352-3; weld possibly
used in, ii.381; workshops, location of,
ii.169
dyepots, pottery, ii.168-70, *ii.3.52*
analysis of, ii.169-70
dyers, iii.138
occupants of excavated tenement,
iii.95
Dyers' Hall, site of, iii.94, *iii.53*
dyer's rocket, ii.348-9

Eadgar *see* Edgar
Eadmund, moneyer, ii.340
Eadmund *see* Edmund
Eadnoth, bishop of Crediton, ii.335
Eadred, king, coins, ii.291, ii.310
Eadred, moneyer, ii.342
Eadric, king of Kent, ii.413
Eadwald, king, lead objects with official
coin types, ii.338, *ii.4.7*
Eadwi,
king, lead objects with official coin
types, ii.340, *ii.4.7*
moneyer, ii.342
Ealdulf, moneyer, ii.287, ii.309, ii.338
earthfast foundations, i.71, *i.61*
summary of types, *i.62*
earthfast wall construction, i.83-4; with
posts, i.77-82; for stave-built walls,
i.75-6; at Fish Street Hill-Monument
Hill (FMO85), i.51; Milk Street (1-6;
MLK76), i.55; Pudding Lane (PDN81),
i.48; Well Court (WEL79), i.62, i.64
earth walling, *i.70*
timber-retained in sunken-floored
buildings, i.81-2, i.100-1, *i.98*
East Anglia,
Ipswich Thetford-type Ware (THET)
pottery, ii.38; mint, ii.331, ii.338, *ii.4.9*
Eastcheap, i.8, ii.421, iii.75-6, iii.124,
iii.130, iii.133-5, iii.137
coin of Ethelred II, ii.296; date of,
i.112; streets around, iii.75, *iii.43*
East Kent, importance of as centre of
sceat currency, ii.282-3
East Saxons, ii.284, ii.412-3

obscuring waterfront structures, *iii.41*; wattle panels on, iii.67

medieval, and waterfront alleys, iii.124

Forest glass *see* glass , potash

Forestry Commission, timber yield tables by, i.83

forging, techniques applied to knives, ii.131-2, ii.134

foundations for buildings, i.64, i.71-4, *i.52, i.61, i.64, i.66-9*

'bed' type, i.72-4, *i.61, i.64*; chalk, iii.43, iii.45; chalk on timbers, iii.43, iii.46; earthfast, i.71, *i.61, i.62*; floor and ground-level construction, i.71-2, *i.61, i.63*; ragstone and gravel, iii.47; summary of types, *i.60*

Fragaria vesca see strawberry

France, pottery imported from north, ii.45

Frankish,

axe forms, ii.135; goods from graves in Kent, ii.414; pottery *see* pottery, Frankish

Fresh Wharf, iii.74-5

Frisia, trade and coinage, ii.282-3

Frisian, merchants, iii.15

in York, ii.144

Frothric, moneyer, ii.340

fruit, ii.380-1

pips in pits, ii.348-9

Fulham, iii.16

Fulk, Count of Anjou, ii.232

Fumaria officinalis see fumitory

fumitory, ii.380

furniture, finial, ii.242, ii.276, *ii.3.127*

Gale, R, analysis of cordage by, ii.247

gaming pieces, ii.205

bone, ii.205-7, ii.265, *ii.3.87*; whalebone, ii.207, ii.265, *ii.3.87*

Ganiaris, H, analysis of oyster-shell palettes by, ii.170

gardens, in Saxon London, ii.353

Gardiner's Corner, coin of Stephen, ii.302

Garlick Hill, iii.18-9, iii.76, iii.125, iii.128, iii.131, *iii.65*

date of, i.112; *see also* Bow Lane

Garlickhithe, iii.19, iii.125, iii.128, *iii.65*

Garrick Street, gold finger-ring, ii.415

Garvin, moneyer, ii.300, ii.315

gastropods, inclusions of in Local Greyware (LOGR), *ii.2.60*

gate, use of term, iii.125, *iii.65*

gates,

?in riverside wall, ii.434, iii.97-8, iii.107, *iii.55*; Roman, post-Roman history, iii.14

Gault clay, matrix of Early Medieval

'Chalky' Ware (EMCH) similar to, ii.44

Gdansk, iii.135

jetty, iii.103

Gefrei, moneyer, ii.318

George Alley, iii.94, *iii.53*

Germany,

use of dendrochronological curve from, iii.156; *see also* Cologne; Haithabu; Hamburg; Lübeck; Worms

Germeyneslane, iii.129

gilding,

on casket mount, ii.151; on copper alloy mounts, ii.255; on silver pins, ii.120, ii.150

girdles, ii.240

embroidered, ii.122

glass, ii.172-4

beads, in early Saxon graves, ii.173; bowl, from burial at St Martin-in-the-Fields, ii.415; Carolingian, in London, ii.172; finger rings, ii.123, ii.172; furnace, at York, ii.123; inlays, ii.123, ii.144, ii.172-3; Islamic vessels, ii.172; jar, ii.173; lead, ii.123, ii.172-3; from Lime Street, falsely identified as Saxon, ii.172; linen-smoothers, ii.122, ii.173, ii.260, ii.431, *ii.3.54*; manufacturing waste, mid 17th-century, from Aldgate, ii.17; potash, ii.123, ii.172-3; production, ii.123; Roman, in Saxon contexts, ii.172; manufacture of spindlewhorls in London, ii.173 soda, ii.172-3; spindlewhorls, ii.173, ii.260, *ii.3.55*; textile implements, ii.173; vessels, ii.260; windows, i.91-3, ii.123, ii.260; X-ray fluorescence, ii.172

glass-working, ii.172

furnaces for, at Lincoln, i.99

Glastonbury, hooked tag, ii.150

glaze, on pottery,

chemical composition, ii.32; *see also* pottery, Saxon/early medieval, glaze

Gloucester,

bossed decoration on Stamford-type Ware (STAM) pitchers, ii.30; botanical remains, ii.352; footwear, ii.214; glass-working, ii.172; mint, ii.301, ii.317; pottery, ii.30, ii.42, ii.43 'early' Saxon still produced in late Saxon period, ii.38; Late Saxon Shelly Ware (LSS), ii.41; production centre, ii.39 stone spindlewhorls, i.165; strap, ii.240

Goathurst Common (Kent), ball-headed pin, ii.150

goatskin, footwear, ii.222, ii.225, ii.232

'God', moneyer, ii.313

Godred, moneyer, ii.301, ii.316

Godric, moneyer, ii.297-8, ii.312, ii.314, ii.324, ii.345

Godwine,

Earl, iii.76; moneyer, ii.344, ii.346

gold,

brooches, ii.124

in St Mary-at-Hill hoard, ii.432

finger rings, ii.151, ii.415

Gold of pleasure, ii.380

goldsmiths, occupants of excavated tenement, iii.95

Goltho (Lincs), buildings and structures, i.76, i.78, i.81

goose, flute made from bone possibly of, ii.207, ii.265

goosefoots, ii.380-1

Gosferth, portreeve, ii.334

Gotland, strap-distributor, ii.148

Gracechurch Street,

coin of Ethelred II, ii.296; coin hoard, ii.292-4, ii.320; date of street underlying as continuation of Fish Street Hill, i.114; pin-beater, ii.205

grain,

carbonised in ovens,

Botolph Lane (Peninsular House; PEN79), i.33, i.99; Well Court (WEL79), i.62, i.98; West Stow, i.98

import of, iii.18

Gramineae see grasses

grapes, ii.348, ii.353, ii.381

Grascherche,

Robert de, iii.76; Thomas de, iii.76

grass, floors, i.49, i.85

grasses, ii.380

with cereal remains in oven residue, ii.351

grassland plants, ii.380

Grateley Decrees, ii.289

gravel,

as drainage course below wall cladding, i.50; floors, i.49, i.85

Gravesend, coin hoard, ii.286, ii.320

Great Fire of London, i.49, iii.73, iii.77, iii.95, iii.138

Great Tower Street (34), glass, ii.172

Great Trinity Lane *see* Trinity Lane

Green porphyry, reused in Saxon London, ii.155

Greensand *see* Lower Greensand

Greensted-juxta-Ongar (Essex), church of St Andrew, i.67, i.76

Grege *see* silk

Gregory, pope, ii.412, iii.14

Grenewychelane (= *Frerelane*), *iii.65*

Gresham Street,

Frankish pottery, ii.415; Merovingian pottery, ii.20

Grimes, W F, on Saxon London, i.116

of Cnut, ii.297, *ii.1.11*; of William I, ii.301

combs, ii.199, *ii.3.79-80*; dyepots, *ii.3.52*; footwear, ii.213-9, ii.219-21, ii.223, *ii.3.98, ii.3.100*; hone, ii.155; horn comb, ii.122; leather scabbard, ii.211-3, *ii.3.94*; leatherworking waste, ii.211; medicinal plants (possible), ii.349, ii.353; metalworking debris, ii.152; parasite remains, ii.387; pottery, ii.430;

pottery assemblages,
   dated by dendrochronology, *ii.2.3*;
   from pits quantified, *ii.1.2*
roof shingles, ii.244; silk, ii.122, ii.430; stave-built vessel, ii.242; stone lamp base, ii.161; waste from manufacture of wooden vessels, ii.240; wooden vessels in pit, *ii.1.10*; woolcomb, ii.135; woollen cloth, ii.430
Milk Street (7-10, MIL72), dyepots, *ii.3.52*
Miller, L, New Fresh Wharf (NFW74)
   excavations supervised by, iii.22
Milne, G,
   Botolph Lane (Peninsular House; PEN79) excavations supervised by, i.13; Pudding Lane (PDN81) excavations supervised by, i.16
mineralisation, of botanical remains, ii.354-5
Minster (Thanet), abbess of, iii.15
Mitcham, early Saxon pottery, ii.20
molluscs, inclusions of in Early
   Medieval 'Chalky' Ware (EMCH), ii.70
moneyers,
   10th-century, iii.133; at London mint, ii.418; possible identity with portreeves, ii.334; possible workshop at York, ii.335; regulations of Grately Ordinance, ii.433; Adelard, ii.302, ii.319; Adelbert, ii.338; Aegelwine, ii.315, ii.324; Aelfgaet, ii.334; Aelfred, ii.317, ii.322-3; Aelfsige, ii.334; Aelfwi, ii.297, ii.312, ii.340; Aelfwold, ii.311; Aestan, ii.340; Aethelm, ii.311; Aethelnoth, ii.312; Aethered, ii.323; Aethestan, ii.311; Albert, ii.291, ii.310; Alfdene, ii.286; Alfred, ii.301; Algar, ii.345; Alief, ii.342; Aura, ii.340; Baciager, ii.322; Bate, ii.345; Beagstan, ii.321; Bertold, ii.331, ii.345; Blacaman, ii.311; Boga, ii.297, ii.313; Bruninc, ii.324; Brunman, ii.298, ii.314; Byrhtlaf, ii.311; Cenred, ii.321; Cethewulf, ii.321; Cormes, ii.305; Deorwald, ii.290, ii.310; Diarelm, ii.322; Diormod, ii.309; Domences, ii.323; Dudinc, ii.342; Dulfsi?, ii.324; Duning, ii.299, ii.314, ii.318; Dunn, ii.309; Eadmund,

ii.340; Eadred, ii.342; Eadwi, ii.342; Ealdulf, ii.287, ii.309, ii.338; Edwi, ii.331-2, ii.342, ii.344; Edwine, ii.297, ii.312; Eoba, ii.284-5, ii.308; Ethelmod, ii.286, ii.309; Ethelwald, ii.284; Ethelwold, ii.308; Folcaerd, ii.301, ii.316; Frothric, ii.340; Garvin, ii.300, ii.315; Gefrei, ii.318; God, ii.313; Godred, ii.301, ii.316; Godric, ii.297-8, ii.312, ii.314, ii.324, ii.345; Godwine, ii.344, ii.346; Grimwald, ii.291, ii.310; Gunricus, ii.305; Hartholf, ii.342; Hebeca, ii.309; Hugered, ii.309; Ibba, ii.285, ii.308; Leofnoth, ii.311; Leofred, ii.312; Leofstan, ii.297, ii.313, ii.334; Leofwine, ii.312, ii.324, Lifinc, ii.340; Liofwold, ii.311; Lulla, ii.338; Manna, ii.340; Mannecin, ii.291, ii.310; Ordgar, ii.342; Pendred, ii.284, ii.308; Rathulf, ii.340; Regnald, ii.338; Rogier, ii.302, ii.319; Saeberht, ii.285, ii.308; Sarthe, ii.305; Siferth, ii.301, ii.316; Sigehelm, ii.323; Snedi, ii.301, ii.317; Swan, ii.297, ii.313; Swetman, ii.314; Swigen, ii.317; Tilewine, ii.286; Udd, ii.308; Werbald, ii.308; Wihtred, ii.338; Wilebert, ii.310; Willelm, ii.303; Wine, ii.297, ii.312; Winedi, ii.316, ii.345; Winman, ii.346; Wulferth, ii.309; Wulfgar, ii.291, ii.310, ii.315, ii.334; Wulfmaer?, ii.324; Wulfnoth,ii.324; Wulfred, ii.297, ii.313; Wulfwine, ii.324; Wulgar, ii.345; *see also* coins
money supply,
   9th-century, ii.287, ii.289; 11th-century, ii.296
Montfichet's Tower, ii.434
Monument Street, i.16
Moore, D T, thin-section analysis of hones by, ii.155
mooring posts (?), at Swan Lane, iii.81, iii.84
mooring rights (*statio navis*), iii.18
Morden, Gilbert de, *iii.65*
Morley St Peter, Ipswich Thetford-type Ware (THET) vessel containing hoard, ii.40
mortar,
   floors, i.85, *i.81*
     at Pudding Lane (PDN81), i.42, i.46-7, i.48, i.49; Watling Court (WAT78), i.61
   wall foundations, i.74, *i.67-8*
     at Pudding Lane (PDN81), *i.27*
mortars, ii.161, *ii.3.45*
   of Caen stone, ii.257
Mortlake, mid Saxon chaff-tempered pottery, ii.20

Morus nigra see mulberry
motif-pieces, bone, ii.120, ii.123, ii.178-84, ii.261-2, ii.432, *ii.3.57-70*
   date, ii.179, ii.180, ii.184; function, ii.180; inscribed *Aelfburh*, ii.184, *ii.3.65*; motifs, ii.179-80, ii.184, *ii.3.71-4*; with Trewhiddle-style ornament, ii.179
moulds,
   bronze-casting, late medieval, at Fenchurch Street, ii.17; for metal objects, ii.166-7; possibly used in manufacture of Saxon pottery, ii.25; Roman tile reused as, ii.166-7, ii.259, ii.432, *ii.3.50*
     XRF analysis, ii.389
   stone, ii.167
mounts,
   bone, ii.210, ii.267, *ii.3.93*; for caskets, ii.151, *ii.3.34*; copper alloy, ii.151-2, ii.255, *ii.3.34*; gilded, ii.255; iron, ii.139, ii.252, *ii.3.19*; ring, ii.151; straps associated with, ii.240
Mucking (Essex),
   cemetery, ii.414; Chaff-tempered Ware (CHAF), ii.48; early Saxon cemetery and settlement, ii.88, ii.412; sceattas, ii.88
mudstone,
   spindlewhorls, i.165, ii.258, *ii.3.49; see also* siltstone
mulberry, ii.381
mules *see* coins, mules
Museum of London,
   formation of Saxon pottery collection, ii.19-21; location of archives, iii.12; reference collection of Saxo-Norman pottery, ii.47; trust funds, iii.77
Myres, J N L, on dating of early Saxon pot from Drury Lane, ii.20

nails,
   copper alloy, ii.152, ii.255, *ii.3.35*; iron,
     from door at Pudding Lane (PDN81), i.89-91, *i.84, i.86*; on wood patten, ii.244, ii.277
National Gallery site, sceattas, ii.283
Nazingbury, Chaff-tempered Ware (CHAF), ii.48
needles, ii.203
Netherlands, imitation coin of Conrad II, Duisberg from, ii.303, ii.320
nettles, i.17, ii.380
Neutron Activation Analysis, of Late Saxon Shelly Ware (LSS), ii.54
Nevers, Count of, ii.333
Newbury (Berks),
   botanical remains, ii.352; source of clay similar to that used for Early

padlocks, ii.141, ii.252, *ii.3.20*

padstones,
in wall foundations, i.37-9, *i.66*; for walls, i.73, i.81, i.100-3, *i.23, i.25, i.29, i.64, i.101*

pail, wood, ii.242, ii.276

Painted Tavern Lane, *see* Three Cranes Lane

painting, shell palettes as evidence for, ii.170

palettes, oyster-shell, ii.123, ii.260
containing vermilion, ii.170-1, *ii.3.53*

Palmereslane (= *Cookeslane*) (Emperors Head Lane), iii.129, *iii.65*

Papaver somniferum see opium poppy

parasite remains, ii.386-8
as evidence for human waste, ii.9; processing and analysis, ii.386-7; results summarised by site and date, ii.387

Paris,
lead objects with official coin types, ii.332; mint, ii.329

parish boundaries,
in bridgehead area, *iii.43*; definition of, iii.95

parishes, late Saxon, and waterfront area, iii.136

partitions, in surface-laid buildings, i.97

Pas-de-Calais, 7th-century coin of London mint, ii.415

paths, cobbled,
11th-century, *iii.11*; 12th-century, iii.42-3

pattens,
medieval, ii.244; wood, ii.244, ii.277, *ii.3.129*

pattern-welding, on knives, ii.127, ii.131-2, *ii.3.3, ii.3.6, ii.3.7-9*

Pavonazetto marble, reused in Saxon London, ii.155

pearlite, in knives, ii.134

pearls, in St Mary-at-Hill hoard, ii.432

pears, ii.381

peas, ii.381

pegs, wood, ii.277, *ii.3.130*

pen-case, ivory, ii.202

Pendred, moneyer, ii.284, ii.308

Peninsular House, excavations at *see* Botolph Lane

pennies, ii.282
broad silver, ii.284

Pentecost Russel, lane of, *iii.65*

perforated pig metapodia, ii.208, ii.266, *ii.3.90*

Perring, D,
Watling Court (WAT78) excavations supervised by, i.26; Well Court (WEL79) excavations supervised by, i.28

Perth, wattle buildings, i.83

Peterborough, school of stone-carving near, ii.153

Peter's Hill (PET81), iii.124, iii.130
assemblages used to define Ceramic Phases, i.11, *i.3*; Badorf-type Ware (BADO), ii.99; Chaff-tempered Ware (CHAF), ii.48; coin and pottery dates compared, *ii.2.4*; coin of William I, ii.301, ii.424; comb, ii.194-5, *ii.3.75*; Domburg-type/Low Countries Greyware (DOMB), ii.114; dyepots, *ii.3.52*; location of excavations, *iii.1*; post-Roman erosion, iii.97; pottery, ii.424; property development, ii.427; strap-end, ii.145-7, *ii.3.26*; Thames Street based on riverside wall, iii.99

Pevensey, cordage possibly of willow, ii.247

pfennigs *see* coins, pfennig

phials, glass, ii.172

Phleum sp see timothy/cat's tail

photomicrographs, of pottery, ii.119

phyllite,
hones, ii.155, ii.257, *ii.3.42*; *see also* Blue Phyllite

Picardeslane (= *Brodelane*), iii.129, *iii.65*

pig,
bones, motif-pieces, ii.178, ii.261
fibula,
implements, ii.207; pins, ii.265-6
perforated metapodia, ii.208, ii.266

pilgrimages, to Rome, souvenirs from, ii.155

pin-beaters, ii.123, ii.205, ii.430

pine-marten, i.108

Pingsdorf, pottery kilns, ii.20

pins,
bone, ii.203, ii.207, ii.265-6, *ii.3.85, ii.3.89*
with zoomorphic head, ii.122
copper alloy, ii.150, ii.255, *ii.3.32*; ring-headed, ii.150; silver, ii.150; silver-gilt and ball-headed, ii.120, ii.150

pintles, ii.141, ii.252, *ii.3.21*

Pisum sativum see peas

pitch, from pits at Milk Street (1-6; MLK76), ii.152

pits, i.12
as cess pits, ii.348-9; botanical remains, ii.348-9, ii.380-1 summarised, *ii.5.1*; character and function, ii.13-15; distribution,
as a guide to growth of settlement of late Saxon London, ii.424, ii.427; in Billingsgate study area, *i.4*; near Fish Street Hill, i.112; used to date streets, i.12; at Watling Court (WAT78), i.112-3

for compost in Southampton, ii.353; function, ii.348-9, ii.353, ii.387-8; limited use for dating Saxon pottery, ii.22; linings, ii.15; medieval, reuse of compared with Saxon pits, ii.15; number as guide to duration of Ceramic Phases, ii.24; parasite remains, ii.386-8; pottery assemblages increasing in size in early medieval period, ii.43; residual material, i.11; stratification, ii.14-5;

site list: Botolph Lane (Peninsular House; PEN79), i.16, i.19, i.37, *i.4*
10th to early 11th-century, *ii.8.11*; 11th-century, *ii.8.12*; botanical remains, *ii.5.13*; distribution, *ii.8.8*
Fish Street Hill-Monument Hill (FMO85), i.21, i.116, *i.4*
10th to early 11th-century, *ii.8.11*; 11th-century, *ii.8.12*; distribution, *ii.8.8*
Ironmonger Lane (24-5; IRO80), i.32, ii.15
botanical remains, ii.348, *ii.5.15*; distribution, i.113; in sunken-floored building, i.64, *i.53*
Miles Lane (ILA79), botanical remains, *ii.5.12*;
Milk Street (1-6; MLK76), i.23, i.55, *i.14, i.15*, ii.14-15
Alexanders (culinary herb) from, ii.381; alignment, *i.16*; axe, *ii.1.11*; botanical remains, ii.348, ii.353, *ii.5.4-7*; coin of Cnut, *ii.1.11*; dendrochronology, ii.406-7, *ii.7.2-3*; distribution, i.113; leatherworking waste, ii.211; metalworking debris, ii.152; plank-lined, *ii.1.8*; pottery, *ii.1.2*; section through, *ii.1.12*; surviving levels OD, *ii.1.6*; waste from manufacture of wooden vessels, ii.240; wattle-lined, i.82; wooden vessels, *ii.1.10*
Pudding Lane (PDN81), i.17-21, i.49, *i.4, i.9, i.10, i.11*
10th to early 11th-century, *ii.8.11*; 11th-century, *ii.8.12*; 11th to mid 12th-century, *ii.8.13*; distribution, *ii.8.8*; Roman residual pottery, *ii.1.5*
Watling Court (WAT78), i.26, i.29, i.56-7, i.61, i.93, *i.17, i.59*
barrel-lined, *ii.1.9*; botanical remains, ii.348, *ii.5.9-10*; wattle-lined, *ii.1.7*
Well Court (WEL79), i.28
timber-lined, i.64
Wood Street (St Alban's House; ABS86), waste from manufacture of finger rings, ii.175

plait-stitch, on footwear, ii.231, *ii.3.116*

planks,

objects with official coin types of
Ethelred II, ii.335, *ii.4.9*; mint, ii.301,
ii.316, ii.318, ii.340, ii.345, *ii.4.9*;
pottery bowl stained with madder,
ii.168; pottery kilns, ii.45, ii.89, ii.92;
saint-brooches, ii.145; stone
spindlewhorls, i.165; woolcombs,
ii.135

thin-section analysis,
of crucibles, ii.390; *see also* pottery,
Saxon/early medieval, petrology

thistles, ii.380

Thornback ray, remains of from well in
Lower Thames Street, ii.138

Thorney Island, ii.419

Threadneedle Street,
coin hoard, ii.291, ii.320
catalogue, ii.322-3
comb and comb case, ii.199

Three Cranes (Painted Tavern) Lane,
iii.125, *iii.65*

thrysmas, ii.280-1
from London mint, ii.280

tiebeams, in walling, i.101

Tiel, merchants of, iii.129

Tilbury (Essex),
lead objects with official coin types,
ii.4.9
of Burgred, ii.328, ii.331, ii.334

tiles, Roman, i.53, i.62, i.64-5
in foundations, i.37-9;
in hearths, i.47
at Botolph Lane (Peninsular House;
PEN79), i.33
in ovens, i.98-9, *i.92*; as padstones for
walls, i.73; reused as moulds, ii.166-7,
ii.259, ii.389, *ii.3.50*;
in Saxon street metalling,
at Botolph Lane (Peninsular House;
PEN79), i.16; Well Court (WEL79),
i.29;
in stone lining for sunken-floored
buildings, i.52; on surface of 11th-
century embankments, iii.34

Tilewine, moneyer, ii.286

timber framing,
for hearths, i.97; ovens, i.98-9, *i.94*,
i.96

Timberhithe/*Timberhithstreet* (High
Timber Street), iii.18-19, iii.125, *iii.4*,
iii.65

timbers,
degree of working on
dendrochronological samples, iii.154;
sapwood, revised estimate, iii.156;
shapes and sizes in Saxon buildings,
i.79; unworked, used in 11th-century
embankments, *iii.12-14*

timber-working, in structures from
London, i.83

timothy/cat's tail, ii.351

tin, coating,
on buckles, ii.253; iron buckle-pin,
ii.3.22; iron mounts, ii.139, ii.252;
strap-distributor, ii.147

Tobert, N, experiments by in
replicating Saxon pottery, ii.25

toggles *see* perforated pig metapodia

tolls *see* customs dues

tongs, i.38, ii.135, ii.250, ii.432, *ii.3.13*

tools,
iron, ii.135-8, ii.250-1; for
metalworking, *ii.3.13*

top-bands, for footwear, ii.219, ii.221-4,
ii.236-8, ii.270, ii.274-5, *ii.3.108*,
ii.3.113, ii.3.122-4

topography, of Saxo-Norman London,
i.110-6, *i.109-11*

Torksey, pottery kilns, ii.89, ii.92

Tottenham Court,
chaff-tempered pottery, ii.22, *ii.417*;
stamp-decorated pottery, ii.28

Totternhoe (Devon), equal-armed
brooch, ii.143

Tower, Postern next to (waterfront
alley), *iii.65*

Tower Hill, Roman silver ingot, ii.411

Tower of London, ii.434
original entrance, iii.76; Roman
defences, ii.409

Tower Street, iii.75-6, iii.124

'Tower Street', brooch, ii.416-7

town planning, Saxon, i.110

trade, i.108
coin evidence, ii.289-90, ii.415; goods
mentioned in 11th century, iii.134;
of London,
11th to early 12th-century, *ii.8.17*;
with Baltic, ii.299; with Dorset,
ii.155; mid Saxon, *ii.8.16*; with
Scandinavia, ii.296
post-Conquest, ii.303
with Scandinavian communities in
England 10th-century, ii.291
long-distance, iii.16; pottery as
indicator, ii.433-4, iii.137;
in pottery,
in 10th-century London, ii.41, ii.419;
in 11th and 12th-century London,
ii.45-6; in later medieval period, ii.41
in silk and luxury goods, ii.122; in
stone, ii.121-2

trade networks, iii.133

trades of occupants,
at New Fresh Wharf, iii.74; Seal
House, iii.95; Swan Lane, iii.95

trading shore (*ripa emtoralis*), Saxon,
iii.16

Treasury site London,
Ipswich-type Ware (IPS) pottery,
ii.38; shell-tempered pottery, ii.38

tree-ring dating *see* dendrochronology

tremisses,
catalogue, ii.305; Merovingian, ii.305

trenails, ii.277, *ii.3.130*

Trewhiddle hoard, ii.147

Trewhiddle-style ornament, on bone
motif-pieces, ii.179

trial-plates for coins or objects with
official coin types, lead, from Lund
and Hungary, ii.336

Trichuris sp *see* whip-worms

Tricitum aestivum s see wheat, bread
wheat

Trig Lane, iii.19
as '*Fysshwharfe*', iii.125, *iii.65*

Trig Lane (TL74),
Badorf-type Ware (BADO), ii.99; river
levels, iii.119-20

Trinity Lane, iii.17, iii.18-19, iii.130,
iii.4
date of, i.112

Tripleurospermum maritimum see scentless
mayweed

Trondheim,
Andenne Ware (ANDE), ii.105;
Crowland Abbey-type bowls (CROW),
ii.111

trough, wood, ii.240, ii.276, *ii.3.126*

turf, walling, i.100

Tyburn, river, ii.419

Udd, moneyer, ii.308

undercrofts *see* buildings, stone

Urnes (Norway), stave-built structure,
i.76

Urtica spp *see* nettles

Uxbridge, ii.47

Valerianella dentata see corn salad

Vannereslane, iii.129

vermilion,
on oyster-shell palettes, ii.123, ii.170,
ii.260, *ii.3.53*; use of in wall-painting,
ii.170

Verulamium, late and sub-Roman,
ii.411-12

vessels,
glass, ii.260;
wood, ii.275-6
in pit at Milk Street (1-6; MLK76),
ii.1.10

Vicia faba see Celtic beans

Vicia hirsuta/tetrasperma see tare

Vikings,
artefact types introduced by, ii.122;
coins, ii.286
imitations of Alfred's monogram,
ii.289; probable hoard from Thames
foreshore, ii.291, ii.323; from
Cornhill, ii.289-90